W9-CKD-302

Worldly Teachers

Worldly Teachers

Cultural Learning and Pedagogy

MARTHA HAWKES GERMAIN

BERGIN & GARVEY

Westport, Connecticut • London

0027i0s

Library of Congress Cataloging-in-Publication Data

Germain, Martha Hawkes, 1942–
   Worldly teachers : cultural learning and pedagogy / Martha Hawkes
Germain.
      p.   cm.
   Includes bibliographical references (p.   ) and index.
   ISBN 0–89789–572–X (alk. paper)
      1. Teachers—United States—Attitudes.   2. Teachers—United
States—Intellectual life.   3. International education—United
States.   4. Teaching—United States.   I. Title.
LB1775.2.G47   1998
371.1′00973—dc21   98–13657

British Library Cataloguing in Publication Data is available.

Copyright © 1998 by Martha Hawkes Germain

All rights reserved. No portion of this book may be
reproduced, by any process or technique, without
the express written consent of the publisher.

Library of Congress Catalog Card Number: 98–13657
ISBN: 0–89789–572–X

First published in 1998

Bergin & Garvey, 88 Post Road West, Westport, CT 06881
An imprint of Greenwood Publishing Group, Inc.

Printed in the United States of America

The paper used in this book complies with the
Permanent Paper Standard issued by the National
Information Standards Organization (Z39.48–1984).

10 9 8 7 6 5 4 3 2

For Frank

To all of the wonderful students and colleagues I have worked with over the years in K-12 schools and in the university, you have made teaching and learning a joy for me: to you, my friends, and my family.

Contents

0027105

Preface: My Story

In a former life, as a secondary school teacher for twenty-eight years, I taught seventh- and eighth-grade language arts and social studies, eighth- through eleventh-grade English, American history, modern Asian culture, Russian history and culture, modern European culture, and American government. During this life, I thought it important to become better educated about the world in order to guide the learning of my students. Every few years, I returned to school to take history and geography courses about China, Russia, and Europe. I loved introducing my students to this knowledge via great varieties of fiction and nonfiction, which we discussed in our big circle, so that we might look at each other when making our points. Essays and interpretive papers allowed students to express how they related to, for example, Tolstoy's story, *The Death of Ivan Illych*.

It was not until I attempted to deepen my understanding of Chinese history and culture by studying Chinese language for four years to enrich my modern Asian culture course that I became fervently involved in an effort to promote cultural and international learning in Michigan schools. Contacts with colleagues in many school districts and my work for the Michigan Department of Education in 1988 to survey all of the approximately 990 school districts in the state showed that very few schools in Michigan had strong international education programs. Only a tiny percentage of these schools included non-Western cultures in their curriculum. I was asked by officials in the state Department of Education to lead a statewide effort to internationalize the curriculum, and especially promote East Asian studies, while developing a model Center for Chinese Studies in my school district, Warren Consolidated Schools. The effort culminated in three statewide conferences, targeted to teachers and administrators, to raise awareness about the need to integrate international and cultural studies into the curriculum. The fourth year of the program, we initiated a pilot first- through eighth-grade Chinese and Spanish language program in six elementary and three middle schools in my district.

I gradually became a more public advocate of the need for international and cultural study in the schools. My core beliefs that human beings must understand each other in order to promote human dignity and mutual respect among individuals and cultures drove this inquiry. Study of works such as *The Mass Psychology of Fascism* by Wilhelm Reich (1946) had convinced me that rigid patriarchy, ignorance, and negative stereotyping had combined to thwart human potential in almost every culture. Intensive study of Chinese language and culture then was the impetus for an activism that centered mainly on teachers as the most important players in any effort to change the focus and content of the school curriculum.

In the process of writing state and federal grants to support our efforts to internationalize the curriculum, I looked for research that would help make the case that teachers need help to understand the world if they are to be effective teachers. I asked researchers at the American Forum for Global Education and other organizations for suggestions. They could not point to any work which would help me support my position. This study evolved out of that experience.

In-depth cultural learning enriched my life and classroom practice tremendously. It led me to probe the issue of teacher learning in the College of Education at Michigan State University. This is because as a teacher advocate for many years, I agree with Milbrey McLaughlin (1990) that teachers are "key players" in the schools. Grass roots efforts must be supported among teachers who work to improve their knowledge of their subject matter and share this knowledge with colleagues. Knowledge about the world and other cultures is crucial in our increasingly multicultural society and interdependent world.

For two years I explored the international experience and cultural learning of six veteran teachers. This study is based on in-depth interviews with these veteran teachers, the definition of veteran being five to seven years (Nemser, 1983). To understand how a veteran teacher's in-depth international study has affected her* pedagogy, I have relied on each teacher's narrative, the stories of her experiences. I have limited this study to veteran teachers because, to a great degree, they personify the school environment in which novice teachers develop their teaching personae. I have intensively studied teacher learning from the perspective of my long experience in teaching, and I

---

* I have chosen to alternate gender pronouns whenever I refer to teachers in general.

hope that this exploration of the way international experience affected these six teachers will generate further work on the impact of cultural experience on a teacher's classroom practice and life.

Acknowledgments

The environment in which I began this study, the College of Education at Michigan State University, was a challenging and nurturing place where intellectual rigor and the warmth of family entwined. Global efforts continue there to promote self-efficacy and human dignity to better guide the untapped human potential in the United States and the world. Leaders in this effort, Jack Schwille and Lynn Paine, who encouraged me to develop my skills through deepened understandings to connect my long experience to a larger audience, are among the most thoughtful and giving people I have ever known. They and Jack Williams, Director of Asian studies, helped me to internationalize the curriculum in the state and then mentored me as a doctoral student.

In addition, I am indebted to Judy Locher and Nancy Fenstemacher for their careful, painstaking efforts to assess issues of style and content; Nancy Fox for computer work entailing many late nights, and my cheerleaders: daughter Beth, Mother, my dear late father, and especially, my helpful and patient husband, Frank.

Introduction

This study is about teacher (K-12) cultural learning—the extent to which intensive international study and experience affect veteran teaching practice. Analysis of narratives from interviews with six veteran teachers is the basis of this work. These teachers describe their lives and experiences before, during, and after their international experience, which they all believe has profoundly affected their lives and work. This study of how intensive international study or experience affects a teacher's pedagogy helps us understand why and how teachers learn, specifically in the area of what I call cultural learning. The latter reflects learning about a society, vicariously through books and articles and in person, interacting with individuals and through observations.

A *New York Times* edition of *Education Life*, "What Does it Take to Teach?" (Section 4A Jan. 7, 1996), conjures up an alarming specter of overwhelmingly white middle class females who are preparing to become teachers of an increasingly diverse ethnic array of students as a great problem that must be addressed in education today. To help solve this problem, former Peace Corps volunteers are being encouraged to teach in difficult inner-city school environments because of their presumed heightened cultural awareness. According to the work of educational anthropologists George and Louise Spindler (1974, 1994) on "cultural therapy," teachers can be helped to become more aware of their biases to improve their relationships with students of diverse ethnic backgrounds. Their study shows that experience living among and working with the people of another culture for an extended period can enhance a teacher's sense of cultural self-awareness and empathy with students.

I interviewed six teachers over a period of two years about their international experiences. Two of them lived and taught in China and four of them in Japan. The teachers, ranged in age from forty to sixty-five, included three males and three females, five Caucasians and one African American. They lived in the Midwest and on the East Coast. Two teach elementary school, one teaches middle school, and three (the males) teach high school. Five returned to their jobs teaching in public schools and one to her job in a private New England preparatory school. Four of the public school teachers taught in mainly white suburbs, two in very affluent areas, while the fifth teacher, who is white, taught all African-American students in a public charter school in an inner city. All had learned about the area before going, while three (the females) had studied the language formally as part of their preparation. Four of the six are married, one of these without children. Two were accompanied by their wives, while one woman's husband visited and traveled with her in China for two weeks in the midst of her teaching exchange. Two are single, one of them being divorced with three children. They all considered their experience to have been personally and professionally transformative and give many examples of how their teaching practice has changed. They describe how they grappled with "culture shock" abroad as well as in the United States after they returned.

In my sample of teacher narratives, there is a link between in-depth international experience and cultural awareness and sensitivity. An educative international experience at least promotes awareness, which is a first step toward cultural sensitivity and respect. This is why former Peace Corps volunteers might be likely candidates to teach among students who have been forgotten by many in affluent America (Kozol, 1991; Grubb and Lazerson, 1982). I argue that in-depth international experience often generates in veteran teachers introspection, empathy, and the desire to learn more. Any personally transformative experience that serves to energize and motivate teachers is worth exploring. I have learned from the teachers as they told their stories about early influences on their lives, their motivations to study, their international experience, and how this experience has affected their teaching practice and professional lives.

CONTINUALLY LEARNING TEACHERS

It is crucial that teachers make an effort to increase their understanding about the world in order to be effective in teaching students about the world. There is hardly any school subject that does not involve some international component. Because teachers are the key players in schools, they must be educated and encouraged to participate in the continual improvement of classroom practice. They must model lifelong learning for children in order to encourage them to do likewise. Effective teachers must have in-depth knowledge of the subjects they teach and be life long learners (Ball and McDiarmid, 1990; Nemser, 1983). Israel Scheffler (1967) views teachers as intellectuals, engaged in continuous learning so that they can make a sense of the world, guide children toward deeper understandings, and be models for the children. Teachers who have lived and worked abroad and connected with individuals in another culture are more likely to live up to Scheffler's (and my) idealistic model than are those who remain within the safe cocoon of their own culture.

Studies suggest that school context is generally conservative and thus inhibiting to the creative and reform-minded preservice academic background of many novice teachers (Goodlad, 1984; Huberman, 1989; Lortie, 1975; Nemser, 1983; Tyson, 1994; Waller, 1967). This was certainly my experience. This book presents a different and more positive view of veteran teacher learning than those studies, which emphasize the negative, constraining effects of the school culture on novice teachers. Because most veteran teachers are generally beyond the struggle to develop a teaching persona and to establish control in the classroom, they are secure enough to evaluate and try to improve their pedagogy and knowledge of the subjects they are teaching. Veteran teachers, such as those in this book, can be examples for young teachers of professional growth, transformation, and lifelong learning, and useful as mentors for novice teachers.

As there are different ideas of what is educative about an experience, there are different kinds and degrees of in-depth experience or study. I have accepted the following criteria for in-depth international experience: (1) the length of time in country or engaged in study must show commitment, that is, a time period of more than six months; (2) the experience must involve significant face-to-face relationships and friendships with individuals within the culture; for example, teaching for a semester, year, or more, living with a family, or attempting to learn the language; and (3) the experience must include reading and studying about a culture for a period of years.

All of the teachers I interviewed had studied the culture (with three learning the language) for at least one year before they traveled abroad. Most had studied the culture of Japan or China for several years in order to expand their knowledge for the courses or units they were teaching. One of these teachers studied the issue of U.S.-Japan trade relations for eight years before he went to Japan. The time dedicated to this study reflects a considerable commitment for veteran teachers, who function within the constraints of jobs and family responsibilities. I considered in-depth experience a criterion for my choice of participants because it would eliminate superficial experiences, such as flying to Hong Kong to shop or the "been there, done that" scenario described by one of the teachers in this book. I do not claim that people cannot learn from such experiences. However, in-depth international experiences are more likely to generate the kind of personal growth and transformation that these teachers describe.

I interviewed veteran teachers because I wanted to understand the teachers' perceptions of their teaching style before and after the international experience. I was interested in teachers whose professional lives were not initially dedicated to international experience, such as foreign-language teachers. The teachers I interviewed were initially generalists—elementary teachers, secondary English or social studies teachers—rather than cultural or language specialists. This approach was necessary to help me understand how cultural learning and experience might be transformative for a veteran teacher.

I used my protocol mainly as a guide. Kathleen Casey (1993) asked the "open-ended" question: "Tell me the story of your life," in her research about women teachers engaged in radical political activities. By that standard, I consider my interviews to be flexibly structured. I asked the teachers about formative family, community, and school influences on their decision to engage in intensive international study. I also explored the nature of the international experience and how they believed their teaching practices had been affected by this experience. I was very interested in whether each teacher thought that this experience was personally and professionally transformative and why.

My analysis of the narratives of these teachers has allowed me to gain greater insight into my own experience. These narratives opened up different ways of looking at this experience as I move forward composing my life along the way, just as my teachers do (Bateson, 1989). I agree with Ivor Goodson (1995, p. 97) that these stories, although they have a beginning and an outcome, are never finished. Who is to say where the impact ends? While we may be gone, the stories evolve into new forms, becoming part of the experience of others, enriching their lives. Those who have continued learning and growing—for example, John Dewey in his life and thought—have profoundly affected the lives of others (Lamont, 1959; Ratner, 1939; Westbrook, 1991). And in the critical theoretical positions of Giroux (1993) and Freire (1970), carefully interpreted stories can motivate people to social action.

I have engaged in this study because I am concerned about the ability of teachers to create an environment that acknowledges and upholds standards of respect and human dignity in the classroom (Byrnes and Kiger, 1992; Cushner et al., 1992). Because of the increasing diversity in the American classroom and society, James Lynch (1989, 1992a, 1992b) believes that it is essential that American teachers be better educated about world cultures that are reflected in the many faces of children before them. This is one major reason that I am interested in teachers' stories about their efforts to develop knowledge about another culture.

The world is very close to all of us. Within and beyond our man-made boundaries the world is reflected in our senses and in our attempts to understand and make sense of our lives in connection with others. Kindness, compassion, caring for others, and cooperative, productive work can flourish as we struggle to understand each other. The work of teachers is paramount in this worldwide human effort. This is why it is most important that educators and policymakers learn from teachers' stories about the meaning they make of their efforts to understand cultures different from their own.

CHAPTER ORGANIZATION

In Chapter 1, I will discuss the theoretical perspectives that have helped me shape the narratives of these teachers into a meaningful framework. In Chapter 2, I discuss issues of voice and relationships with the participants in this study and include a brief introductory vignette about each of them. Chapter 3 explores the experience of these teachers before they traveled abroad, including their family background, K-12 schooling and undergraduate influences, their postgraduate and early teaching experiences, including how they characterized themselves as teachers before their international experience, and each of their learning styles throughout their lives before they traveled to China and Japan. Chapters 4, 5, and 6 analyze the content and context of their international experience. Chapter 4 concentrates on the school experience of those who taught abroad, Chapters 5 and 6 on their experiences out of the classrooms, especially the connections they made with people in the host country and their learning within that country. Chapters 7, 8, and 9 explore the degree to which these teachers believe their teaching practice and their lives have been affected by their international experience, with Chapter 7 exploring the changes they found when they returned home and in their classrooms in Chapter 8, and Chapter 9 analyzing their personal and professional transformation. Chapter 10 presents ways that international education could be integrated within the school reform movement.

This research has provided background for my recommendations in the concluding Chapter 11 relating to exchange programs for teachers to promote international experience that will foster the kind of personal growth and transformation in veteran teachers that John Dewey envisioned. Surpassing what was thought to be possible just decades ago, our age of increased connections across borders has made international education an essential element in school reform.

1

Crossing Borders: Opening Minds

This study is a qualitative analysis of veteran teachers' narratives about their international experience. I have analyzed these experiences to explore the elements that might facilitate a teacher's personal growth in the Deweyan sense. I listened to the stories of teachers who have been "border crossers," not necessarily in the radical political context of Henry Giroux (1993) but possibly in the context of the work of anthropologist Mary Catherine Bateson (1994). In her long-term efforts to connect with others in varied cultural contexts, Bateson eventually learns a great deal about herself. Bateson's view that "experience is structured in advance by stereotypes and idealizations" helped me analyze the reactions of each teacher to his or her experience abroad (1994: 5).

Most important to this study is the work of educational anthropologists who explore the individual cultural contexts of teachers. The teachers' understandings of this context often define their effectiveness with students from different cultural backgrounds. Other works that have helped me choose questions to draw out teacher experience and make sense of their narratives are by anthropologists Mary Catherine Bateson (1989, 1994), Susan Florio-Ruane (1994), and George and Louise Spindler (1974, 1987, 1994).

John Dewey's work (1925, 1938) on the issue of experience and education is key to this book. Self-reflection is necessary for the kind of personal growth that Dewey believes is necessary in effective teachers, whose experience he would consider to be "educative." Dewey illuminates educative and miseducative experience, the former leading to personal growth and transformation, the latter fostering stagnation or degeneration of thought and work. International experience and study that fosters a life long passion to learn and understand would be educative in the Deweyan sense. Conversely international experience which enhances a teacher's sense of cultural superiority, seals a closed mind, deepens the chasm between self and other, or promotes negative stereotyping of people would be an extreme form of Dewey's concept of miseducation.   This book includes examples of educative and miseducative aspects of international experience.

Effective teachers must engage in experience that is the wellspring of personal growth and transformation. The mind informed by educative experience is open to new knowledge, insights, and ways of understanding, from the simple to the complex. Intellectual curiosity combines with the will and discipline to learn. Transformative learning is always reflective; the mind changes as it looks at itself from new perspectives. It is this aspect of international study or cultural learning that can provide new insights about the world and ourselves. I agree with Dewey (1916) that the mind-world dichotomy is false. The mind transforms itself and the world by looking inward and outward simultaneously and by praxis, action to change the world. Transformative international experiences for teachers must begin with awareness and exposure to the cultural worlds within the United States as well as the world beyond our national boundaries.

Dewey (1902) eschewed the idea of a retreat into the world of the mind, of knowledge for its own sake without purpose. He believed that educative learning is transformative and that this personal transformation is necessary for the transformation of society. He did not view the individual human being or the individual school outside a social context, a widening web of connections, relationships, and responsibilities in the world. Meaningful human existence is in the connections, literally displayed in his use of conjunctions: *The Child and the Curriculum, The School and Society, Experience and Education*. To Dewey, isolation wastes human potential. In *Experience and Education* (1938) which Dewey wrote at age seventy-nine, he criticized simplistic "either or" thinking. His earlier works had emphasized mastery of a teacher's subject matter to enable her to relate this knowledge to the child and guide him toward more complex understandings of knowledge as it is organized in the disciplines. The goal of education is what he calls "a fully integrated personality," one who is able "to extract meaning from his future experiences as they occur" (1938: 49). "Education as growth or maturity should be an ever present process," he wrote. The teacher's experience and mastery of his subject matter are the necessary precursors to Dewey's goal of education.

Teachers who study and experience another culture as veteran teachers are often curious and love to learn; hence they are continually deepening their grasp of their subject matter. Bateson considers this knowledge to be embedded in "layers of awareness" reflecting insight, "that depth of understanding that comes by setting experiences, yours and mine, familiar and exotic, new and old, side by side, learning by letting them speak to one another" (1994: 14). If this international experience is to be educative in the Deweyan sense, teachers will want to be as unbiased as is possible; they will question their own assumptions; they will pursue books and articles to put their first-hand knowledge into a broader context. The more they know, the more they are aware that they do not know. They are not arrogant or prejudiced; they are open to experience, and their work as teachers would be to help themselves and others become better human beings.

This is the Deweyan ideal of educative experience, applied to teachers as "directors of the soul life" (Dewey, 1904: 321). This continuum of personal growth lasts a lifetime and is a model to all future generations. This is what it means to be a great teacher-guide, whose depth and commitment to learning transcends narrow national boundaries. Education in the Deweyan sense is not isolated but is activist in terms of social responsibility. Teachers like the six in this book, who have lived and taught abroad and studied international issues, often are actively engaged in promoting international understanding and breaking down cultural barriers and negative stereotypes.

TEACHERS AS "BORDER CROSSERS"

Discussing how teachers can become examples of the educative or transformative power of international experience brings up issues of cultural understanding. Does knowledge about the world promote cultural understanding? Is there a link between understanding the world and how teachers might work with students in an increasingly diverse multilingual society? Is there a link between a teacher's knowledge about the world and how teachers cope with the failure of desegregation in the American north, where overwhelmingly white middle-class students constitute the student bodies of most northern U.S. suburbs and black and Hispanic students are concentrated in poor, often dilapidated urban ghetto schools? According to Jean Anyon (1981) and many other scholars and journalists, these students and schools are worlds apart (Delpit, 1995; Grubb and Lazerson, 1982; Kozol, 1991; Spindler and Spindler, 1994).

This book provides some examples of how individual teachers might begin to bridge this gap. By their example as "border crossers" in the sense developed by Henry Giroux (1993), teachers of all races can encourage their students to break down the social barriers of race and class, to empower and transform themselves into activists for social justice. Teachers like those in this book, engaged in the Deweyan concept of educative international experience, could by their example help their students to understand and respect differences, and hear the often silenced multiplicity of voices constituting American society (Delpit, 1988).

The United States has become a multilingual, multicultural society, a microcosm of world cultures, with students of some cultural groups living in what many consider to be Third World conditions in the inner cities, while the mainly white affluent Americans live in the suburbs. Teachers who have taught abroad will bring a different perspective to these cultural realities. They have experienced minority cultural status and they have depended on connections with others from different cultural backgrounds. The teachers in this book give credence to the idea that international experience can affect a teacher's sensitivity toward foreign or minority children in her classroom.

Demographer Harold Hodgkinson exhorts Americans to think about the consequences of high birth-rates among minority population compared with the white middle-class population. He predicts that by the year 2020, in many areas of the U.S. South and West, a majority of "minority" cultural groups will reside. The separation of the white middle class from the despair and decay of mostly black and Hispanic inner cities gives a special cogency to Giroux's argument. Those engaged in the "culture wars" debate, who propose that schools emphasize traditional, European-based American values rather than multicultural values, may unwittingly be building the separating walls even higher (Bloom, 1987; Finn, 1989; Gitlin, 1995; Hirsch, 1987; Hunter, 1991; Levine, 1996; Ravitch, 1983; Ravitch and Finn, 1987).

CULTURAL LEARNING

Cultural learning and the cultural analysis of schooling can shed some light on the possibilities of educative international experience. Vivian Paley, a first-grade teacher, discovers and confronts her biases as a "White Teacher," the title of her book (1979). She is humbled and mortified when she realizes that she had been viewing her black girl students as a group and her white girls as individuals. Negative childhood memories of being treated this way as a Jewish child exacerbated her feelings. She asks, "Was I still so acutely aware of color that I could see children as individuals only as they became close to being my color and using my speech?" (1979: 137). One can more easily connect with someone whose experience is similar to our own. Paley, as teachers who experience minority status in another culture, became aware of her interaction with the black girls because she was able to connect her own experience to those of her students.

Anthropologists George and Louise Spindler have studied the questions raised by Paley for many years. They contend that without reflection about who we are, without a deeply probing personal and professional look at ourselves, we will unconsciously treat people differently. We will tend to be more open and generous with people like ourselves. Their work on this issue began during the 1950s with what they call the "Roger Harker syndrome." Harker was considered by himself and others to be a good teacher, fair and unbiased toward his students. When the Spindlers shared data with him that indicated otherwise, he left the meeting, unable to accept the idea that he reacted more openly and generously with students from his own class and cultural background than he did with students from other backgrounds. Harker subsequently returned to work with the Spindlers to become aware of his cultural biases and to improve his connections with students from minority backgrounds (1974, 1994).

Today the Spindlers call this work "cultural therapy" (1994) in a professional rather than a personal, psychological sense. The Spindlers encourage all teacher-educator programs to engage teachers in a process of reflection on their "enduring selves," the core values and cultural traditions embedded within the family and cultural life of all humans. The effort is to understand who we really are from that standpoint. The next step is to understand the "situated self," how the self adapts to contexts similar to or different from those of homes and community. They bring up the question: is it necessary for teachers to probe deeply into themselves in order to better understand others from different cultural backgrounds? Part of the "culture shock" in the teachers' narratives in this book involved a similar introspection, which the teachers believe affected their classroom practice.

The Spindlers contend that to the extent that a child or adult develops a sense of "self-efficacy," he can become a self-actualizing individual. However, a failure to adapt, in which the conflict or the barrier is too great for some children or teachers, causes an "endangered self" to emerge. This is a person who actively or passively acts out his alienation by withdrawal or overtly self-destructive behavior (such as the use of drugs, violence). Dewey's conception of educative experience could be the precursor to this sense of self-efficacy. The example of miseducative experience in this study is a teacher who has not engaged in the introspective self-analysis that the Spindlers recommend and is alienated from colleagues and family. For example, when Ellen Stacey* returned from three years of teaching English in Japan, she described a sense of malaise and isolation in her personal and family life: "Before I went to Japan, I was always in the social scene, always. Now I've been back from Japan and I have cut off all my friends. I distanced myself from everything, including family. I think I went through a period of deep depression when I returned from Japan."

---

*Names and places have been changed to protect participant anonymity.

The Spindlers can provide one framework for understanding how a teacher's international experience might promote empathy with another point of view, another "cultural" way of viewing reality; or conversely, it might be the basis for rigidity, prejudice, and alienation. The Spindlers, John Dewey, and many others in the past and present reform movement encourage educators to listen to their students, to try to step outside of their subjective experience and understand the context and environment of all of their students' family and cultural backgrounds. The curriculum must connect with or "draw out" whatever aspects of the enduring self of the child will help her develop self-efficacy (Dewey, 1900/1902/1990). This curriculum must include international issues because they constitute the real world of students today. The teacher who has become a learner, a student again, of other cultures and who cares about the world is likely to develop a curriculum that puts a priority on international issues and understandings. The teacher has developed a sense of self-efficacy about the world, thus becoming a model for his students.

Lisa Delpit (1988, 1995) demonstrates cultural learning for efficacy by challenging teachers to openly confront the dominant power issues by teaching poor or minority children the code words and traditions of the culture of power, not from a perspective of inferior status but from the perspective of tools to open the doors of opportunity. Gatekeepers represent the values and beliefs (enduring selves) of the majority in power. Formal English language and culture could be taught as a separate and equal second language, not as a superior language and culture. A teacher of native Athabascan children suggested that the class plan a formal English dinner and then contrasted this with their own dining practices. This is an example of children learning another way of thinking and acting, learning to know and understand the culture of power without encouraging a rejection of their own culture. This is also exactly how white middle-class children can learn about the cultures of the world. Some of the proponents of the much maligned Ebonics movement had a variation of this sort of cultural learning in mind (Leland and Joseph, 1997). According to Oakland, California school board member Toni Cook, "African-American students come to school with a home language other than English. We're going to bridge that gap and make sure our children learn" (p. 78).

Teachers with international and cultural experience in more than one culture are best equipped to introduce authentically the study of world history, geography, world cultures, and languages to their students. Two of my participants, Ed Donovan and Paul Vandemere, used the simulation game Ba Fá Ba Fá (Shirts, 1977) in their classes after they returned from China and Japan, respectively. Paul started each new class with this game to promote cultural understanding in his classes.

Very early on, the very first days of every semester with my beginning students, I would put them in an exercise where they were members of two different cultures, with different norms. They had to send visitors to the other cultures to learn those norms. They had to become observers and then see how they were treated as outsiders while they were doing this. . . . You have to suspend your judgments of other countries as you are now learning about them. You have to not be quick to make those judgments.

Paul used this game to get them involved in thinking about how and why structures and practices are different from those in the United States, with the goal that the students will begin to question and understand the background to their own cultural traditions.

The work of E. M. Forster and Edward Said, however, cautions people from the privileged, developed world, for example, middle-class teachers from the United States, to be aware that they are part of a culture of imperialism deeply embedded in Western culture. Connections between these fortunate people in the world and what Said (1993), in derision of Western chauvinism sometimes calls the "natives" of an indigenous culture, can be fraught with great complexity. As in Delpit's work, the culture of power "holds the cards," thereby forcing those out of power to learn the ways of the oppressors. A superior-inferior scenario develops that could skew many friendships and connections. E. M. Forster in a *Passage to India* (1924) shows how a well-meaning young woman, who wants to get to know a "native" Indian person as a representative to her of all of India, precipitates a near disaster in human relations. Her fears and cultural phobias cause her to falsely accuse an Indian doctor, who had gone out of his way to assist her in her quest to experience "the real India," of a sexual assault. When Forster writes "Only Connect," it is emblematic of not expecting much in the way of human intimacy when differences in ethnicity or class exist. This prescript to *Howard's End* (1921) could also mean that connecting is the only hope for humans.

The relationships that develop between the six teachers in this book and individuals from their host countries are most important and meaningful to each teacher. None of them would consider their experiences "in depth" without these connections, however fraught they are with the negative entanglements of Western cultural imperialism that Said describes.

Delpit's vision juxtaposed with that of the Spindlers could provide an alternative for people who felt they had to go through a period of painful alienation from their own family and cultural roots in order to cross cultural barriers. Richard Rodriguez (1982) describes this partly as a profound sense of loneliness, a feeling that he had to reject part of himself in order to break into the dominant culture. Some scholars view schools as places where the cycle of poverty and despair might be broken by pedagogy and curriculum that exposes the children to knowledge that opens up other worlds of opportunity to them, just as several teachers in this study do by sharing their international experience with students (Floden, Buchmann and Schwille, 1987).

This practice might counter the cases of lowered expectations and less demanding curricula for lower social and economic segments of society (Anyon, 1981; Kozol, 1991; Resnick, 1987a). Teachers equipped to compare diverse cultures can present alternatives to children mentally locked into one particular cultural world view. For example, Denise Green found that as an African-American teacher, her experience helped her students, many of whom were African-American children, dream impossible dreams and expand their ideas of what is possible. Green became a model to them, her postcards and coins precious symbols of things they might do some day. When she returned from Japan, she gave them a writing assignment:

> Describe the perfect classroom, describe the perfect teacher, and the perfect field trip, three separate assignments. The perfect field trip, I never had a response like this. The kids talked about going in a spaceship to outer space. . . . I just kept reading them over and over and I was just truly amazed because their teacher, someone they knew, someone they could touch (this is my belief) had taken some kids on a field trip to Japan. They thought that I could take them any place. They thought the ideal field trip could be anywhere. When I had given them that assignment in the past in other grades, it was nothing like the response I got to this.

SELF-REFLECTION TO BROAD CONNECTIONS

Teachers who move out of their own familiar context, their own cultural comfort zones, can become cultural learners. Bateson (1994) considers the value of multicultural learning to be in how we view ourselves comparatively: "Seen from a contrasting point of view or seen suddenly through the eyes of an outsider, one's own familiar patterns can become accessible to choice and criticism" (p. 31). This is an example of how international experience can contribute to the personal growth and transformation of teachers. Israel Scheffler and John Dewey believe that teachers must be thinking people in the deepest, most self-reflective sense (Scheffler, 1967). A teacher "fairly saturated in subject matter" models by the example of her life and being the attributes of student and thinker to her students (Dewey, 1904: 320). Knowing facts without the context was not Dewey's concept of worthwhile knowledge. The teacher must "psychologize" the subject matter in the context of cognitive understanding, relating and connecting this knowledge to the realities of life, from the perspective of the learner (1902).

This mental turning over of knowledge through constant inquiry is the basis of a self-reflective mind, the kind of mind that exhibits "reflection in action" (Schon, 1987). It is the ideal of Oakeshott's (1989) "grand adventure," describing mankind's sometimes agonizing "predicament of self-disclosure." This self-reflective ordeal of consciousness distinguishes humans from other mammals. The essence of being human is the self-reflectivity of a thinker.

Dewey hoped teachers would nurture in the minds of children this respect for the dignity of the human mind. The ultimate goal of promoting international experience for teachers is to promulgate this basic respect irrespective of cultural backgrounds as an example to young people. Cultural learning does affect the self-awareness and empathic sensitivity of some teachers. In the affective areas of tolerance, thoughtfulness, and mutual respect, they are better mentors for their students than they were before their international experiences.

A teacher's international experience could be understood as a break with experience, in that when she crosses that border, she will have to give up some preconceived notions and assumptions about the culture she is studying and perhaps some assumptions about her own culture. Teachers who study other cultures than their own, with the self-reflection of thinkers and learners, can demonstrate their growth and exemplify the Deweyan ideal of educative experience in action. In *Democracy and Education* (1916), Dewey advocates social action for the betterment of society as the natural outgrowth of educative experience that promotes personal growth.

Dewey's ideal is evidenced by the many teachers who want to establish connections with others in different cultures and are part of a network of people who wish to build a better world. They are among the people who link up across boundaries, often as part of interest groups known as international non-governmental organizations (INGO), such as the YMCA, the International Red Cross, and Amnesty International (Boulding, 1990). While Bellah et al. (1991), Gutmann (1987), and others consider how we can build a better democratic society within the United States, people in INGOs work to connect across cultural and national boundaries for a better United States and world. Worldwide anti-nuclear movements, Doctors Without Borders, and endangered-species activists are grass-roots movements dedicated to working with others to "make a better humanity," as was Dewey. This work gives meaning and purpose to life, the key to understanding Dewey's educative experience. The connections of human understanding and mutual respect, according to Boulding, rest on many one-on-one relationships, the friendships across borders of people who are committed to being responsible for the consequences of human actions on this earth. The connections of these teachers with people and families become part of a broader network of people who work to improve the lives and potential of children around the world.

WHOSE VALUES? WHOSE HISTORY?

My review of multicultural and global literature shows it to be fundamentally at odds with the work of scholars who feel that this multicultural emphasis is threatening to basic values embedded within their conception of the American cultural and historical tradition, a position that gives credence to Said's interpretation of western cultural imperialism. Allan Bloom (1987), for example, is disturbed that today young Americans "know much less about American history and those who were held to be its heroes" than in the past (p. 34). His work, *The Closing of the American Mind*, was on the *New York Times* best-seller list for ten weeks and sold over one million copies, indicating the wide influence of his argument (8/21/96: 14A). Bloom believes that ethnocentrism is a positive value because humans need to center upon their own values and culture in order to have a basis on which to make judgments. He describes uncentered students who no longer can feel moral outrage at man's inhumanity to man, because they respect all values, even those that would cause people to throw a grieving woman upon the funeral pyre of her husband (1987: 26). He writes:

> The study of history and of culture teaches that all the world was mad in the past; men always thought they were right, and that led to wars, persecutions, slavery, xenophobia, racism, and chauvinism. The point is not to correct the mistakes and really be right; rather it is not to think you are right at all. The students, of course, cannot defend their opinion. It is something with which they have been indoctrinated. The best they can do is point out all the opinions and cultures there are and have been. What right, they ask, do I or anyone else have to say one is better than the others? (p. 26)

Bloom considers this loss of values, knowledge, and centeredness a result of the premium placed on openness, diversity, multiculturalism, and emphasis on non-Western cultures in the schools. His answer would be to open the American mind by returning to and acknowledging the superiority of Western cultural traditions and values. This ostensibly would bring back a dedication to values of right and wrong, good and evil, and a nationalistic sense of who we are as Americans. International and multicultural education is Bloom's foil because he believes it promotes relativism and takes time out of the curriculum that would be better spent giving students a more thorough grounding in Northern European-derived cultural values.

Bloom and E. D. Hirsch, author of *Cultural Literacy* (1987), both describe John Dewey's philosophy and multiculturalism as causes of the general cultural and historical demise of what is traditional and good in American culture (Hirsch, 1987: 31). What is "traditional and good" in American culture depends on "whose values" are American values, a question Henry Giroux (1993) pointedly asks. Harold Hodgkinson (1991) indicates that one-third of American children in American schools will be minority children in a few years. Giroux's question, "whose history?" is salient to this projection (1993). He considers Ravitch, Hirsch, and Bloom examples of a "new form of nativism in the guise of transcending issues of race and class." Giroux would educate young people to proclaim diversity and empower themselves to work toward creating a better world. Teachers who have become cultural learners as envisioned by Bateson, Spindler, Delpit, or Paley and within Dewey's concept of an ideal teacher are more effectively equipped to accomplish Giroux's ideal.

TOWARD AN "OPENING OF THE AMERICAN MIND"

I began this study with the idea that the goal of multicultural, development, and international areas of study in education is to end injustice and inhumanity, and to empower teachers to work toward a better world. I agree with Edward Said that multicultural education should not be characterized as a "Lebanonization" of education, a separation (1993). It is an integration of the narratives of individuals in formerly excluded groups that have contributed to society and culture. Teachers who deepen their understandings about others, who begin to think in terms of an all-encompassing "we," may transcend "the restraints of imperialism or national or provincial limits" (p. 335). To teach respect of cultures is to teach respect of individuals within cultures and their "enduring selves."

Four of the teachers in this book discuss their opposition to the views of Bloom, Hirsch, and others who would limit international and multicultural perspectives in the school curriculum. The teachers' arguments involve trade, environment, and health issues that require international cooperation. Mary Ehrhardt, a second-grade teacher who lived in Beijing with a Chinese family and taught English at a key middle school, expressed her concern.

I really think that's the closing of the American mind. I think it's a narrow view and ignores the fact that in the twenty-first century the international relations are going to be even more I think a part of our daily lives than they have been in the twentieth century. . . . I would have to side with the vision of the founders of the League of Nations and of the United Nations, but it's only through learning to negotiate and understand and accommodate our political wishes that we are going to be able to work cooperatively in the world.

Paul Vandemere argues that "Amway would not be the number one door-to-door sales company in Japan if it had a mindset that said that any American they send over doesn't need to know about Japan or the Japanese. Chrysler would be shooting itself in the foot for it to say,'We can be as successful in China with Americans who are clueless about China and Chinese language.' " More important to Paul,

> We ignore, if not discredit, the contributions of so many people and so many cultures to what makes up America and what makes up this world. We neglect, we lose a resource, a strength that this country has. We should consider our diversity a strength. The Japanese consider their homogeneity a strength. That's OK for them. Although certainly the homogeneity can be taken to extremes, there are differences in groups, etc. within Japanese society. But we have a real strength here. We can't let the strength divide us. But the great contributions that different ethnic groups have made, that different societies have made should be understood and relished.

The work of Bloom and Hirsch on culture sets up a superior/inferior perception that fuels anti-immigrant, nativist sentiments bordering on xenophobia. Bateson (1994) describes a basis for this bigotry: "Each community believes that its understanding is not simply good, not even better, but best. We cannot all be right, so whatever is different is wrong" (p. 179). Bateson, like Said, would attempt to eliminate the superior/inferior perception that Bloom and Hirsch promote.

> The basic challenge we face today in an interdependent world is to disconnect the notion of difference from the notion of superiority, to turn the unfamiliar into a resource rather than a threat. We know we can live with difference. . . . Men and women, for instance, have lived together throughout history. We know we can benefit from difference. But the old equation of difference with inferiority keeps coming back, as fatal to the effort to work together to solve the world's problems as the idea of competing for a limited good. (Bateson, 1994, p. 233)

It is important for teachers to learn from other cultures in such a way as to eliminate negative stereotypes and encourage mutual respect among individuals of all cultural backgrounds. Whether teachers respond this way to their international experience is one area this book explores. My argument is that if the international experience of veteran teachers is educative, teachers with these experiences will be more capable of encouraging students to work and live cooperatively with those people in this world who are different from themselves.

Ed Donovan thinks that Americans cannot appreciate their own culture if they have nothing with which to compare it.

> How can they appreciate it [American culture] if they don't have anything to compare it to? I think that you have to have something to compare it to. I admire the whole system of rocketry; that was German. The invention of gunpowder was a wonderful thing for the United States, just ask the gun boys. That came from China. This is stupid, this idea that we encompass everything. And nothing else should get in.

Lawrence W. Levine, a cultural historian at the University of California at Berkeley, has written *The Opening of the American Mind* (1996), which rebuts Bloom's thesis on the basis that multiculturalism, an anathema to Bloom, is "the inevitable and praiseworthy product of constitutional democracy . . . [and] means that in order to understand the nature and complexities of American culture, it is crucial to study and comprehend the widest possible array of the contributing cultures and their interaction with one another" (Honan, 1996: A14). In a *New York Times* interview, Levine discussed his disappointment in his own undergraduate education during the 1950s at the City College in New York. "We studied Northern and Western Europe. . . . Nothing on Africa, Asia and Latin America. Even Canada was a great blank. My own father was an immigrant from Lithuania and my grandparents were from Odessa, but we talked only about Northern and Western Europe. There's something wrong with that" (p. A14).

Bateson argues that the study of culture stimulates creativity and insight: "We know that difference stimulates creativity. When we talk about going beyond the traditional canon, we are talking about opening up a library not of great books but of versions of humanness—some of them never written down in any form at all" (1994: 171). Levine also stresses the positive aspects of multicultural and international study, arguing that opening "America to great diversity . . . has not lead to repression as Bloom argued, but to the very opposite—a flowering of ideas and scholarly innovation unmatched in our history" (Honan, 1996: A14).

   The literature on multicultural and international education includes concerns about creating classroom environments that celebrate diversity and uphold standards of respect and human dignity (Byrnes and Kiger, 1992; Cushner et al. 1992). This literature does not include much work on teacher learning, but on the creation of curriculum such as global education projects and organizational structures such as "international schools," which will promote multicultural and international understanding (Enloe and Simon, 1993; Freeman, 1986; Rosengren et al. 1983; Tye and Tye, 1992; Wilson, 1993). Angene Hopkins Wilson's work on international experience in the schools includes interviews of teachers and former Peace Corps volunteers who have become teachers about the meaning of their international experiences. In almost every case, as in this small sample, they believe that they are better teachers because of their international experience.

   I hope my analysis of interview data in this study will begin to fill a gap in the research literature about how we might view a teacher's learning about cultures different from his own. I hope that the teachers' stories in this book will help educators and policymakers understand the possibilities of educative international experience. How a veteran teacher analyzes her work in the classroom, within the context of her own personal and professional growth, can add to our understanding of the precursors to and ramifications of a veteran teacher's cultural learning.

2

Voice and Relationships

I became interested in other cultures initially when I read Fyodor Dostoyevski's *Notes from the Underground* in a philosophy class during my sophomore year in college. From the time I began to teach in 1964, I used autobiographies, biographies, and novels to augment textbooks in every social studies class I taught until 1993, my last year of teaching secondary school in Michigan. I hoped that the personal perspectives of others might imbue my presentation of the dry American history textbook, for example, with humanity and passion.

During the early 1970s I encouraged my white, middle-class students to read personal accounts of what it felt like to grow up in a majority white, racist society; we read, for example, *The Autobiography of Malcolm X* (1965) and Sammy Davis Jr.'s *Yes I Can* (1965). We also read novels such as *Johnny Got His Gun* (Trumbo, 1939) and *The Ugly American* (Lederer, 1958) for a different perspective on U.S. foreign policy. For political history, we read Mike Royko's *Boss* (1971) and the political novel, *The Last Hurrah* (O'Connor, 1956). I believed in empowering students (before we used such a word) to think for themselves. We used the text with these books to look at history—that is, human life—from different perspectives. In the Russian history and literature course I developed, we started our exploration of Russian history and culture with Nicholai Gogol's satirical novel, *Dead Souls* (1842/1961). The version that I used included a section that was censored by the Czarist government about corruption and inefficiency in the bureaucracy. My students realized that the book was a brilliant satire exposing the Russian upper class and government as essentially being mindless fops, worthy only of mirth and derision. The character Manilov, in *Dead Souls*, had bookmarks on page 14 of every book in his voluminous library. It was Gogol's perspective on

Russian life and society, which differed from that of the government and upper class, that I wanted the students to begin to grasp.

I was consistently curious about other cultures and ways of viewing the world. The first writer who really moved me, after Charles Dickens in *Great Expectations*, which I had read in high school, was Dostoyevski. I became fairly obsessed with his writings, which led me to seek out undergraduate senior thesis credits to write "A Comparative Study of Dickens and Dostoyevski." Authors such as these represented to me an elucidation of the human struggles and dilemmas in nineteenth-century societies, which were controlled by forces that negated what I believed to be the inherent dignity of every individual. Twentieth-century struggles of the disempowered resonate within a similar context.

LEARNING ABOUT CHINA

In this research on the cultural learning of veteran teachers I am promoting experience which I felt was inaccessible to me during the 1960s and 1970s. When I stepped off a plane in 1981 in the middle of a very dark night at a tiny airport, for the thirteen million people in Shanghai, I took a blurry picture, capturing evidence in the print of my shaking hands. This was fifteen years after I began my study of Chinese history at the University of Michigan in the summer of 1966.

I am promoting the kind of international experience that might affect a person's perspective as it has mine. Living and learning in a culture that I had studied and taught for fifteen years were almost overwhelming to me. For two years before I traveled to China, I had studied the Chinese language to expand my knowledge of Chinese culture.

This ten-week experience of studying Chinese in Shanghai emboldened me to study the language for one and a half more years and to incorporate this study into my teaching. The experience in China, in addition to many years of study about China, greatly enriched the course I had developed and taught for ten years, "Modern Asian Culture." The Chinese language introduced me to a very different perspective: an exquisitely beautiful human expression, the music of finely spoken Mandarin, and the grace, elegance, and balance of written characters. Because I felt I was becoming transformed in the process of learning this language, a part of my own ethnic and cultural background came to the fore: the New England preacher and missionary. Two of my great-grandfathers were ministers, one Episcopalian and the other Baptist. Many of my ancestors were Quakers. Biblical names such as Ezekial and Jedediah are common first names in one branch of my family tree. Some of my ancestors were missionaries in Hawaii and other lands. Transformation in life often inspires advocates somewhat akin to ministers and missionaries. True to this part of my family tradition, I became an advocate of gaining and sharing international experience and knowledge with students and colleagues in the schools.

Learning Chinese was a gift, a luxury for me, as Russian literature had been earlier. I wanted to share this gift with students and colleagues. My students seemed to enjoy this gift, especially the seventh-grade learning-disabled and emotionally disturbed students I taught in a "basic" social studies class in 1982. They liked the language much better than the world geography book with big print. My colleagues thought I was weird, practicing characters on memos during faculty meetings about schedules and assignments. Some parents and colleagues criticized me for using Chinese to elucidate the few paragraphs on China in the geography textbook.

COMING HOME

Like some of the participants in this study, the most difficult part of my study about China and the world was the isolation and alienation I felt when I returned from China in 1981. The school principal, who had been trying to expedite my involuntary transfer out of the building because of my union activities, assigned me to teach basic English classes instead of the modern Asian culture course I had developed. Three weeks into the semester, he was overruled by a central office administrator, who informed him that North Central Accreditation would not accept another teacher's single Russian history course twenty years earlier as qualification to teach modern Asian culture. I was abruptly returned to that class for the rest of the year, where I had a wonderful time sharing this experience in China with my students.

A new superintendent and the principal of another high school, who believed that my teaching and work in Chinese language merited a second look, encouraged me to develop a Center for Chinese Studies in the school district. When the state Department of Education officials learned about this, grant applications mysteriously appeared in my mailbox. After we filled in one application and were notified of its acceptance, state officials asked me to lead an effort to develop a network of educators who would promote international education in the schools, focusing on education about East Asia. I eventually accepted this responsibility, which was part of my own personal and professional transformation, from classroom teacher to director of a center for Chinese studies, an academic magnet for four high schools, and chairwoman of the Pacific Rim Consortium Steering Committee. The latter evolved from including thirteen to thirty-eight public and private schools, intermediate school districts, community colleges, and universities in the state. The last statewide consortium conference was a joint effort with the Michigan Council for the Social Studies and attracted some 600 educators from Michigan and Midwestern states. High school students were encouraged to participate with their teachers via a scholarship program administered by the Michigan 4-H Youth programs and funded by twenty-three Japanese banks and corporations and Ford Motor Co. I also directed a first- through eighth-grade Chinese and Spanish language program in nine elementary and middle schools in Warren Consolidated Schools.

During these activities, I continued teaching Chinese history, culture, and language to ninth to twelfth-grade students in the Center. My students helped me raise $15,000 for five students in the center to live with a family and study Chinese language and culture in Beijing. International study and experience had significantly transformed my personal and professional life. I, like Mary Catherine Bateson, included my eleven-year-old child, Elizabeth, in this experience by taking her to China with me during the summer of 1985. I worked with educators to promote different perspectives in the schools, especially the inclusion of non-Western cultures in the curriculum. Bateson (1994) describes the awareness she has developed because of her experience studying, living, and working in other cultures as like the gift I feel that this experience has been for me.

VOICE

I include some of my experience because I want to make this chapter clearer about who I am. I began this study in 1994 by engaging in a life history project during my graduate course work. It is important to consider Donald Polkinghorne's discussion of criteria for life histories "to include a recognition of the role the researcher had in constructing the presented life story and the effect the researcher's views might have had in shaping the finding" (1995: 19). I came to this research with a point of view that evolved out of my background and experience. I frequently argued vehemently against intolerance, bigotry, or negative stereotyping. The rawest wound I suffered during my formative first year of teaching junior high school in 1964 was inflicted by my colleagues. They banded together to forbid my suggesting to some eighth-graders that they read John Howard Griffin's *Black Like Me* (1961), to understand from a white person's perspective what it was like to live in the prejudiced, white-dominated society of the South at the time. I was appalled that although none of the teachers had read this book, they were quick to judge it inappropriate as supplementary reading material.

Literature concerning qualitative research methodology frequently states that we must be clear about ourselves as researchers, about what has caused us to engage in our studies and the lens through which we try to understand and make sense of our data. Bruner (1990), Emihovich (1995), Krieger (1991), Goodson (1995), and Clandinen and Connelly (1994, 1996), among others, provided insights on the issue of voice. It is important that my strong voice not overwhelm those of participants and that it makes clear who I am: that I am a long-term public advocate of international study and experience, especially for teachers who can profoundly affect the "soul life" of children (Dewey, 1904), and that I believe in racial, ethnic, and religious tolerance.

RELATIONSHIPS AND VOICE

Doctoral work helped me to reconcile my longterm role as a teacher advocate and union leader with the judgment role entailed in analysis of the stories of my participants. Sitting on the bargaining team of a teacher association in 1970 as the first woman elected vice president pushed me into becoming what others considered a radical teachers' union leader. The preppy, freshly scrubbed lawyer for the administration and school board characterized the only useful function of teachers as enforcing the following conditions in the classroom: straight rows, no paper on the floor, and quiet. My proud profession in his view was akin to that of a warden or animal trainer, to keep the "little beast children" in control. As a result, I began my career as a union activist for the next ten years until I felt that teachers as role models for children were being treated with the respect and dignity they deserve.

This union movement culminated in teachers obdurately facing police in riot gear while on a picket line to promote their livelihood and dignity. A society that used the majority female status of the profession to deny teachers fair living wages, benefits, and control over their professional lives made this action necessary. I felt proud that we won contracts for teachers that became state and national models.

My strong identification with teachers from the perspective of advocate is not diminished. A deeply embedded teacher persona enabled me to interview teachers in the context of a collegial conversation. I did not consider myself an authority or superior in terms of knowledge over what they had to tell me in spite of the fact that I had had what I consider the luxury of time to read widely in the international, multicultural, and cross-cultural literature. This egalitarian relationship, my respect for them and their profession as teachers, enabled these interviews to contain personal and highly descriptive information.

I had known four of these teachers for more than eight years because my work enabled me to attend and participate in many state and national conferences, such as the National Council for the Social Studies or the American Forum for Global Education. I consider my participants friends and colleagues. One of these teachers was recommended to me by an administrator colleague in graduate school, and another through a friend who knew about my study. All of these participants knew of my work in promoting international education, including the two that I had not known personally.

Before each interview, I discussed with each of them my research question: In what ways and to what extent does a teacher's study of other cultures shape his or her pedagogy? They understood that I wanted to learn from them and that I was an advocate for international education. The transcripts of these interviews, which averaged about four hours each (the range being between two and six hours), reflect very little talk by me except with references to things I had experienced that resonated with their experiences. They were very open, expressive, and enthusiastic about the opportunity to share their experiences. This interview experience was not an exchange between a "subject" and an academic authority, which places the interviewer in a superior position to the interviewee. The collegial conversation worked well. We learned from each other. I cared about their international experience and what it meant to them. They felt secure that I, as a veteran teacher and colleague, would treat them and their words with the respect and dignity they deserve.

In *Acts of Meaning* (1990), Jerome Bruner encourages us to look more seriously at the way people construct meanings through narrative style. Bruner writes that we can learn not only from what we do, but from what we say about what we do. I have enjoyed hearing teachers in their own voices describe how they have learned from their lives and work (DiShino, 1987; Paley, 1979; Stumbo, 1989; Wigginton, 1986). Bruner's view of the importance of narrative in an individual's "meaning making" of his experience goes deeper than just an individual's interpretation of experience, and enters into the essence of culture itself: "Our capacity to render experience in terms of narrative is not just child's play, but an instrument for making meaning that dominates much of life in culture. . . . To be in a viable culture is to be bound in a set of connecting stories" (Bruner, 1990: 96-97).

Clandinen and Connelly explore Dewey's concept of the connectedness of life that is related to their work on narrative inquiry. They write: "For Dewey, education, experience, and life are inextricably intertwined. In its most general sense, when one asks what it means to study education, the answer is to study experience" (1994: 415). The effect of international experience on a teacher's classroom practice cannot be completely separated from the effect of experiences on a teacher's life. Therefore, in this study I have included the teacher's life abroad outside of the classroom and the teacher's self-analysis of personal as well as professional transformation.

A SOCIAL PURPOSE

An unanalyzed story could be just an interesting tidbit of information. Nancy Zeller (1995: 76) considers the real dilemma to be whether the goal is to interpret or present the data. Ivor Goodson (1995) argues that telling stories, such as emancipatory narratives, without theoretical frames and contexts of meaning plays into the hands of the economic and political power brokers in this world by failing to analyze critically the structures that are the context for these individual stories. In only telling the story of a teacher's life and allowing it to speak for itself, we may be ignoring "these contextual parameters which so substantially impinge on and constantly restrict the teacher's life" (p.96). For example, when one of the teachers in this study returned from abroad, the principal of her school showed little interest in her experience, expecting her—like another of my participants—to go back into her "slot" as if she had just returned from a weekend trip, not an intense life-transforming international experience.

I agree with Goodson (1995: 89-98) that to have meaning, stories must be told in context, "stories of action within theories of context." Stories then can be the beginning of a collaboration, an analysis of the social context in which we live as a first step to changing that context—in this case classroom practice—for the better. Therefore, it is my choice to interpret these narratives rather than simply to present them. This interpretation is within the purview of critical theory; that is, with a purpose to gain understanding about teacher cultural learning, to help educators work toward a more creative and democratic learning environment in the schools.

The teachers in this book demonstrate how "we make the road by walking" (a poem by the Spanish poet, Antonio Machado). Their personal and compelling descriptions enhance our understandings of the pain, pleasure, and challenge of discovering themselves in another cultural world. One of the teachers, Ellen Stacey, laments her insistence on fixing her damaged tire in Japan, saying, "I was too American, too Westernized. I had to take care of the matter right away." Ellen acknowledged that her "American" proclivities bumped up against the Japanese way of handling problems. The Japanese had wanted to take care of her in their own way, but she admitted: "I didn't allow them." Mary Ehrhardt laughed about being "shelved" along with many Chinese travelers on the three-tiered hard seat sleepers from Shanghai to Beijing. Denise Green, who has relatively light skin for an African-American, made sure her Japanese students were aware of her race by showing the kaleidoscope of skin color in her family and classroom with slides.

As a researcher and colleague, I walked in their shoes for awhile, sharing their memories. I have worked to portray their stories within the framework of what I have learned from them that has value for educators and school policymakers. I organized their stories into another perspective, one that means a great deal to those who believe that the connections among humans irrespective of cultural or national boundaries are most important. In the tradition of peace activists such as Elise Boulding (1990), for peace and cooperation to supplant war and strife, we need to encourage "worldly teachers" to model for their students, colleagues, and communities the kind of connections among people that will lead to a better world for us all.

INTRODUCTIONS

Because this chapter sets the stage for a thematic analysis of data in the following nine chapters, it is important that the reader have a clear view of each participant within the context of his or her work and life. Below are descriptions of six special teachers who chose to study and experience a culture very different from their own and share their experiences with others.

*Ed Donovan** is sixty-five years old and not talking about retirement yet. He is a pale, blue-eyed Caucasian of German and Irish ancestry, of medium build. His head is Yul Brynner or Michael Jordan bald, depending on your generation, and he smiles often. He speaks slowly and precisely, clearly thinking about what he is saying unless the emotion of the moment overtakes him and he says something like, "It was a ball!" referring to his experience returning to visit friends or traveling "hard seat" on a train in China. Ed is married with four older children and several grandchildren.

He works in a high school in a wealthy suburb on the east side of Detroit surrounded by trees, lovely green grounds, and large houses, which reminded me of Jean Anyon's (1981) description of the executive elite school in a study of the effect of social class on schooling. In his curriculum vitae is the statement that this school was "cited for excellence by the National Commission of Education." During my visit to the school, I noticed that it was very clean and the classrooms had many large windows, which always impresses me because I taught for

---

*Names and some details have been changed to protect participants' anonymity.

ten years in a "fortress" high school without windows. The classroom in which I interviewed Ed was a clean, light, and airy, with a minimum of student graffiti on desks. Ed had taught at this school for thirty years, before that having taught writing and American literature for five years at a rough training school in Detroit, where only two of 400 students did not have juvenile police records. Ed currently teaches in what he refers to in his CV as a "team taught, humanities-oriented course with special emphasis on writing and ritual reading."

Ed has been an active member of the Michigan and National Council for the Social Studies, an officer in the local parent-teacher association and the local teacher association, with the elected positions of vice president, executive boardmember, treasurer, and representative of the state teacher organization, the MEA. He has been chosen the school district's Teacher of the Year, received recognition from the University of Chicago as "an outstanding high school teacher," has been a member of the North Central Association evaluation team and a consultant for a large school district in northern Michigan. Although I had known Ed through the international education network, I knew nothing about these achievements and activities before I interviewed him.

Ed is the son of a doctor who studied and worked in Germany during the 1930s. Ed's father was accompanied by his wife, who traveled to Russia during their years in Europe. His description of maids from abroad who had helped raise him indicates that he was brought up in a family of some means. Ed's schooling through college was in private Catholic schools.

Ed's international study and experience began early in his career, when he was asked to teach about China within the humanities framework. He educated himself informally and formally in anthropology to prepare for this work. His first experience in China was a yearlong English teaching assignment at a medical college in Kunming in 1986-87, accompanied by his wife Heather. Subsequently, he taught during the summers of 1991 and 1995 at a provincial university and a teacher's college. During 1995, he traveled widely from Beijing to Hainan Island to see friends with whom he had been communicating for nine years since his first yearlong experience in China.

Mary Ehrhardt is fifty-four years old and also not discussing retirement. She is a pale Caucasian of German descent, blue-eyed with short, curly light brown hair. She has a slight build and is in good physical condition, as her description of living in China will attest. Mary speaks rather softly but with near perfect diction, her descriptions being precise and full of detail. Often in telling a story her eyes sparkled and she laughed quietly, or in the case of her concern for individuals in China, her face became deeply serious and thoughtful. I interviewed Mary in her house, although I have visited her school and classroom. She provided refreshments of Chinese tea, a gift to her from a Chinese friend in Beijing, which went well with the homemade chocolate chip cookies she had prepared.

Mary teaches second grade in an old, well-known New England preparatory school, where most students' families pay high tuition and other students are given scholarships to provide some demographic and social balance. The school is in a lovely, hilly, wooded section of a small town. Its buildings feature high ceilings and cozy rooms adequate for small class sizes with tables or desks in circles, and large windows in every room. Mary's bulletin boards are full of colorful and interesting pictures and student work. Mary has taught at this school for nearly thirteen years, which qualified her for a yearlong sabbatical to use as she wished. This was her opportunity to experience China as a teacher and learner, a subject she had taught and for which she had developed curricula for nine years.

Mary majored in English at Oberlin College and received an Ed.M. degree at Harvard University's Graduate School of Education. During the 1960s she taught third grade for six years in Oberlin, Ohio, and Ann Arbor, Michigan, where she was a "cooperating teacher for student teachers" and "devised a plan for multi-aged grouping and team teaching." Mary then devoted herself to raising two children and being a docent at a local art museum until she returned to teaching, first as a parent volunteer in 1976 and in 1984 as a full-time teacher. As a parent volunteer, she coordinated "Creative Arts" from 1976 to 1978 in which, according to her CV, she administered an enrichment program on a "budget of $900 which provided cultural experiences to augment the curricula."

During the summers of 1985, 1987, 1990, 1992, 1993, and 1994 she attended summer institutes in the following areas: elementary math, teaching writing in the elementary school, reading and writing, computer usage, and Chinese language. During 1991-92, she took a yearlong multicultural training course at her school. She has been active in the PTA boards, school committee elections, the Whole Language Association and the Unitarian Society. Before I interviewed Mary, I thought I knew about her accomplishments until she gave me her CV.

Mary lived in Beijing with the family of a Chinese teacher at the school where she taught for four months in the winter and spring of 1995. She commuted to school, like most Chinese people, on her bicycle, cycling a half hour each way. Mary taught English to elementary and middle school students and organized a weekly seminar for the teachers at a "key" school (an official term designating a school as excellent and conveying it as an academic track school receiving particular support and carefully selected students). As an exchange teacher with one other U.S. teacher and five U.S. students, she prepared for her experience by studying Chinese with them and planned and supervised with her colleague their trips in China.

Denise Green is a slightly built, light-skinned African-American woman in her early 40s. She has high cheekbones and an expressive face and shining eyes, which widen appreciably when she is telling a story. We laughed together at her funny and creative descriptions of herself, others, and events in Japan. She stood up and acted out the posture and demeanor expected of her as an American exchange teacher in Japan. She filled her stories with a great deal of descriptive detail that helped me envision what it was like to be there. Denise was my first interview in this study and our conversation lasted late into the evening. She spoke so fervently and quickly that I gave up trying to take some written notes and relied on the tape recorder. This interview with Denise helped me feel that I was exploring something worthwhile and meaningful to her as well as to myself, a feeling that has been borne out in all of my subsequent interviews.

Denise teaches reading in a racially mixed elementary school in Indianapolis, Indiana. Before she went to Japan, she had been teaching a third- and fourth-grade split class. She had taught in Little Rock, Arkansas, after graduating from the University of Indiana during the early 1970s. She had taught for twelve years in Bloomington, Indiana, and Indianapolis before she went to Japan during the 1987-88 school year. During Denise's junior year at the University of Indiana, she was a university exchange student in Ghana, where she studied and traveled widely, learning one of the local dialects.

Denise's family came to Indiana from Prince Edward County, Maryland, where her father taught history, losing his job at the height of the Civil Rights crusade. He later received a Ph.D. in educational administration at Indiana University. Denise's schooling was in the public schools of the Bloomington area during the 1960s. The stories she tells about her schooling, unlike those of the other teachers in this sample, are full of the tension she experienced as a minority African-American student in a dominant majority social context. She describes struggles against racism in her school experience, while the other teachers in this study describe a bland, mostly unexciting and uneventful K-12 experience. The key factor in Denise's family background was the consistently strong support of her parents. They encouraged her quest for knowledge including studying languages and her struggle for equal treatment in the schools.

0027105

Denise's experience in Japan was as an exchange teacher of English for seven months under a state-run program that required that she take one year of Japanese to participate. After a six-week training program in Japan, she was assigned to a different school every two weeks for the duration of her five-month stay. She planned and taught English classes with Japanese teachers, and presented slides in talks about American culture, in which she showed family and school pictures portraying the tremendous diversity in American family and school life when compared with Japan. During these self-introductory talks, she made her status as a divorced African-American woman clear, especially when these issues were left out of a Japanese educator's introduction of her. She believes that her light skin had caused many Japanese to consider her white, a factor that she felt made her treatment different than it would have been had she been darker-skinned. The window on American culture that she opened for Japanese students and teachers was quite different from those of the other participants.

Denise has continued to study Japanese language, having studied Spanish and French during her high school and college years. She has presented many workshops and programs for teachers at the state and national levels about Japan as well as other subjects, such as reading.

Bill Notebaum, also in his early 40s, is a tall, large-boned man with a well-manicured beard and intense blue eyes. When I had met Bill several years earlier, he had seemed very different. I hardly recognized him in a dark blue suit on release time working to develop a new charter school in his district in a suburb of Cleveland, Ohio. While in a rather pressure-filled context, Bill spoke in a relaxed and thoughtful way about his international experience and how it had affected him. He spoke more theoretically about his thought processes and evolving ideas as he developed the issues and experiences that were a precursor to his study tour in Japan. He considers the latter to be a catalyst for his subsequent decision to ask for administrative support in 1991 to initiate and direct an international high school with an International Baccalaureate degree.

In the wealthy public school district where Bill taught, many of the homes surrounding this school could hardly be seen through gates and trees. This school would fit well within Anyon's (1981) description of the most elite schools, where some students are being prepared to become CEOs of Fortune 500 companies. There is a relaxed, laid-back atmosphere here, and the rooms have large windows letting in a great deal of natural light and allowing students to look out at wide expanses of green grass and trees.

Bill is married, with two teen-age daughters. He taught English, Advanced Placement economics, and Advanced Placement European history. Bill's most recent project is the International High School, a public magnet school in which five school districts in the Cleveland area have decided to participate, with students and teachers who apply to study and teach there. This school will emphasize international and cross-cultural studies, its curriculum and teachers implementing team-teaching programs with authentic performance-based assessments taking the place of traditional multiple-choice and true-false tests. The curriculum will include many different language and cultural studies courses, including Japanese, Chinese, and Russian.

Bill's CV includes many publications and examples of leadership such as his membership on "the writing team for the Ohio Social Studies Task Force to write a new state core curriculum" and the "U.S. That Can Say Yes" described in Chapter 9, in addition to all of his work making economics presentations and writing papers for educational outreach programs.

Bill's family was from a Dutch Calvinist community in Pennsylvania. He went to private Dutch Calvinist schools from elementary school through college, by which time he was aware of the narrow perspectives inherent in those parochial schools and the community. However, his parents lived in Japan twice for six months at a time while he was in high school in the United States. His father was in a business relationship with a Japanese company.

Bill's Japanese experience followed a five year period of studying U.S.-Japanese trade relationships. While his actual experience in Japan was only a one-month study tour, he credits this experience as being the catalyst for his decision to go forward with the International High School idea. He visited schools and businesses in Japan, where he observed practices such as the Japanese homeroom, which he plans to incorporate into the International High School. I consider Bill an "Abe Lincoln" example because his long-term independent study reminded me of the self-education of our former president. This in-depth international study dominated his relatively short, but powerfully motivating experience in Japan. His experience is different from the others in this regard and provides another perspective on the impact of in-depth international study and experience.

Ellen Stacey is a tall Caucasian woman of Lebanese and Irish descent in her early 40s. Her curly reddish blond hair was pulled back, giving her a distinguished look. She speaks in a low, resonant voice and has a warm down-to-earth manner, often using her hands and arms dramatically to make and emphasize points. She was the most emotional of my participants, expressing strongly positive and negative feelings. She was also the most ambivalent of these teachers about what this international experience meant to her. The contrast between the kind of story she told about her first experience in Japan and her second experience there was stunning. Transcripts of my interviews with her were the most difficult of all six to analyze because of the complexity of and ambivalence she felt toward her experience.

Ellen was educated at private Catholic schools through college. She is single and has taught English with a concentration on writing skills in the inner city of Milwaukee for twenty-four years. Since she is only certified to teach elementary school, she now teaches English and Japanese to eighth-grade African-American students and an evening Japanese course at a local community college.

The description of her work life the year before she went to Japan almost exhausted me: workshops during weekends as a writing consultant for the state; Japanese classes two nights and study group another two nights each week; and responsibility for National Honor Society at her school in addition to teaching seventh- and eighth-graders full time. She has written articles, such as "All the World's a Classroom for Cultural Exchange," for the local newspaper and the reading association. She was chosen the Outstanding Teacher of the Year for the schools of Milwaukee in 1989 and the Teacher of the Year for the school where she worked in 1990. She presented many workshop programs, such as "Japan, Powerful Molder of Young Minds," in addition to the subject of writing.

Ellen's first experience in Japan in 1988-89 was similar to that of Denise Green. It was a state program that required a year of Japanese language study. After her six-week orientation in Japan, she was assigned to teach English and work with teachers one school a month for the next five months. Ellen's second experience in Japan, for three years between August 1990 and August 1993, occurred through a sister-city arrangement rather than the Department of Education. For two years she was assigned to a different school each day, the third year first semester, one school a week, and the last semester to one school every six weeks.

Paul Vandemere is a medium-height, Caucasian man of Dutch descent with wavy, brown hair in his early 40s. He has the deeply resonant voice of a gifted and eloquent speaker, which he is. Paul is well read and knowledgeable about many subjects, but he seems to enjoy most speaking about international issues and experiences, especially his two-year experience in Japan. Paul is an associate principal of a high school in a sprawling suburb of Chicago. The school was built with many windows along corridors brightened by lockers painted royal blue and yellow. He had returned from two years in Japan in 1986 to direct and teach in the newly created East Asian Institute in his district until 1994, when he decided to change his career path and work in school administration.

Paul grew up in a family and community that included teacher union leaders, civil rights activists, friends from Israel, neighbors from Saudi Arabia and exchange students from Nigeria. After studying international relations in college, Paul's first teaching assignment was in Cairo, Egypt, for two years, after which he returned to his home area and began teaching social studies, forensics, and debate courses at the local high school. After ten years of teaching and coaching debate and forensics, Paul attended classes at the Fletcher School of Diplomacy to better prepare himself for teaching international studies. When he saw an ad from a Japanese company that needed an American skilled in forensics and public speaking, he and his wife, a veterinarian, applied and were accepted in the program.

Paul's two-year experience in Japan was unique. He tutored executives, some of which were CEOs of Fortune 500 companies. Although he visited Japanese schools, traveled widely, and participated in cultural events, the part-time work he did with Japanese executives precluded his involvement in the schools, except as an occasional observer. It is interesting that he was as impressed with the Japanese homeroom concept as Bill Notebaum and hoped to influence his colleagues to include it in his high school.

Since Paul returned from Japan, he has participated on numerous state committees to write state-mandated core curriculum guidelines for social studies to include global studies. He has worked hard with his colleagues to include world studies as a required course for all students in the high school. In 1993, Paul was chosen Teacher of the Year for his district and for the state. He was given release time to travel widely in the state to speak at schools and to community groups. Paul incorporated some of his international experiences into these talks as an advocate of international education in tandem with school reform and excellence in education, which his own life and work personified.

We will get to know these teachers fairly well in the next seven chapters. Our focus will be to understand their background and lives before their international experiences in Chapter 3, their experience teaching abroad in Chapter 4 and living abroad in Chapters 5 and 6, their views about the impact of their experience on their pedagogy in the classroom in Chapters 7 and 8, and their perspectives about how their experience might have been transformative for them and why in Chapter 9. In most cases during these chapters, their voices speak for themselves in their narratives.

3

The Person, The Life: Why Go?

Every one of these six teachers seized the moment "jumped at the opportunity," to have this experience. All had studied their respective areas intensively, several for years, before embarking on their international adventure. Five of them had demonstrated an interest in learning about other cultures during their family and K-12 schooling experiences. Their attitudes toward learning and education are overwhelmingly positive. This chapter will explore the backgrounds, home and school environments in which these teachers were educated, college and post-college influences, their early teaching experiences evolving into the kind of teacher they considered themselves to be before the experience, and their attitudes toward learning, what I will call their learning style. This chronology helps to put each phase of these teachers' lives in the context of their prior experiences. The one theme that connects all of these phases and relates to the teachers' decision to engage in international experience and cultural learning is their learning style. An analysis of the latter partly defines these teachers. Who is this person before she embarks on a potentially life-changing experience and how might this identity affect her experience?

WHY GO?

Why in the world would anyone go through such a life-disrupting experience even for one month, much less for three years, when he could have spent a month or more sunbathing, golfing, and shopping on Barbados? Teaching is one of the most stressful occupations in the United States. It would seem that rest and relaxation ought to be the reward for people who are charged with the responsibility of motivating children and young people to learn, some with 150 or more high school students whose part-time schooling competes for their attention and commitment with jobs (for cars), TV, and parties. Reports abound about the "dead wood," the many burned-out teachers shuffling to retirement, hoping their bored and rebellious students won't slip drugs into the strong coffee they use to help them get through each day until stomach ulcers take away that one small crutch. Why would veteran teachers want to take on the daunting task of learning about another culture, when information overload is already causing anxiety and cultural critics are shouting that we are all too ignorant about our own culture to function above a very low level in American society? Wouldn't a teacher be too exhausted after working with often unruly, disruptive, disrespectful young Americans to devote months or years to the study of another culture? Wouldn't a teacher feel too fatigued from working with students who have had too much too soon or too little, too much hurt, too much disappointment, to expand his own knowledge, even to study a second language at age fifty-four? Who are these teachers? What drives them? Why did they go?

THEIR REASONS

"I jumped at the opportunity." Mary Ehrhardt

Mary Ehrhardt used her sabbatical to participate in a student-teacher exchange program between the Chinese students and teachers in Beijing and her own hometown, Cambridge, Massachusetts. Denise Green says, "I jumped at the chance" to participate in a teacher exchange program in Japan run by the state Department of Education in Indiana. "My hand shot up. . . . My colleagues thought I was crazy," said Ed Donovan, when he and his fellow faculty members were asked by a program leader if "any of you guys were interested in teaching" for a year in the People's Republic of China. Bill Notebaum was one of twenty-five teachers chosen out of 800 applicants to attend an all-expenses-paid monthlong educational experience in Japan, which included visits to schools, businesses, and cultural sites. Paul Vandemere answered an advertisement in the Teacher Association paper for an overseas teaching assignment in Japan with an interpreting company to teach English, public speaking and forensics to business executives.

The common motivating factor among these teachers was a desire to improve and deepen their knowledge of the subject matter they were teaching. Most had studied for years the history, geography, and culture of the area they eventually lived in or visited before they decided to go. Paul Vandemere, Mary Ehrhardt, Ed Donovan, and Bill

Notebaum had taught about the area, with little or no formal education about the subject. They each embarked on their self-education projects in order to offer more to students than the text and to enrich their classes. Initially, one might say, the curriculum and text educated the teachers. However, these teachers expanded on and went far beyond this elementary survival stage in teaching a new subject by doing their own research and/or going back to school for more formal education. Several of these teachers were also feeling unchallenged, burned out, or depressed about their lives and work—another motivation for the decision to go.

Ten years before going to China, Ed Donovan had taken summer courses in anthropology at the University of Minnesota "just to pick up something to share" with his students. He viewed his year in China in much the same light. In the 1960s he had been hired to teach a humanities curriculum that included a unit about China, about which he knew very little. It was then that he began his efforts to educate himself about China. By the time his "hand shot up" some twenty years later, he felt the need "to get my batteries recharged. . . . I was burning out." The only possible obstacle was his wife Heather's feelings about living in a remote area of southwestern China for a year. A Christmas party was held with professors from the sponsoring university and the university in China in which his wife, a nurse who could also teach at the medical college, was "hooked" by the excitement of going on this adventure with her husband.

Denise Green had been fascinated by languages, Egyptian hieroglyphics, and Chinese characters as a young person. She liked to imagine what the strange words might mean and vowed one day to go to China. Denise felt that her experience in Japan and a side trip to China would help her make those places "come alive" for her children. The enjoyment she had experienced learning Spanish and her general interest in other languages and cultures encouraged her to tackle Japanese as a way of qualifying for the state teacher-exchange program in Japan.

After recuperating from surgery, Ellen Stacey learned from a friend about an exchange program similar to the one Denise Green had experienced. "I was really depressed at the time" she said. Ellen entered the program with the hope of qualifying to go to Japan. The prerequisite for the program was a one-year Japanese language and culture course. Ellen found that learning Japanese was "too demanding" and time-consuming in addition to her responsibilities as a reading consultant for the state Department of Education and full-time teaching, but her friend urged her to stay as a study partner. In spite of her ambivalence about these classes, Ellen was one of three out of fifty teachers in the program selected to teach English in Japan for seven months. Ellen expressed less enthusiasm about going abroad than the other five teachers. This becomes more significant as we explore her experience there.

Paul Vandemere, like Ed Donovan, was feeling somewhat "burned out" by heavy professional demands. He had been teaching international relations and non-Western civilization in addition to coaching winning teams in debate and forensics. He, like Ed Donovan, felt the need to educate himself more fully about the non-Western world. Therefore, he took courses at the Fletcher School of Diplomacy at Tufts in the summers of 1983 and 1984, where he became motivated by East Asian scholar William Perry to learn more about East Asia. Perry made this area "come alive" for Paul Vandemere, and Paul, like Denise Green, aspired to use his study and experience to do the same for his own students. He and his wife, a veterinarian, chose to accept a 40 percent cut in pay to go to Japan for two years.

Because he was low in seniority at the high school, Bill Notebaum was asked to teach economics. He had majored in history in college and had not taken economics. Unfortunately, this is a common occurrence in U.S. high schools (Powell, Farrar, Cohen, 1985). Bill began his own crash course in the area the summer before he taught it. This began a six-year course of self-directed study spurred by his students' questions about the trade imbalance between the United States and Japan, especially in the automotive industry. Like Paul Vandemere and Ed Donovan, his effort to educate himself led him to study the U.S.-Japan trade conflict with as unbiased an approach as he could. Bill was not comfortable with his students' assumptions about U.S.-Japan trade.

> The principal point of view of my students, I think, would reflect the prevailing view at that time, particularly among automobile executives, that Japanese competition was unfair, it was unbalanced, that it was a result of extremely inexpensive labor costs in Japan, that their industry was overly both protected and subsidized by government. Being the normal social studies teacher that I am, I always wanted to make sure that I bring some balance to any position the students take or even that I take. I just wasn't comfortable with what was assumed to be true.

He formed a liaison with an official in the Federal Reserve Board to present workshops to educators on the U.S.-Japan trade relationship. The workshops fulfilled part of the Reserve Board's educational mission. Bill was granted a fellowship to visit Japan for one month, the high point of his international study and experience.

The desire to educate herself in the area she was to teach drove Mary Ehrhardt to begin a ten-year study of China. This culminated in her living with a family and teaching for four months in a key elementary and middle school in Beijing. Just as Ed Donovan, Paul Vandemere, and Bill Notebaum felt they had to be better prepared in their subject matter before teaching it, Mary Ehrhardt felt she needed to delve into the subject matter first before she taught her second graders. "I had to be a learner first" in order to construct a curriculum for her students, she said. She researched in the library, "read a very great deal" about China, viewed and took copious notes on the BBC *Heart of the Dragon* (1984) series shown on PBS in the United States. She used the "wonderful materials from Stanford," the SPICE program—a nonprofit organization that specializes in teaching materials about East Asia. After several years of teaching the China unit, she did all the preliminary work for a Fulbright-Hays grant in order to deepen her knowledge to share with her students: "I was ineligible as an early elementary teacher for a Fulbright-Hays grant. But the networking that I did to achieve that actually turned out to be very, very helpful when I had the sabbatical and knew that I wanted to try once again."

The ten-year effort she put into learning about China helped Mary decide that she wanted to live with a family and experience life as a Chinese person might as much as was possible. She felt "shaky" about her knowledge of issues such as the communist system and the place of religion within the society: "There were enough little seeds of doubt in my mind about what I was doing that I really felt I needed the reassurance of first-hand experience." She felt that she must know the subject matter well before she could appropriately develop the curriculum for her second-graders. Deborah Ball and G. William McDiarmid (1990) suggest that a teacher must know his subject matter well before he can effectively translate it into curriculum for students. Mary wanted to know her subject matter well enough to be able to teach it to her second-graders and to have a clear view of what she expected the students to know and understand:

> I guess that my educational training, especially in science and social studies, primary sources were so important that I felt I needed to really delve into these topics and become a learner myself. I was not going to use the textbook. Therefore, I needed to learn a lot and then develop a curriculum that would be appropriate for children at the grade level that I was teaching.

Dewey promotes this kind of knowing in the concept of a teacher's "psychologizing" the subject matter, the way a teacher translates his in-depth knowledge to connect with the understandings of a small child and helps him build and develop his own knowledge base. Perhaps this is what Paul Vandemere and Denise Green mean when they talk about making the area "come alive," a fascination with learning about another culture, another country, and other people in which the strange becomes familiar to themselves and to their students.

Finally, they traveled abroad to learn, to break out of the cobwebs restricting the mind, to know a little more, to understand the complexities and dilemmas others face within a society different from their own, and a family different from their own. Considering family influences will help us begin to understand their motivations, why they were so open to the chance for an international experience. They each considered family and community influences to have been very important influences on their later interest in international study and experience.

FAMILY AND COMMUNITY

"My parents were 'internationalists.'"   Paul Vandemere

Paul Vandemere's parents were committed members of the United Nations Association, and his mother was also a member of the WILPF. They were politically active charter members of the United Auto Workers and the first teacher union in the state. Close family friends from Israel who visited regularly at Christmas were working with the Rockefeller Foundation to help new governments in countries such as India establish themselves in the late 1940s. These Jewish friends "opened up worlds to my brother and me" and their stories about India and Africa fascinated him. The family also hosted exchange students from Nigeria in the early 1960s. Paul remembers "endless summer nights" on his neighbor's porch discussing world politics and issues in a small, almost rural Midwestern town. Down this dirt road drove a limousine with Saudi Arabian flags flying. His neighbors were a Lebanese family who were host to Crown Prince Faisal, soon to become the king of Saudi Arabia.

Paul Vandemere's father died when he was thirteen years old. His brother went to India for two years as a member of the Peace Corps, and Paul taught in Egypt for his first two years of teaching. Because his family was involved in the Civil Rights movement, he remembers when he was a high school student marching with Dr. Martin Luther King and hearing a version of the "I Have a Dream" speech. Bristling, he remembers when their neighbor forbade her daughters from playing ice hockey with Paul and his brother because they included their house guest, a Nigerian exchange student. The ugliness of the woman's racism stood out starkly for Paul, who was only twelve or thirteen years old, as did his parents' outrage at her behavior. They took him and his brother to lectures about international issues by speakers such as John Kenneth Galbraith.

> My parents were definitely internationalists from their perspective. They were strong members of the United Nations Association before it became controversial, back in the '50s. My mom was a member of the WILPF, Women's International League for Peace and Freedom. My parents had a very strong interest in politics and in social issues and in international issues. We had exchange students from Nigeria, from India, and other places who would come and stay. Good friends of the family would come every Christmas. He [one friend] helped Golda Meir and others set up things in Israel in 1948 and 49. Their friends and their lives opened up on one level worlds to my brother and myself.

Like Paul Vandemere, Bill Notebaum involved himself in the Civil Rights movement by leading a group of high school students to lobby Christian Reform Church (Dutch Calvinists) ministers to speak out about civil rights to their congregations. He was, he thought, reacting to what he called the "mean-spirited, soft racism" of his community. In spite of being vehemently criticized by community members, Bill and his friends volunteered at day care and job training centers in the inner city to do odd jobs painting and fixing up those facilities.

Bill's parents' business experience living in Japan while Bill was in high school significantly influenced his later interest in that country. During his junior year, when his parents left him with his older sister's family to live in Japan for six months, he was "fascinated" by the "crates full of stuff" that kept arriving from Japan.

> My father was in the textile business and when I was in high school, Japan was moving very dramatically into the textile business. It was one of the major areas that they were moving into at that time. His company became involved in a joint venture with a Japanese company and he traveled overseas to Japan. . . . I was a junior in high school, I think. His travel experience in Japan was fascinating to me and we talked on the phone. He sent letters, and he came back with just crates full of stuff. We ate with chopsticks for years. . . . My dad and my mom too were always very complimentary. They were never derogatory. My dad said he was always warmly received and so, I don't remember much Japanese hostility in the '60s, but if there was any, my parents certainly didn't represent that.

The fascination with learning from relatives' travel was not something only Bill experienced. Mary Ehrhardt and Ellen Stacey were also fascinated by the artifacts within their grandfathers' sea chests and their stories about traveling abroad. All of Mary Ehrhardt's grandparents were teachers, although her father became a businessman. Her two grandfathers had traveled widely in the United States, Canada, Mexico, and Europe for their own edification. Ellen Stacey's Irish grandfather had traveled to many places in East Asia, including China and Japan, and "had brought back many mementos from Japan and the Orient when he was over there. My grandmother always wore this beautiful silk robe. When she died, I got it. It's bright blue, and so in my grandmother's house she always had my grandfather's military sea trunk. . . . There was always that mystique."

Ed Donovan's father, a medical doctor, and his mother lived in Germany while his father worked and studied at the University of Berlin for a year in 1933 and in 1936 (Ed was three and six years old). Ed and his siblings were cared for by family members and maids. His mother traveled all over Europe and Russia during these years. He remembers many political discussions at the dinner table in which his father, a great admirer of Harry Truman, chided his "dyed-in-the-wool Republican" wife, by bringing up Harding and Grant. "It was hard to defend Harding," says Ed with a twinkle in his eye. Ed also admired his father and uncles for displaying a sense of tolerance unusual for the time. His father had escorted the first African-American man as a guest into the oldest exclusive white men's club in the city and supported him later as the first African-American man on the Detroit school board.

> The influence for me has always been my father, I think. He was a doctor and was maybe one of the more tolerant people about race particularly. He brought in the first black man to the DAC; he had to bring him in the back door, but he got him in, got him served dinner. This would be in the '50s. His [Ed's father] comment was that "if you need a blood transfusion, it doesn't make a difference what color a guy's skin is. You need the blood, you're going to take it."

Denise Green's family supported her interest in language and cultural studies and provided a powerful example of the importance of struggling against great odds and barriers to get an education. She heard many family stories of her father's struggle against racism as a teacher in Prince Edward County, Maryland, during the 1950s and '60s. When Denise had to fight not to be cast as a maid, being the only African-American in the eighth-grade production, or to get approval to take more than one language at a time in high school, her parents steadfastly supported her. Her father's attainment of a Ph.D. in education in spite of many difficulties impressed on her that there was "no excuse" for her not to work hard at her own education and to succeed. Although her parents did not overtly encourage her interest in the world, when she expressed an interest they supported her. The cultural struggle that her parents had to wage as African-Americans trying to reach their potential in a white racist society could have set the stage for Denise's great curiosity about and interest in world languages and cultures. She remembers feeling humiliated along with three other African-Americans in the majority white early elementary class when the music teacher brought in the score of a Negro spiritual, showing a picture of slaves bent over working in a cotton field. "We knew we weren't like that," Denise said.

The family influences on these teachers represent a complex range of experience, from the curiosity surrounding artifacts and stories of grandfathers' experiences abroad to more intense parental influence in the example of parents who lived abroad for six months to a year at a time during, for example, Ed Donovan's early childhood and Bill Notebaum's teen years.

Paul Vandemere considered his family's commitment to the values of social justice within the purview of the Civil Rights movement to have been influential in his later decision to study and experience another culture. James Lynch (1989, 1992) considers social justice the common element in international and multicultural education. The family experience of Paul Vandemere, Ed Donovan, Bill Notebaum, and Denise Green gives credibility to Lynch's perspective.

K-12 SCHOOLING

"We felt a combination of anger, being offended and shame." Denise Green

There are not many positive examples among the K-12 schooling experiences of these teachers during their "apprenticeship of observation," as is evidenced by Denise Green's statements about her music teacher, who brought in an example of the typical anti-black stereotypes predominating in textbooks and teaching materials of the '50s and '60s. However, where teachers stood out as possible examples, the example did seem to support these teachers' later international learning. Denise fondly remembers only one teacher, an African-American, who taught a black history elective in high school to a majority African-American class in a mainly white school. This teacher functioned as an ombudsman for her students, especially when they were discouraged by white counselors from applying for college. She had been to Africa and taught the students about the great kingdoms in Africa, such as Timbuktu, before their devastation by slavery (Franklin, 1947/1956).

Ellen Stacey, who attended private schools during all of her K-12 and undergraduate education, considered her private Catholic education a positive influence. Ellen's Catholic schooling encouraged in her a tremendous respect for education, which she found reflected later within Japanese society. She said, "We all wore uniforms," not like the public school children, whom she and her classmates considered "outsiders."

Bill Notebaum, also educated in private religious schools, but within the Dutch Calvinist Church, considered the "publics" as "weird" because he and his school mates thought they did not go to church and were poor. In spite of this narrow perspective, Bill believes that the church and church school atmosphere fostered a sense of honesty and integrity in the children: "I went to church more hours than I would like to tell you. I was really brought up in a culture and a group that emphasized honesty and integrity and proper moral behavior, not to be a hypocrite and not to lie or to mislead people." This value system is important as background to his desire to do his own research on the U.S. and Japanese trade situations in as unbiased a way as possible. He later wrote an article, "The U.S. That Can Say 'Yes,' " a takeoff on a popular work in Japan at the time, *The Japan That Can Say No* (Ishihara, 1989) to emphasize the need to understand each other's position more fully.

Ed Donovan credited his Greek and Latin teachers at the Jesuit school with teaching him how to think and challenge text:

> The Greek teacher had been a former all-American football player out in California and had joined the Jesuits. The Latin teacher had been a champion Golden Gloves boxer in California and joined the Jesuits. The guy who was the Greek scholar got me involved in looking at cultures differently. The Latin scholar got me to think. In fact, I can remember him taking a swipe across the top of my head one time, telling me to use my head before he used it as a punching bag.

Bill Notebaum described a "Contemporary Problems" teacher whom he admired and "who actually felt that meaning and understanding were important. . . . He broke us up into groups and gave us topics, let us choose topics and we basically for the most part of the semester investigated those topics, and then did presentations on it and wrote papers on it. . . . I did mine on the Civil Rights movement, the black experience in America." This teacher's methods were progressive for the time because they included group work and investigative research on contemporary American issues such as civil rights. Bill and his friends made in class "presentations on racism," which led to their voluntarily making presentations to church youth groups and ministers after school. Their goal was to raise awareness within the Dutch church about civil rights.

> We started to ask for entry to young people's groups in all of these different churches and societies. You have Sunday school, you have catechism, you have hymn sings, you have young people's associations and all this kind of stuff. And so what we would ask to do is not just to attend but to do presentations on racism and racial views and the issue of the African-American experiences. That kind of branched out to where we started going to ministers and saying that racism and racial relations was an important issue and that they ought to be addressing it from the pulpit and not just speaking silently on it because it was too controversial. . . . We got quite a few of the ministers to give some pretty serious, heart-wrenching sermons and that's when people would challenge their views and we also asked for the right to hold meetings in church basements after church, voluntarily. So we stood up and said our piece and took our shots.

Mary Ehrhardt felt moved by the stories of her seventh-grade geography teacher, a Korean War veteran. These "great stories about the world . . . made it come alive" for Mary. In high school her Advanced Placement world literature class, which included reading the enthralling *Murder in the Cathedral* began her "lifelong love of literature" and influenced her to major in English at Oberlin College. However, the experiential, "learn by doing" approach in the Deweyan-inspired progressive private elementary school she attended in New Orleans helped motivate her to become an active learner, and caused her to seek out an experience in China very different from what most foreigners experience in that country.

Paul Vandemere remembers little about K-12 motivating influences in the public schools. Each of the remaining five teachers could name only one or two teachers who had motivated them to be learners, to seek out study and experience beyond the ordinary. It was college and post-college experience that seemed to be more meaningful than the bulk of their K-12 schooling.

These few examples of K-12 teachers who teachers feel positively affected their development make a rather negative statement about American public and private schooling from the 1940s through the

1960s. In most cases these teachers describe one or two outstanding teachers as exceptions to the rule. The general context of their K-12 schooling seemed of little relevance to these self-described, highly motivated learners. The criticism of Hyman Rickover (1959), James Conant (1959), and others of the lack of intellectual rigor and excitement in the schools of the '50s becomes cogent in the context of this study, as do the criticisms of the 1980s and early 1990s. This is one reason that the motivation of teachers to study another culture is important to analyze. With support, these teachers can change the context of the schools in which they teach by being examples to students and colleagues of vibrant, continuously learning adults. In most cases, the background and support of these teachers were in their homes, not their schools. The few positive examples of teacher models show that schools can have a much greater influence if more teachers are encouraged to take learning risks like these six teachers, to help change schools into authentic learning environments.

UNDERGRADUATE AND EARLY TEACHING INFLUENCES

"I saw what appeared to be a giant pajama party off in the corner of the Cairo airport." Paul Vandemere

An argument could be made that after Paul Vandemere had studied international relations in college and had been brought up among international influences with his family, friends, and neighbors, he would have been comparatively well prepared for his first international experience. His Arab neighbors facilitated a teaching position for him in Cairo, Egypt, during his first two years as a novice teacher. According to Paul, naiveté and ignorance reigned: "I did not study at all." He soon learned that the giant pajama party was actually people in traditional dress for their *hajj*, their pilgrimage to Mecca. He invited some of his Egyptian students over to his apartment for New Year's Eve, "treating them to submarine sandwiches complete with salami." His students were polite; "they didn't tell me about it." He had wanted "to do something very American, that they had never had before," so he offered them a variety of cheeses and meats, which they all ate except for the salami, pork being unacceptable to Muslims. "Egypt opened my eyes," Paul said. Even though learning in his family included world geography and history, this learning did not include cultural norms and customs.

I was in a sense not in Egypt. Literally, I was there, but not figuratively. I was living on an island in the middle of the Nile that was the diplomatic community, in an apartment complex university owned, went to the university and then came back and made occasional forays into parts of Cairo, but on a much more superficial basis than when I was in Japan.

Paul's experience in Cairo shows that many traditional international relations and history courses do not teach much about culture. Bill Notebaum realized this also when he tried to use his learning about U.S.-Japan trade issues as the basis for teaching a more general Japanese language and culture course. Although history and economics are part of culture, they do not constitute cultural learning. The idea of culture includes the way people behave within the context of their history and tradition, thus encompassing the gamut of human life in society. Therefore, to prepare adequately for an in-depth international experience, one would learn about the geography, art, religion, language, history, and cultural practices of the country to be visited. Paul was not adequately prepared, and he did not consider his experience to be in-depth. Paul felt that he was too isolated in what he later called a "Gaijin [foreign] ghetto" to have experienced Cairo in depth, the way he feels he did experience Japan. Being among the people in Japan helped him become more in tune with Japanese culture, for instance, being aware of such matters as how to present or receive a business card. This means that knowledge of specific aspects of a culture is not enough, that there must be a more holistic, Deweyan sense of connections. For example, how does the traditional tea ceremony connect with Japanese art, philosophy, religion, and history? Paul learned from his experience in Cairo that he wanted to know a culture beyond the surface level, which probably helped him do this in Japan.

Denise Green's student-exchange experience in Ghana during her college years was more in-depth than what Paul describes because she lived with Ghanaian students in the university dormitories. She also tried to learn some of the local language, although not formally, as she later did before her trip to Japan. Denise tried to explain her cultural experiences to an Indiana University professor of education and her African-American friends with little success: "How does one describe snow to a man in West Africa, who lived in a home made of scrap metal with a dirt floor and a bare bulb hanging from the ceiling for light, buckets to a community tap for water, and used an open fire with an exhaust hole in the ceiling for cooking?" Denise presented this problem to a University of Indiana education professor, who told her that she should have shaved off a piece of soap to show the man. Denise Green thought to herself, "But then I would be the quintessential 'Ugly American,' throwing away a precious commodity like soap in this demonstration."

During her undergraduate experience, she had tested into third-year Spanish, so she dropped French to concentrate on Spanish. A clerical error misfiling her application caused her to be sent to Africa instead of Latin America, an event she did not regret. She used the year to learn as much as she could from her Ghanian roommate and on side trips. In the process she picked up enough words and expressions in the local language to get by. She learned first-hand about the tremendous pressure on students in Ghana to succeed, causing some who did not to commit suicide every year. She compared this situation with the relative lack of pressure on university students in the United States, who can make up failed courses and who are given second chances.

> Because some [Ghanaian] people were the first kids in that community to go to college, so a lot was expected of them, while they were at the university and once they returned to their communities, to help pull others up. And some students felt very, very burdened by that responsibility. And I was glad I did not have that kind of responsibility. Every year, they told us there were kids who would commit suicide. When I was there, one did commit suicide because he felt he couldn't handle the exams because their exams are at the end of the year. There is one exam for each class. If you passed the exam, you passed the class. You failed the exam, you failed class. And you'd have to take the whole class again. It's not like a semester. And you didn't have a choice of electives like we do. There is a set curriculum. The thing about failing is if you had to repeat that one class, that could endanger your scholarship. . . . And that was a do-or-die situation. I really felt for those kids.

In contrast to Denise's and Paul's first-hand international experience, Bill Notebaum, a history major at Calvin College, was fascinated by the immigrant experience in American history. "Trained as a historian," he found the emphasis on objectivity a great value, that also complemented his strong sense of integrity: "When you realize your point of view and you pose a bias, at least be fully cognizant of it and be in control of it rather than have it control you."

This striving toward self-awareness of biases is basic to the work of George and Louise Spindler (1994), who promote the idea of cultural therapy, the self-analysis of one's cultural core, the enduring cultural selves that we take for granted and of which we are unaware of how strongly it colors our perceptions. Being aware of these biases helped Bill Notebaum analyze the U.S.-Japan trade conflict by trying to understand the Japanese point of view in addition to the ways the United States and Japan are deeply influenced by cultural factors.

Intellectual pursuits dominated Mary Ehrhardt's and Ed Donovan's college backgrounds. Art history, first experienced at Oberlin College, became Mary Ehrhardt's lifelong avocation. The art courses and excellent art museums on campus opened up this new world to her. To pursue this study, she spent one summer studying art in Europe. As a graduate student, she returned with her husband to study "specific works of art." They stayed in a number of family homes in the Netherlands, Switzerland, England, and Italy. These homestays appealed to her as a way to experience a culture, to develop personal relationships with individuals in the culture. It was here that she learned that it was easy to develop international friendships "that have lasted over the years." She still writes to friends and families that she met in Europe over thirty years ago. To Mary, meaningful cultural experience was not the art, the architecture, or the lovely scenery in themselves. It was her connections with the people whose lives included those things as part of their cultural tradition.

Ed Donovan majored in English and philosophy and later earned an M.A. in history. His Russian history teacher was taught by Alexander Kerensky, leader of the first Russian Revolution (February–October 1917) before the Bolsheviks took control under Lenin, Trotsky, and Stalin. After he had tried out the business world for a few years, he decided, as the oldest son of a medical doctor whose younger brothers became attorneys and doctors, that "I would do something really important, like teaching." This was a "tongue-in-cheek" statement, somewhat akin to Bill Notebaum's idea of being "only a high school teacher" when people gave him the backhanded compliment that he should be teaching college. It brings up the point of the low status of teaching in the United States particularly for men in their 40s or older. Ed says this ruefully because he is concerned about the quality of his teaching; however, professional character and status are still conferred on doctors and lawyers to a far greater degree than on excellent teachers.

These teachers felt that influences in their college and post-college lives had foreshadowed their decision to pursue an intensive international experience. Paul Vandemere, Denise Green, and Mary Ehrhardt had international experiences during and just after college, which caused them to seek out further, more in-depth international study and experience as veteran teachers. Ed Donovan and Bill Notebaum experienced a kind of learning in college that encouraged them to think more deeply and look for different perspectives. This exposure has bearing on the kind of teachers they have become and their choice to be cultural learners.

AS TEACHERS AND LEARNERS

"I was hopefully a good teacher." Bill Notebaum

Understanding what kind of teacher a person thought herself to be prior to an experience she considers to be transformative is difficult. These teachers struggled with the question even though they all considered themselves changed as a result of the experience; but determining the nature of the change was difficult for them to describe. I asked them to walk me through the sort of classroom, methods used, and relationships with students that they believed described their teaching practice before the experience. Bill Notebaum and Paul Vandemere considered themselves rather traditional teachers with respect to a teacher-centered approach. Only Mary Ehrhardt and Denise Green, the two elementary-level teachers, described somewhat progressive methodology as a regular feature of their classrooms before their international experience. Bill Notebaum, Paul Vandemere, and Ed Donovan described their approach to subject matter related to international issues as superficial, lacking in depth and a sense of reality before the experience.

Ellen Stacey, an exception in this group on this issue, described herself as a more creative and energetic teacher before her second experience teaching and living in Japan: "The students not only were writing, but they were creating for me. They were making commercials for intermissions on a program that I would, the kids would, write; we would help put it together. . . . I think I was much more creative before I went to Japan."

Denise Green became aware immediately on her first experience in a Japanese classroom of how different her teaching style was from what was expected of a teacher in Japan. She found that posture was extremely important. She described this by standing up in a very straight, rigid pose: "We were supposed to stand straight like this and not move as we lectured to the students." Leaning on something or, worse, sitting on a desk, was totally unacceptable. Even when sitting while another teacher spoke, a teacher was to sit ramrod straight, feet flat on the floor, no elbows on a desk or table.

Ed Donovan's monitor in China would stop him as he moved out beyond the podium to walk up and down the rows as he talked, take his arm and gently guide him back to the podium. The monitor eventually gave up after several weeks of Donovan's forgetting and pacing among the students as he had done for many years in the U.S. Ed and Denise Green came back more aware of how much more relaxed and interactive their teaching styles were than what they observed in China and Japan respectively.

As a teacher in Illinois, Paul Vandemere found himself learning the subject matter of his texts one day or week ahead of the kids on his own time. Students made meals related to each of the regions they studied. He invited speakers on culture from the university to talk to the kids. It was extremely limited and superficial, lacking in authenticity and depth.

> In the non-Western world course that I had developed, I did a section on East Asia. But again, it was primarily staying one day or at least a week or so ahead of the students in those first couple years. Certainly again it was more superficial and more traditional geography and history and the political system. . . . I had meals for each one of the regions that the kids made. I had people come in from different universities and did demonstrations on different aspects of their culture. But again, it was limited.

A picture of Mary Ehrhardt's teaching style before her experience in China emerges in what she chose to bring to China to share with the Chinese teachers and in examples of the China curriculum she developed for her American students before her experience in China. Role plays and many interactive games were a mainstay of her teaching in China, methods she did not observe in any Chinese classroom before her work with the teachers. For the nine years she taught the China curriculum in the second grade, the vehicle for study was a six-week role play trip to China. She described her initiation of the China unit this way:

> Just this afternoon, we have just recently flown to China. . . . It seems that second-graders are still pretty gullible and they do love pretending. They really get into taking the trip and do believe that they are in China and that their hotel rooms might look remarkably like their own homes, their own bedrooms at home. But they come back every day willing to travel on to someplace different. So this afternoon, we visited the home of a Chinese child and learned about the family and their activities and we are in Beijing for a few days now.

Mary Ehrhardt's role is that of tour guide. The students prepare for a month or so by comparing the geography of the United States and China, and they study the art, history, language, and culture of China as a prelude to their "trip." They make up passports, send for visas, plan an itinerary, and read about the places they will visit. Their parents sign permission slips, as is the school procedure for all field trips. "Occasionally, a parent is befuddled too, especially our new parents. They're not quite sure whether to sign this permission slip or not," Mary said. After studying the geography of the places they would visit, they decide what to pack, each child being "responsible for his or her own luggage." On the day of the trip,

> they bring with them, whether it's a backpack or a little suitcase on wheels, what they can manage on their own in China. By that time, they are not quite sure whether they are going or staying. Occasionally, there's a reluctant child, so occasionally a parent will come and have maybe even a reluctant or a teary good-bye because they're not quite sure whether they want to go to China or not. The trip takes about an hour. The classroom is set up like an airplane. . . . We have hexagonal tables and we rearrange them so they stretch them out like the wings of the airplane and I use a slide which we took of the nose of a 747 jetliner so that they actually feel like they are walking into a plane. Then, this is a multimedia event. We use the maps to just follow our route. We actually have tape-recorded a pilot in his takeoff and instructions to the passengers so that they actually do take off and they do hear from the pilot where they will be, what they should observe out of the window as we go across the United States. We land in San Francisco and refuel. We've talked about crossing the international dateline. So the trip proceeds with an in-flight movie and a meal served en route. When we finally land in Beijing, we're met by a Chinese customs official. And usually that is an exchange teacher from China who has been coached to role-play with us, checks the passports, asks the children in Chinese how old they are, what the purpose of their visit is, and how long they will be in China. When we've all deplaned, we then have a whole team of teachers ready to continue through the day and visit a children's palace, which is perhaps PE or art or music, and so we proceed during the day as if we've really arrived and are starting our trip. At the end of the day, the children go off to their respective hotels. It really is quite fun. I think this is a pretty typical social studies practice. I've heard about a lot of other trips, but this one is real even to the point of having seat belts and a little seat pocket in front of you where you can keep your passport and have magazines and things that you can read while you're flying.

This imaginary trip for second-graders demonstrates the kind of teacher Mary Ehrhardt was before her China experience, which she believes transformed her as a person and as a teacher. How she and the other teachers prepared for their own international experience is important to understand, in order to analyze how each of them functioned in a very different environment from the one in which he or she had been raised, schooled, and employed as teachers.

These teachers discussed the changes they perceived in their teaching practice after their international experience. Bill, Ed, and Paul described their pedagogy before their international experiences as being more traditional and superficial, lacking in imagination and ingenuity. Ellen described herself as an energetic, creative teacher before her three years in Japan. Even though Mary would be considered an extremely creative teacher before her experience, she felt that this experience greatly improved and enriched her work with second-graders. We will revisit this subject in much greater depth in Chapters 7 and 8.

THEIR PREPARATION

"I wanted badly to communicate [in China]." Mary Ehrhardt

Ed Donovan and his wife Heather attended several sessions in which program leaders presented "the unromantic side" of living and working for a year in a remote area of southwestern China, "so we were prepared." He feels that his years of teaching and learning about China were ample preparation. Paul Vandemere's teaching about China and his experience learning about Japan and China at the Fletcher School prepared him and his wife, Linda, for their two years of living and working in Japan. Neither Paul nor Bill Notebaum considered learning Chinese or Japanese, except at an extremely elementary level, limited mainly to greetings. Bill Notebaum candidly admits, "I don't think I have the kind of brain that learns languages very well," because he feels he has a learning disability in phonetics: "If you repeat a word ten times, I can't repeat it ten minutes later." His major preparation was the six years he studied economics as it is related to Japanese and American culture.

Denise Green and Ellen Stacey participated in an almost identical program that required the teachers to study Japanese in class from 6:00 P.M. to 10:00 P.M. two nights a week and study with a colleague from the class the other two evenings for one year, a daunting schedule for any full-time teacher. It seems amazing that Ellen persevered in this even though she "kept trying to drop out of it" because the language was so demanding of her time and effort. Denise Green seemed to enjoy her study of Japanese, even to the point of wanting to pursue it as the subject of another degree or to study for a year at Tokyo Christian University, so that she could subsequently teach "Japanese in [U.S.] public schools."

The summer before Mary Ehrhardt was to go to China, at age fifty-four, she took her first Chinese language class taught by the Chinese language teacher at the local high school in the district that had developed the exchange program with China. The other teacher chosen to teach in China had taken Chinese for three years in college. Mary Ehrhardt's classmates were the five high school students also chosen to go, some of whom had taken the Chinese course at their school. "I was a diligent student," Mary said. "I studied every day. . . . I found that it took a great deal of time and effort to acquire some language skills." The course included frequent conversation and used the pin yin form of Romanization, not the characters. She and the five students studied thirty lessons prepared by the Beijing Language Institute and became "pretty well acquainted in the process." They were tutored by Chinese high school students in the United States as part of the exchange program. The Americans befriended these students because, as Mary Ehrhardt noted, "It's pretty hard to be a teenager so far away from home. . . . [This] was the beginning of our exchange experience." Mary's preparation included intensive language study and relationships with individuals from that culture, a true exchange experience even before she took off on her own airplane trip to China.

Mary, Denise, and Ellen participated in rigorous, mandatory language and cultural studies before they flew to East Asia. All of them clearly benefited from this training. Mary considered this preparation indispensable to the character and quality of her experience, especially the language work, which enabled her to communicate with her host family. Neither Ed nor Paul thought their preparation, which did not include language work, was inadequate. Bill felt that the preparation and follow-up of his study tour in Japan was excellent. A more rigorous preparation including language may likely have dissuaded Bill, Ed, and Paul from engaging in this international experience. Nevertheless, they did miss out on the kind of experience that Mary and Denise describe.

LEARNING STYLE

"I just became fascinated. I knew that I wanted to learn more." Paul Vandemere

The picture that emerges of these teachers is one of people who were committed to improving their teaching, who were interested in learning, who saw the experience as a way to develop and invigorate themselves. These factors relate to a key issue in who these people are and why they chose to learn about another culture: the learning style of each person. Each of them evidenced a love of learning at some point in their lives. Some seem to continuously reflect this quality. Their enthusiasm bubbles up just in the way they describe "jumping at the opportunity" to study and experience life in another country. There is a persistent strain throughout these interviews of wanting to know and experience more, reminiscent at times of Dewey's ideal of the teacher as learner. This ideal teacher will work to grasp a deep knowledge of subject matter and then connect his knowledge to the understanding of a child and take her from the starting point of her own awareness as far as she can go.

Terrific courses at the Fletcher School motivated Paul Vandemere to further study and answer that ad for a Japanese company. Ed Donovan took anthropology courses in the summer at the University of Minnesota "just to pick up something to use in class." One example he used in class was an anthropologist's observation of the way many Americans walked, taking up a lot of space with arms swinging, reflecting a luxury of space. The anthropologist compared this walk with that of many Chinese who walk with one foot ahead of the other and elbows pulled in close to the body, reflecting a lack of space in China. During another summer Ed participated in an archaeological dig organized by Northwestern University because "I was curious. What it did was teach me to look at things differently." Since he had an M.A., he did not take these courses for another degree but because he was curious and wanted to know more to share with his students.

In *The Inquiring Mind*, Cyril Houle (1961) studies adults who continue to learn, distinguishing between those who learn to improve job skills, to work toward a goal such as another credential, and those who learn for the sheer delight of learning. These latter are people who have never lost their childlike curiosity and wonder. Learning is a pleasure to them. All six of these teachers display elements of the foregoing in their narratives to differing degrees. Mary Ehrhardt's study of art history led her to choose art as her avocation. In addition to teaching full time and raising a family, she became a docent at an art museum that specialized in New England modern art. She had found the interdisciplinary study in art history "very exciting" and continued with this approach in her teaching and docenting work. To educate herself about China she continually looked for new sources and ideas. She learned about the Chinese folk tradition of shadow puppets and established a tradition telling a Chinese folktale with the children performing as the puppets.

We use a king-size sheet with screens on either side and we do this in the performing arts center so that it can be totally darkened. I would love sometime to share the video with you because this

year, even the children who were more challenging to work with,
their performance and the musical sound effects which they create
and the overhead transparencies which become the scenery were
really amazing, I thought. It's very beautiful and very compelling
and magical.

Before she taught the Chinese unit, she "spent a long, long time
reading, just to get a handle on what one would teach second-graders."
She found a Chinese bilingual class in Boston, whose teacher agreed to
communicate with Mary's class as pen-pals when she began the China
unit nine years ago. Mary Ehrhardt reveled at the "chance to become a
student again," especially when she learned brush painting and
calligraphy in China from a Master. This was one way she felt her
experience in China became "richer and richer day by day."

Denise Green displayed intellectual curiosity as a small child when
she became "just fascinated" with a "little girl down the street" who
spoke Spanish. Denise kept "bugging and bugging her" to speak
Spanish with her and explain what those sounds meant. When she
saw cereal boxes that advertised books about the world for a dime, she
sent away for the books. When they began to arrive, her surprised
parents asked her how this had happened. They only admonished her
to ask them first before she sent away for anything and allowed her to
keep them, including her prize, *The Seven Wonders of the Ancient
World*. Denise Green later described her desire to learn the language
and culture of another country. She admired her eighth-grade teacher
for making the students talk to each other using Spanish words and
phrases, helping them to be comfortable using the language. She
described how she and each of her three children "would have three
books going at once," amazing her teacher sister. She hoped that one
day she could work on a degree to study something that she just wanted
to know more about, like law or Japanese, with no professional purpose,
loving learning for its intrinsic value—the quintessential "Inquiring
Mind."

Bill Notebaum responded to his students' questions "by doing my own
reading and research, subscribing to journals. . . . I felt the need to
become more informed." In this process the subject of economics really
hooked him "because it was answering more questions about what was
going on in terms of the changes I was seeing in the world." He could not
accept the prevailing view that Japanese competition was unfair
because it was based on cheap labor in government-subsidized
industries. He immersed himself in the work of W. Edwards Demming,
who was initially rejected by American industry, but who took his
message to Japan and was greatly influential there.

Of these six teachers, only Ellen Stacey displays some ambivalence about learning and does not talk about going to Japan to improve her teaching. She said her interest in the Japan program developed because she had just had an operation and felt "depressed."

However, Ellen describes her Catholic education this way: "We all came out educated with a love of education." She felt her first seven months in Japan had "reunited" her "with that fire of the love of education." She admired the Japanese because they had "the same tremendous respect for education that I grew up in." Their students wore uniforms as she had done in the parochial school system. Even though she dropped French after two years of it in college because "English was easier," she showed me in her bookcase books on how to speak Arabic, Spanish, French, and German. In 1996 she was teaching Japanese to seventh and eighth-graders as well as community college students in the evening.

Family, community and schooling influences, the times, university experiences, and the first years of teaching helped create the person who decides to disrupt his or her life and career to study or work abroad. Some of these descriptions remind me of Abraham Maslow's *Toward a Psychology of Being* (1968), in which he studies people on a continuum of basic survival to self-actualizing behavior, in part as an antidote to the preponderance of work on abnormal psychology. The stories of these teachers are also reflective of Mike Rose's *Possible Lives* (1995), in which he describes his interviews with exemplary teachers to give some balance to the overwhelmingly negative depiction of teachers and teaching practice in the education reform literature of the last twenty years.

Teachers who are learners are the major building blocks of meaningful school reform. Teachers who are exposed to colleagues who display an enthusiasm for learning may catch the fever of deepened knowledge, a heightened sense of self-efficacy, and more sensitive and humane relationships with students. These teachers give examples of how some of their family, friends, and former teachers have motivated them to stretch their boundaries and explore what it means to study about, live, and work in another culture by experiencing this themselves. Their learning style, in connection with the motivating influences of others, helped each of them to realize more fully their potential as teachers and as human beings. Making schools into places of continuous learning, led by continuously learning teachers, will do more to improve education than all of the standardized testing humans can devise.

In much the same way that Mary Catherine Bateson describes six phenomenal women in *Composing a Life* (1989), these teachers have chosen to study or experience another culture in depth as a means of exploring and developing themselves into continuous learners with gusto and enthusiasm. They are an example to their students, colleagues and the community of how humans can grow and learn through life always in the process of composing themselves, the way an artist composes a painting or a composer a symphony. The quality and character of the international experience, the subjects of Chapters 4, 5, and 6, are crucial to how this composition plays out. We will consider how this international experience affects this human composition, this self-directed work of art, in Chapters 7, 8, and 9.

4

Creative Classrooms

Experience affects individuals in myriad ways. A new experience, such as experiencing another culture in depth, can cause people to feel that it has profoundly changed them. This is the case with all of the veteran teachers who participated in this study. Who the person is and her life before the experience will play a role in how she is affected by the experience. International experience can encourage learning, cultural awareness, and respect for other lifestyles and viewpoints among many teachers. Just as a creative teacher can construct a child's experience in the classroom to promote the development of his knowledge and understanding, so also can teachers construct their own experience to the same end.

This chapter examines three dimensions of their experience: a description of their work during their international experience, focusing on their pedagogy within another culture and how their pedagogy differed from that of their host school's teachers; their professional work-related contributions in the schools; and their observations about the schools and what they learned. We will focus on the four teachers who taught in the public sector: Ellen, Denise, Mary, and Ed. The possibilities for in-depth teaching experiences abroad are increasingly available to teachers and have great potential for providing a comparative basis for changes in pedagogy. How they lived in the culture, the connections and friendships they made with people in the culture, and their observations about the culture are the subjects of Chapters 5 and 6.

Five of these six teachers taught for significant periods in the host country (four months to three and a half years). Ed Donovan taught at a medical college in Kunming, China, for one year. Paul Vandemere tutored business executives in forensics and public speaking for two years with a private company in Japan. Mary Ehrhardt lived with a family in Beijing and taught English to elementary and middle school children in China for four months.   Denise Green and Ellen Stacey taught English in different public schools for five months in Japan. Ellen Stacey returned to Japan to teach English for three years.   They all taught English, although Paul Vandemere also taught forensics and public speaking. Unlike the other teachers in this study, he worked for a private company. His students included CEO's of Fortune 500 companies. He used his skills as a debate and forensics coach to teach these CEOs and company executives to perform well in English, to give presentations and speeches. Because Paul and Bill Notebaum, who only visited schools and businesses, did not teach in the public schools in Japan, their experiences in the teaching arena are not comparable to those of the other four.   Their unique experiences are discussed in Chapters 7, 8, and 9.

THEIR WORK: DIFFERENCES IN TEACHING PRACTICE

"What upset the Chinese most is that I wouldn't stand behind the podium." Ed Donovan

Denise, Ed, Ellen, and Mary used teaching methods that surprised and sometimes upset their hosts. They all eschewed rote learning and lecturing behind the podium, which they viewed as the norm in their respective countries. They all found ways to resist teaching in the traditional manner, even when being physically steered by a monitor back to the proper place behind a podium, as Ed Donovan was. Ed and Denise described their teaching in the United States as considerably more relaxed than what they had observed in China and Japan, respectively. Denise said sitting on desks, standing, or leaning against a wall were unacceptable in Japan. Ed described his classroom in the United States as a place where students participated more freely in discussions and where the seating arrangements sometimes differed from the traditional rows.

By his own description, Ed was not the kind of teacher who could tolerate standing behind a podium and lecturing to his students. When Ed's Chinese class monitor diplomatically tried to steer Ed back toward the podium, he found himself again walking among the students.

Every time I would come down off the podium to come down the aisle, the class monitor would take my arm and say, "But Mr. Ed, you should be behind the podium. This is where the teachers are." I'd forget the minute I got going again. So he had a very difficult time with me for a week and a half. After that, evidently he talked to one of the leaders who said "forget it."

The most traumatic event for his adult students was Ed's insistence upon a seating chart that put women with men in the front of the class.

It was interesting that when they first came to my class, most of the women never sat in the front seats. It was one of the things that I became aware of within the first week. I made a seating chart. It did make them uncomfortable. What I did was put girls in the first two rows in half the room, the first two sets of seats; then sprinkled throughout the room. That was very uncomfortable. They were used to sitting girls on one side of the room, particularly the back side, and men in the front. I upset that pattern. They didn't say anything for two or three months. Finally my monitor said, "You did very much upset us." I said, "Why, because I came off the podium and walked down the aisle?" He said, "Oh, that was pretty bad, but when you mixed the women and the men together in the room, everybody was very worried." I said, "What do you mean?" He said, "You don't do that in China." It was something that was kind of counter-culture for them.

Denise Green, like Ed Donovan, had trouble standing behind a podium in Japan: "They wanted the teacher to stand up in front of the room and pretty much stay there. It was hard for me to just stand in one place. You know, I'd start wandering around and the kids would actually start laughing. They weren't used to it and they would start giggling." She attributed the strict atmosphere in the classroom to the pressure on children to prepare for entrance examinations. Denise also found the way students in Japan were expected to recite answers to be much more formal than her American classes were; "I do find the English classes to be more formal. When you ask a question, you have to go through all that, pushing in your chair, saying the answer and then sitting back down. What kind of discussion is that? It isn't."

Ellen Stacey felt that she was initially expected to function as a tape recorder in the Japanese classroom, however, she soon began to improvise.

Well, when I first went there, they only wanted me to be a recorder, a tape recorder. Repeat after Ms. Stacey: "The Titanic went down." [And the students would repeat] "The Titanic went down." And so I would try and diversify the questions so I would be the translator for the text because I knew that was important. But when it came time for questions, I would go back into the textbook, use some of the vocabulary. If the textbook didn't say it, the teacher wouldn't teach it. So they taught "brothers and sisters" and then I would say, "Well, how old are you? How old is your brother? How old is your sister?" And it was like, oh that's a very good idea. But it wasn't in the book that way, so we never thought of it. That part was good.

Ellen also brought some innovations in style into some of the teaching of English, as did Ed, Mary, and Denise.

Mary Ehrhardt used teaching methods based on her enthusiasm for experiential learning, which intrigued the Chinese students and teachers. She had brought from the United States "a hockey goalie bag full of books and tapes and activities for my teaching." She had given her Chinese ninth-grade English class an assignment to put a wordless children's picture book into sequence and write the story. These students voiced their perceptions about her teaching practice.

I taught these many classes and actually it probably was the highlight, the kinds of interchange that I had with the students. I had no expectations that they would improve particularly with my weekly visits. But after about four weeks, the ninth-graders, one particular ninth-grade class, and it just happened that I had given them a writing assignment that came out of putting in place or sequencing a picture book, a children's book, a wordless picture book. They had to put the book in order and then write the story. Just that experience, working with a partner in a small group, several students said, "Oh, we get it—what you want us to do. You're different. You're not like our Chinese teachers. You want us to talk. You want us to write. You want us to ask questions." It was an amazing breakthrough in their level of verbal, of speaking and in their willingness to try writing, to do more than just a grammar exercise from their book.

The pedagogy that each of these teachers modeled to the Chinese and Japanese students and their teacher colleagues seemed very different from the norm in China and Japan. These United States teachers apparently enjoyed exposing their hosts to methodologies that were at least a little different. None of the United States teachers felt that their methods might have been lacking except Ellen Stacey, who admired and learned from the interdisciplinary work between math and physical education teachers, and the map learning exercises she observed in Japan. Denise Green was concerned about fitting into the structure of what was expected of her in Japan more than modeling a change in teaching practice. They all were secure in their belief that they were making positive contributions in the schools.

THEIR CONTRIBUTIONS IN THE SCHOOLS

"They [the Chinese teachers] had not, for example, ever heard of Piaget or Dewey or Vygotsky." Mary Ehrhardt

In addition to modeling a different style of teaching in China and Japan, Ed, Mary, Denise, and Ellen enthusiastically described what they felt were their main contributions to the schools of their host countries. All four of these teachers were proud of their work and seemed to feel as though they had made a difference in the schools and classrooms where they taught. Their delight in talking about this was independent of the response of students and teachers. In this regard Ellen Stacey described her experience as fulfilling, even though she rather negatively portrayed other aspects of her experience. These American teachers at the least left these countries feeling as though they had accomplished a great deal, even though they sometimes viewed the need, as in the case of China, to be almost overwhelming. Mary Ehrhardt captured this feeling of need in her work with Chinese teachers in weekly seminars.

While planning for and teaching fourth to ninth-grade students, Mary Ehrhardt and her colleague, Jackie Sonnenday, organized weekly seminars for the Chinese elementary and middle school teachers of English. The seminars were based on issues of greatest interest to the Chinese teachers. They started with the physical, cultural, and economic geography of the United States.

> They wanted to know where different places were. In our exchange of views of stages of the human beings' life, we compared child-rearing practices and marriage customs and our salaries and working conditions and health benefits, insurance and taxes, and voting. They were very interested in health education and teaching about human growth and development. There's nothing in their curriculum for students as they grow and physically mature. We talked to the teachers about pedagogy and things as detailed as the kind of thinking that goes into a room arrangement of a classroom.

Mary explained the reasons that she arranged her classroom in certain ways. For example, she gave them a rationale for why she would use desks in a circle to have a face to face discussion among students. "I showed them how my tables were arranged so they could be used as activity centers for children to move about the room and have materials accessible to them."

She found the youngest teachers in their 20s, who were familiar with child psychology, to be most receptive to new ideas about teaching practice: "They were eager to perhaps try to do skits or carry on some role plays or have a debate if they just had a little practice in knowing how to do that. Those are the kinds of things that we tried to show them—how to use other kinds of methods."

The Chinese teachers took the opportunity during the weekly seminars to discuss issues about which they felt ill-prepared, for example, human sexuality, a subject that had been prohibited by the government authorities in earlier years.

> What they were primarily interested in was the American courses in teaching human growth development and sexuality, relationships, because that is really foreign. There is no China official developed curricula in human sexuality. They were very interested in knowing how teachers actually interfaced with students about those issues without offending and without being embarrassed themselves, without embarrassing their students. They really see the need and I think at this point it's really a level of curiosity because so much of that aspect of life is regulated by the government. They are beginning to think about just how you talk about relationships and issues that come up and their bodies changing.

Mary's colleague, Jackie, had taught the human sexuality curriculum, so she modeled a lesson for the teachers. Mary and Jackie later followed this up by sending books after they returned to the United States.

> Starting with the idea of a question box in the classroom and asking them to submit any question that they had about anything in this area; then Jackie took two or three questions and modeled how an American teacher would respond. What we've done just recently is we've sent them two books that we actually asked our American students what they remember from sex ed classes or health and development classes, or their family discussions that were most helpful. We got two books on human development. One is "Where Did I Come From?" and another is the sequel to that. It may not be called "All About Me," but it is about puberty and adolescent development. Actually, both are done in a cartoon fashion. Both also have very accurate and specific diagrams and information. We've sent them to our colleagues in the department

to see and actually we sent them as gifts to them and their children and to use it at their discretion personally to try them out with their own children.

Many of the weekly seminars explored methods of teaching based on the works of Dewey, Piaget, and Vygotsky, among others. Mary described how enthusiastically the Chinese teachers discussed substantive educational issues. "In fact, we got them so riled up about our conversation about educational philosophy and how it really impacted the way we arranged our classrooms, that they said, 'We need to revolt. We need to have a revolution.' " Mary believes that the hard reality of the examination system in China greatly diminishes the prospects for change. The motivation to teach to the test, a phenomenon that is observed in many American schools, is very powerful in China when teachers' wages are dependent on their students' performance on national examinations.

The greatest hindrance to putting any of this into practice is that they teach for national exams and the responsibility of the success of their students lies on their shoulders. If their students do not pass, they may be docked in pay or it may impact where they are on the waiting list for getting a better apartment. So these teachers worked tirelessly to prepare their students for the exams. The exams are basically grammar. They teach this sentence after sentence, in this rote manner, and they're bored, the students are bored. They have practice books, lesson books piled like this on their desks, grading these every day. Then they have students who need extra help coming in their hour and a half lunch period or after school for special help. They just feel tremendous pressure to make their students successful. Perhaps the pressure is even greater in the school because 98 percent of the students who do last through the school go to higher education of some kind.

In addition to this work in the weekly seminars, Mary and Jackie spent a day taping stories and lessons in an American accent. They used the well equipped language laboratory in this key school.

We recorded a story so that our students could go to the language lab and listen to English with an American accent. They're very lucky to have a tape recorder, a VCR and an overhead projector in every classroom. They do use audio-visuals for instruction. But it is a Chinese-developed curriculum by teachers who speak with a British accent. At the moment, they are very eager to learn American English. We taped stories and did lessons which were listening lessons and then comprehension from listening to just show the teachers how lessons would sound in English with an American accent.

Ellen Stacey, like Mary, enjoyed input from the Japanese teachers who welcomed her help.

> They also had me check the tests and write the test that they would give. They [the Japanese English teachers] would call me up and say, "We have this question with this sentence. Could this sentence really work or are there other ways that you could answer this question?". . . Sometimes they would sit beside me and say, "I'm teaching this and I'm thinking about this and do you have any ideas?" I would have input. Those were the happier days for me because I would really be able to work together a lesson, especially when it came to reviews . . . before the big test and stuff; that was really nice.

However, in some schools, there was little preparation or collegial sharing of ideas between Ellen and the English teachers:

> I would walk into a whole school and no one would even speak to me until it was five minutes before my class. They were trying to teach me their lesson on the way up to the classroom. I had the one teacher, whenever I was to teach in his class, I was assigned for his class, he didn't come to school. . . . Because I had to teach five classes, they would say, "Go on up into that room and someone will be there to help you."

Ellen's contributions in Japanese schools included sharing more flexible methods with Japanese teachers, such as using word games like "Pictionary" and mentoring some of the less-experienced foreign-exchange teachers. They came to her and said, "We're having problems. What do we do in this situation?" She replied, "Try this idea, maybe that will work." Feelings of "power and confidence" heightened in Ellen.

In her sixth-grade English class, Mary Ehrhardt, like Ellen, also used innovative techniques, introducing children's literature such as *Caps for Sale* by Slobodkina (1940) to help the Chinese children role-play in English. She brought it to China in a small book and big book format and transformed it into a play in the sixth grade, using part of it to help the Chinese children understand the past tense in English.

The main character is a peddler. The child who became the peddler was really the most proficient in that class in English. He had a few English books and he would bring me his books so that I could see what he had. . . . He would save his questions about the peddler until I came, and then we'd talk about that role. Each child had a sentence to say and after we practiced and presented to the class, we actually videotaped the play. . . . The lesson allowed us to work on past tense. Since Chinese does not have tenses, the students found it very difficult to say words that ended in "ed," so it gave us an opportunity to learn that "ed" can be three different sounds.

Role-playing this story turned the traditional teacher behind the podium into something quite different, even perhaps a little revolutionary.

Then, in addition to the peddler, there are a set of monkeys. The peddler sits down; he has his whole stack of caps on his head, and he is discouraged because he doesn't sell any caps. But he eventually walks out into the country and sits down under a tree and falls asleep. While he is sleeping, these monkeys come out of the tree and they each take a hat and climb back up into the tree. When he awakens, he has no hats. So then the peddler has to convince the monkeys to give him back his hats. He says: "Give me back my hats." But all the monkeys do is imitate him. "Give me back my hats." He goes on to get so angry that he stamps his feet and they stamp their feet. He gets so very angry that he takes his hat off, his own hat, and flings it on the ground and he says, "Give me back my hats!" And they all fling the hats down on the ground.

The sixth graders' roles in this performance were quite different from anything they had ever experienced in school.

This interchange was so hilarious for the class because I painted a tree and pasted it to the teacher's desk. Now the teacher's desk is a podium on an elevated cement platform and normally the teacher lectures from the podium and the children feed back what the teacher says. But the tree was attached to the teacher's podium and the monkeys climbed up on top. They performed from on top of the teacher's desk. This was unique in all of Chinese education, that children would be allowed to climb on top of the teacher's desk. In fact, this class sends me a whole class letter

about once a month because they thought this was just so different
and so significant in their beginning to speak English, doing a play.

Students and teachers alike in China made it clear that they valued
what Mary offered. Even though her methods were different and
challenged the status quo in the school where she taught, the time and
effort she put into this work, as well as the response of students, helped
to encourage some teachers in China to change their traditional
teacher-lecture, student-recitation methods. A seventh-grade class
Mary worked with, for example, gave up its ten-minute break and
fifteen-minute eye exercises to engage her in discussions on topics of
their choice about the United States.

> One topic was the NBA basketball because that was what they
> see on TV. They can get the NBA. Another time they wanted to
> know about teen-agers of America, how they dress and what music
> they like. Then they liked to know something about families. So
> each week we picked a different topic. They asked me questions,
> all in English. We had a discussion about America. . . . Some
> certainly did not understand my responses. There was some
> interpreting on the part of the Chinese teacher. I think the fact
> that they really wanted it, they wanted the dialogue and were
> willing week after week to do it, they got something out of it.

She asked her husband and son in her weekly phone call to give her the
NBA standings and to teach her about the NBA organization so she
could share it with her seventh-grade Chinese students.
     An improbable event, such as recognition of her birthday, became an
opportunity for sharing cultural knowledge. When celebrating her
birthday, her class asked about her age, which initiated a controversy
and discussion in the classroom on different perspectives, Chinese and
American, on aging.

> They knew when my birthday was and they made cards and
> wished me a happy birthday, and then the follow-up question
> was, "How old are you?" There was kind of a moment, an
> awkward moment because some students thought that was an
> inappropriate question. It's not in China, the older you are, the
> more revered you are. I said, "But in America, you don't ask. . . .
> You probably wouldn't ask a person my age their age because in
> America the culture tells that to be young is better than to be
> older." So we had a discussion about birthdays and about age.

Mary demonstrated here that not only was she able to plan the sharing of cultural knowledge, but that she could flexibly use this situation to promote cultural understanding about different approaches to the subject of age. In this case, Mary models an ability to engage in what Donald Schon (1987) describes as "reflection in action." As applied to the classroom, this means that she can spontaneously adapt the surprises that often occur in classrooms to enhance learning, in this case cultural learning.

Cultural discussions were also a major aspect of Denise Green's work in Japan. Her knowledge of Japanese seemed to break the ice with students and allowed her to engage in a more in-depth cultural sharing at times because they were more spontaneous with their questions in their language.

For example, Denise showed her ability to defuse, with humor and a little language, a potentially difficult situation. After the late arrival in class of the son of one of her Japanese friends, Denise broke the tension with just a few words in Japanese.

> He was late to his class, which was supposed to be a no-no. As he walked in, he bowed to the teacher. And I was in the middle of saying something. The phrase we were working on was, "What do you want to be when you grow up?" They were supposed to answer this question. So he came in late and he sat down. Then instead of sitting there quietly and trying to figure out what was going on, he whispered something to someone, then to someone else to make them giggle. I said [to myself], "OK, I've got to get on this one." So I looked at him and said, "What do you want to be when you grow up?" And in Japanese style when you answer a question, you stand up because you're sharing. If you don't know the answer, you can hang your head silently and wait until you're told you can sit down or you can confer with people around you and give an answer that you think is OK. Well, he stood up and he thought about it and said, "OHHHH?" which is like, you know, "What?" He was trying to be silly and the kids giggled. So I repeated it. So then someone told him in Japanese what it meant. He didn't think that I knew what they'd said. Then he said, "Yakuza." It meant gangster. So he waited for the giggles and so I waited for them to stop.

Her response to the boy in Japanese surprised and delighted the students.

> So I said, "Yakuzasan. You may sit down." I said it all in Japanese. He was stunned. So I told him to sit down again. Then later on

when we were doing something else in the class, I looked at him and I called on him. So when he answered in English correctly and sat down, I told him in Japanese, "You did very well, Mr. Yakuza." He blushed and the class cracked up. It was funny. Even the teacher laughed.

Some of the most interesting experiences for Denise occurred, as with Mary Ehrhardt, when the students were allowed to ask questions about Denise's life in the United States.

The ones [classes] I liked best, and these usually occurred the first day I was in the class, that I would initiate a self-introduction in either Japanese or English, depending on the teacher's request and then the students were free to ask me questions. That was the most fun because they could ask anything and I could handle it however I wanted. Then when we got to the more formal part of the instruction, it was more cold. . . . After the first couple of questions, you could almost make a list of the stuff they would ask. First of all, if they were asking in English, you knew about how much they knew. If they were free to ask in Japanese, they would usually ask more questions.

Denise felt that elements of her exchange responsibilities emphasized the cultural part of the exchange as well as proficiency in English. In this case she preferred to use Japanese, so the students could ask more questions than their level of English allowed.

Some teachers looked at it as more of a cultural than language exchange. You could almost tell which ones, because the ones who looked at it as a language exchange demanded that the kids only speak English. "Do you have children? How old is your son?" But if you could ask in Japanese or English and you could ask anything, they would ask anything. "Do you have a car? Do you have a Japanese or American car? How big is your house?" They would ask more normal-type questions for a kid who's talking to someone who lives in another country and "Do you have . . ." and he might mean a comic book character. They wouldn't ask that in English. Part of it was that they hadn't had that much English so there was only so much that if they had to ask in English, that they could even ask. . . . If they could ask in Japanese, a lot of times the conversations were clear.

When she was more concerned about sharing cultural perceptions, she often used pictures of her family and her classroom. She brought up the issue of her African-American heritage and showed many different hues of skin color in the photographs of her family as well as those of her American classroom. The Japanese teachers were reluctant to discuss this issue, probably fearing embarrassment to Denise about race.

I would bring it up, but they wouldn't. Even in their classes I would bring it up and if I did, because the culture clubs would meet after school once a week, sometimes I would be invited to the English culture club. They would give me the Pen-Pal club or the English speaking club. . . . Sometimes I would show a photo album or show some slides. It wouldn't be very long, maybe twenty minutes. Just to say this is what my house looks like, this is what my neighborhood looks like, this is what my school looks like, what my classroom looks like. These are members of my family. . . . I would talk about it very freely then. They would see in my classroom children of Asian descent. I would say this one, her family speaks Spanish at home. They would be able to see the different races in my class. But also, my family. I would bring out the fact that we were African-American and would talk about the different skin colors.

Both Mary and Denise show that cultural knowledge is learned and shared through much more than simple exposure to a different style of teaching or a person of another culture. Meaningful exchanges often occur during unplanned moments of frank discussions.

Ed Donovan, in contrast to Denise, focused more on teaching English in the classroom than on his role in a cultural exchange. He felt that the use of the Socratic method with his adult students was very effective and provided a respite from the traditional lectures from the podium given by most Chinese teachers. Ed uses the term "Socratic" to mean that he promotes a dialogue. One student responds to another, in contrast to an interchange, in which the instructor dominates by asking a question to which a selected student responds: "I used a Socratic method mostly before I left. It fit in very well with their style of learning. Question, answer, repeat. I did very basic things with them. It made me very aware of the language that I used." He was pleased to know that some of the Chinese teachers he had taught earlier were using his teaching materials and techniques.

I had a letter from a gal that took a course from me this past summer and she said, "I've used tongue twisters, and I've used sayings of famous people." They had put on a play because we had suggested that that might be one of the things that they could do. She learned them in school and I would give them copies of all this stuff. Then they could use it in their own classes and the whole idea of starting a story with one person and then having every person continue it. It's all these different kinds of techniques that we kind of use without thinking too much about. It is something that's brand new to them because their idea of teaching is standing up in front of a room and lecture. I noticed the last time I was there that a young man who had sixty-six people in his class, in his English class, was using a Socratic approach. He would walk up and down the aisles and he would tap kids on the shoulder or tell this one to say something to that one, tell that one to respond. These are kinds of techniques that we've used and that we've taught since 1991 particularly.

These teachers felt they had made significant contributions to their Chinese and Japanese students. They felt their contributions helped their colleagues in other countries see a different way of teaching based on more student-teacher interaction and less on lectures from a podium. They seemed not to question that the methodologies they promulgated were better for students and teachers. It was an assumption based on their deeply held beliefs about what is good teaching practice, almost as if the exposure to something different was a good thing in itself. Mary Ehrhardt, for example, strongly believes in experiential learning for herself and her students, as evidenced by the elaborate role-play trip to China that she uses in her second-grade U.S. Classroom. Ed Donovan is also committed to a pedagogy that emphasizes interactions among students in a classroom. Mary and Ed hope that the pedagogy they have introduced in China will be in some way adapted to Chinese classrooms.

THE SCHOOL ENVIRONMENT

Before we focus on what these teachers have learned from their teaching experience abroad, we must consider the content and context of this experience. Under what conditions did these teachers work? What were their schedules and responsibilities? Their narratives show a concern about the length of time each teacher was assigned to a specific school. This issue is important because it affects the kinds of connections and relationships that can develop among colleagues and students, relationships that take time to develop.

Denise Green and Ellen Stacey found that being assigned to schools for short periods was counterproductive. Ellen's situation was much more difficult because she was assigned to one school a day during most of her three-year experience. She remarked in disgust, "I was show-and-tell." Denise enjoyed working with students but found that it was hard to develop relationships with students and teachers when she was in one school every two weeks.

> In terms of relationships with the students, it was hard being at the school for such a short time. Some students would come right into the teachers lounge and they would feel very comfortable coming up standing. And you always knew they wanted to talk to you because they'd stand there and giggle and look at you from a distance or maybe at a desk close to yours or stop and talk to another teachers. The other teacher would grin and say, "They want to practice their English, is that OK?". . . Some of them would come up on their own . . . sometimes to practice their English and sometimes to ask you questions. Sometimes I'd see them on the streets in my travels and I always know if I had been at a school where I taught, not because of their uniforms, because the insignias would be so small, I wouldn't be able to tell. But because the group would stop and giggle and point. Sometimes they'd yell, "Hi sensai!". . . Sometimes they would actually come up and speak to me. Then I'd know that I'd been to their school and they just wanted to chitchat for a little while. I think, however, that if I had been at fewer schools for longer periods of time that it would have been different.

Denise was faced with the same obstacle in her connections with teachers. Speaking of developing a friendship with a teacher, she explains, "But once you leave that person's school, your schedules conflict and it's hard to get together again." She would have preferred being in one school at least a month: "I would have preferred that, I really would have preferred that. But then like I said, I was in a position that I couldn't say anything about it. That was decided."

Denise thought about the Japanese teachers who had come to Indiana as part of the state exchange program and were assigned to a different school each day. Denise had commiserated with two of them after her experience in Japan: "I don't know how you're doing this, but I pity you." In the schools where she had been assigned one grade level, Denise taught the same students every day for two weeks "because I would be the eighth-grade teacher or ninth-grade teacher or seventh-grade teacher. I would develop a close relationship with that teacher and felt like maybe I'd done something with the students." However, scheduling in other schools allowed her to visit many classrooms only once. Denise and Ellen were the only two teachers who faced relatively short periods in one school; while Ed and Mary had more continuity. Both Denise and Ellen disliked this aspect of their work. Such an arrangement often precludes the development of the in-depth relationships that Mary and Ed enjoyed. In some ways, their experience was superficial, just as the visits of Japanese teachers to U.S. schools for one day at a time can only be superficial.

CASE STUDY: ELLEN STACEY

Among these four teachers, Ellen Stacey describes her experience in Japan in the most detail. Because she lived and worked there twice and for a much longer period, her case is complex. This is true not only because of the length of time she lived and taught in Japan but also because of the quality of her experience there. A more thorough analysis of Ellen's experience abroad can help us understand how a teacher's learning can be affected by such an experience.

During Ellen's first teaching experience in Japan, after six weeks of Japanese language and cultural studies with her five American colleagues, she was assigned to a different school each month from August through December. Each morning, after she attended the morning meetings with all the teachers, she would be assigned to an English teacher: "I'd go into the classroom with the team teacher, usually we would plan together, and then my job would be part of a lesson plan. So I was the English version of what the book had said or an English translation for a story, or I would have to listen and interview the kids and have them talk to me."

Her second teaching experience in Japan was very different from the first. Until the third year, she was assigned to a different school every day. The first year, however, she had to work only a few hours each day: "They treated me like a princess." During her second year, when the foreign-exchange teachers were asked to edit and proofread the English speech contest, all four of her students won the contest. When the students wrote their speeches in Japanese, their teachers would translate them into English, which the students would memorize for the contest: "My job was to take the Japanese thought process, edit it into a speech for that child, so that the child could memorize the speech with vocabulary that he knew, challenging him maybe with only two words instead of a whole list."

By the third year, Ellen was working twelve to sixteen-hour days, which included social obligations centered on her work: "They expected me to be a Japanese teacher. They expected me to be up at 7:00 and in the school by 7:30. They expected me to be home around 10:00 and do some entertaining. It was too hard for me, too hard. I was teaching five classes a day and their teachers were only teaching fifteen to twenty hours a week." She was hospitalized for exhaustion three times during the third year, "just from overwork." She called her illnesses "stress related," the result of extreme tiredness. Describing her third year, she said:

> It tired me fast. Especially when I ended up in the hospital three times. That part was terrible. Because in America when you're sick, you stay home. In Japan I was sick, and every morning they would call me at 6:30 and see if I was OK and if I was ready to go back to school. I wasn't so [sick that] I had to go to the doctor's every morning. The doctor was not next door. I had to take an hour train to get to the doctor.

In spite of her stress and exhaustion, Ellen considers the work she did with the Japanese students and teachers and the exchange teachers from other countries to have been valuable for her own confidence as well as for those with whom she worked. "Every year my job was to teach them how to teach as a team."

The third year she led the exchange teachers in persuading the Japanese authorities to allow herself and three exchange teachers from other countries to stay in one school for six weeks.

> The first year I was there, I was in twenty-five schools in twenty-five days. A school a day. How effective could I be, a school a day? I was show-and-tell. I can't do this; it's too hard on me, it's too stressful. I was learning to ride on the wrong side of the street, number one. My car was over in ditches every time I turned around. I was lost every single day. I have no sense of direction. I tried to say, "You can't do this. If you want me to be effective, you have to keep me in a school longer."

Getting the exchange teachers to work as a team was a daunting task: "The first time there was just John; the second time there were four of us. I tried to get the four of us to work as a Japanese team because if I would go and say, 'It's too hard for me to do this,' they [the Japanese authorities] would say, 'It's too difficult for us. You do it anyway.' "

The third year they worked together toward the goal of teaching for a longer period in each school. Ellen had been assigned to supervise the group, so she worked with a colleague from the year before, Robert Barry, to determine the feelings of the others and then they planned their strategy.

> I called every one of the teachers that were there, the foreign teachers and I said, "Are you happy in going to one school a week?" Now instead of one day, it's a week. We're at one school and then we're transferred to another school. Every one of us had

to go through twenty schools in a semester. It's still not any good. I said, "Are you happy with that situation?" They all said, "No!" They wanted to stay longer [in each school]. So I said, "All right. Meet me at 4:30."

The four of them presented a united front to the Japanese authorities and achieved a change in policy: each would be assigned to one school every six weeks instead of one school a week. Ellen described their strategy:

We said [to Robert] "This is the problem, you are a man, you state the problem. We will all back you up." And we all agreed on what our dialogue was going to be. He came up, he meaning Robert, because he had the most seniority; he was the man. Robert said, "We are not happy with this situation." Laurie said the same thing, "Yes, I agree with Robert. I feel the same way. It's too difficult." Joel said the same thing and then they looked at me. And I said, "Yes, we've decided that this is too hard." The next semester, we were at a school for six weeks. One school. They divided five schools among four of us.

Many of Ellen's negative impressions of Japan may have been formed by the difficulty of changing her schedule over three years from one school a day to one every six weeks. She also talked at length about the positive aspects of the schools in which she worked, reflecting her ambivalence about schooling in Japan. She is extremely complimentary about what she sees as a family atmosphere of concern and caring between students and teachers, which she had not experienced in her public school teaching in Wisconsin. She also admired the fact that art and music especially were such a priority in the Japanese schools. She admired the way government and business worked together to make sure the schools were well equipped with high technology, such as computers. However, she seemed appalled at the way marginal students behaved in school and were treated by the authorities. She was amazed at the extent of physical violence in the schools, an observation corroborated by David Berliner (1993), who quotes from Japanese newspaper accounts of teacher and student violence that might shock many Americans.

It is important to understand that Ellen's teaching experience in Japan included schools that encompassed "problem" students. Thomas Rohlen in *Japan's High Schools* (1983) also documents conditions in some Japanese schools in which most students were not on the university track. Minority Burakumin and Ainu children are generally not found in schools where a majority of the students pass university examinations or in schools where many American educators would be encouraged to observe. According to Ellen, "these were the schools where these kids were not earmarked for the better schools." She describes students whom she calls "misfits," who wreak havoc in the Japanese school system: "These were the kids that were probably going to be trained for custodial work or maybe train personnel, or maybe factory workers. That's what these kids were trained for. They weren't going to go on to college."

During her first experience, she was placed in inner-city schools. Her first impressions were of graffiti on the walls. She felt that there were "just as many problems and rebels" as in the inner-city U.S. schools with which she was familiar. Describing one of the rough schools she was assigned to during this first experience, she said, "I saw a teacher holding on to a windowsill for his dear life and the student slammed the window on the teacher's hands and broke them. . . . The teacher came to school the next day with both his hands in casts. . . . I saw teachers literally beat up children." Ellen believes that "any misfit can live in America and get lost in it," while she considers this "impossible" in Japan.

> Those kids that did all that destruction in that school that I went to the first time and saw them burn down the building and tear out half the walls, they're already earmarked. And because they don't fit into the Japanese way of life, if they ride motorcycles and are killed, they are not even counted as statistics. If they don't learn to read a newspaper because it takes eleven years of study to read a newspaper, and if these kids don't learn to read a newspaper, then they're not Japanese, so they're not part of stats.

The last semester of her third year in Japan, Ellen taught for six weeks in a very "rough school." She describes one Burakumin seventh-grader and her understanding of what it means to be a Burakumin.

> I met him in seventh-grade; he was a nice kid. He had no friends though. . . . [A Burakumin] is basically someone who's unclean. The history of it goes back to where they wore leather, what do you call it when you skin animals, so therefore the Japanese don't wear leather and they don't wear suede. Because this is a trait of the Burakumin. Their hands were dirtied by the blood, so they were ostracized from the rest of the people. They had the lowliest of jobs. This kid's ancestry, maybe it goes back about 2,000-3,000 years, who knows how far back. But he's born to this family, now he's into the school. The first year everyone gets to know that he is a Burakumin. So they ostracize him, so he becomes a rebel in his

own cause. By his second year, eighth-grade, he has found two buddies that he can cohort with and they're going to be a little gang. By his third year they slept in the school; busted every window inside the school out; they trashed all the rooms; they throw beer bottles all over the place; they smoked on campus right on the property. I was there teaching, and they tried to intimidate me as a teacher. I was walking out and they walked right up to me and bumped me and tried to intimidate me in that way. They would come up to me with cigarettes on the playground during the school day and blow smoke in my face. They would come up with their beer bottles.

The principal and teachers, according to Ellen, did not seem able to deal effectively with this problem.

The way the teachers dealt with it? They would not allow them in the regular classroom. They had a special classroom for these bad kids. Now it's up to twelve kids. The principal has called in the police on the incident with the busted glass. The community ostracized the principal because the principal did not need to involve the police. He should have handled it with the community before going to the police. So now the principal has lost face. The principal invites this speaker from Tokyo, who is a champion Olympic star, to speak at the school. The bad kid, the Burakumin child, finds out that this is the schedule of what's going on, the agenda for the presentation, sees that the principal is going to be the last speaker, gets his little buddies up behind the stage, and there was a change in the agenda. But the bad kids didn't get the change. So now the speaker is the last speaker and they are in the back of the stage making all kinds of noises, disrupting the whole assembly and everything, and they don't do anything about it.

The fear Ellen had for these students surpassed anything she had experienced in her inner-city Milwaukee school.

It affected me because it put a tense fear in me. I never felt that kind of a fear because I had never been intimidated by a student. They were still children but they hated anybody in authority. I was sitting in the teacher's room and there are windows in all the teacher's room, and one of the kids came up and said to the teacher that was sitting to my right, "Come here, come here." He was calling and beckoning him outside the room. And the teacher wouldn't move, and the teacher would say, "Come over here, come

over here." The kid picked up, I'm not kidding you, a huge stick—
it was a tree, it was a log—and was going to heave it through the
windows. I don't know, from the corner of his eye, he saw me there
and he put it down. So he [the teacher] was telling him to go over
to where the gym clothes, the smaller lockers were. So the kid
comes over that way. I'm hearing all this rumble. The next thing I
hear is, "OW!" Then I see this kid is being carried out by three
teachers. He's all limp and they're dragging him across the field.
The next day he comes to school with a cast on his arm. They
busted his arm.

In stark contrast to her fear and concern for these rebellious
Burakumin children was her description of the creative ways they
expressed their rebellion.

The kids have to wear uniforms. These [Burakumin] kids would
put purple velvet on their trims of their uniforms; they would put
patches on their uniforms. The ribbons for girls, because they've
got girls into the group, the ribbons for girls can only be navy blue or
dark brown. These girls were putting red on and they would wear
red lipstick, anything to break the rule. The one kid, he was
really a nice kid, they were sniffing glue and stuff and their brains
were all messed up by that time, he put a tuxedo stripe down the
side and then he embroidered his name. Really beautiful, creative
things, but they were not part of the group.

Ellen criticized the Japanese procedure for dealing with problem
children.

If they had a problem child, they would sit there and they would
talk about this problem child. The way it would go is, the child
was the problem, the first teacher who had the problem would
talk to the head of the seventh-grade house. Then they would
present it to the whole group. In the bigger school that I was at, it
would have twelve, thirteen, or fourteen teachers involved in this
discussion of this one child. They would come up with some
alternatives. This is what we could try, this is what we could do.
After they came up with this decision, then the department—the
seventh-grade house chairman, the grade leader—would go to the
assistant principal and say, "We are having a problem with this
child, and these are some alternatives." Then the assistant
principal would sit in and give his information or input. Then
after that was settled with the information or input with the
assistant principal, then the principal would be asked to come in.

By then they've already solved all the steps they were going to
take to change this child's behavior. By then, this has gone on for
a week.

To put Ellen's criticisms into context, it is important to understand
that she was treated as a Japanese teacher by her third year there.
She gained a different perspective about the responsibilities of
teachers in Japan. To Ellen, Japanese teachers have many different
responsibilities, compared with American teachers. For example, the
meeting schedules seemed difficult to her.

A teacher in Japan cannot really have friends outside of the
teaching field because I would pass [by the school] at like 5:30 in
the morning to get to my school that might have been an hour
away from my apartment. There would be students out there
practicing with drums and their musical instruments by the lake.
There would be students already in the school in competition,
preparing for sports activities, at 5:30. A teacher did not leave a
building at 3:00 or 4:00 even though the day is done at 4:00, even
though all activities are finished. Teachers would be there
sometimes 9:00, 10:00. Then if they had a group meeting, forget it.
This group meeting, if they could not agree on some activity or
behavior about a child, everybody in this teaming (it was a
seventh-grade house, an eighth-grade house, a ninth-grade house)
all sat together in the teacher's room and they all had to decide on
what they were going to do. Their March activity, their end of
the school year activity—they had to plan some activity every
month.

Ellen described how a young Japanese teacher's commitment to work led
to disastrous consequences.

There was a woman there that sat across the table from me, our
desks were right together, and I spoke to her when I first went
there and she had a cold. I said, "You know, you should take some
time off with that cold." "I just had a baby and I think I'm just a
little run down." Well, that means more of a reason to stay home.
She died of pneumonia. She was only twenty-six years old.

Nevertheless, Ellen again found a good deal to admire about the
content and context of Japanese schools: the relationship among the
schools, the town administration, and local business; the emphasis on
the arts and music from the earliest grades; the encouragement of
students to take responsibility for their learning without ready answers

from the teacher; and the close mentoring relationship she witnessed between many students and their teachers, a factor she found missing in her experience in the United States.

The partnership between the schools and the community also encouraged teacher artists, for example, to pursue their art and excel. Next in line after the mayor for political power is the superintendent of schools.

> So usually they're a good partnership, the Superintendent of the school and the mayor. The mayor knows that he cannot be re-elected if he does not do something for the schools. So in these schools, you have huge artworks by the artists who live in the community. The teacher who is a teacher in the school, is pushed to excel and do artwork so it can be displayed in other parts of Japan's schools. So these teachers are walking around with artwork, sculptures, art, whatever is displayed here or there, and they have a great honor for the arts. Musicians, what they do with those people is phenomenal. When computers became a thing, which they are, the mayor said, "Every school will have a computer center." Air-conditioning is an extremely expensive thing because all of these things are imported. Every school must have spent at least over a million dollars to have an air-conditioned computer room.

The emphasis in Japanese schools on music amazed Ellen.

> Every student knows how to read music. When you start in school, you are taught do-re-mi-fa-so-la-ti-do. You are taught, you don't have an instrument in front of you. You will have a keyboard that is pasted on your desk. . . . You are practicing on this desk, pretending it's a piano. That goes all the way through elementary. If you have a preference for musical instruments, they are available. These kids also had competitions throughout all of Japan. Every junior high student, seventh grade, every class, has to perform a song. One of the students in the class has to play the piano, the other group has to sing, and one of the students is the conductor. All the seventh-graders in every school compete against all of the other seventh grades.

Robert, a teaching colleague from Oxford University and an accomplished organist, told her, "These kids are running rings around me in their ability." To Ellen, it was "just phenomenal" that "they practice five days a week, sometimes six, sometimes seven depending on the competition. They practice every morning before school and every afternoon after school."

Ellen observed Japanese students taking on leadership roles that would be extremely rare in the United States. She perceived the math and gym departments to be "almost one and the same" because of the way they worked closely together. The way Japanese teachers worked together to teach responsibility and skills in art and sports events was another opportunity for her to learn and admire their methods.

The math department "origami" teaches the geometric figures from preschool on up. When you are in junior high, your job is to set up a sports activity in September. Your whole school has to be part of this sports activity. It is your job to measure out how far it is for a high jump, measure how far you need or what the diagram has to be for a baseball diamond. And then after they put all these measurements, they have to go back and then say to the teacher, "We're having problems with this. How would we do this?" He would never tell them the answer. He would say, "Well, look at this dimension and you'll see your error." Then they had to go out and draw it. Then after that, the day before the sports meets, all the kids in the whole school were out in the field. If you go to Japan, none of the schools had grass on their fields. It's all sand. Everyone had to go out there and pick up any rock or pebble that they thought their classmate might stumble or trip on. Everything is ready. The teachers do not present the awards. The kids keep all records. At the end of every match, the kid has the name of the winner and one of the calligraphers, the student, writes the name on it and presents the awards to them. The kid doesn't present, the kid writes it, gives it to the teacher; the teacher turns around and hands it to the principal; the principal gathers everyone together and says, "So-and-so won this award. Congratulations. This class won this award, congratulations."

Ellen was so impressed with the way Japanese teachers taught map skills that she tried their method (unsuccessfully) when she returned to Milwaukee. (She describes this effort in Milwaukee in Chapter 7.)

Every school, every grade in Japan has map skills. Their job, and it takes them maybe three months for all the teachers to figure out a map skill, they write out the whole map. They tell the students, "We will meet you at the train station." They all get to the train station; they don't care how they get there. Once they're at the train station, they sit with their teacher and have a very good time. The teacher tells them, "This is your map, this is the schedule, this is what you have to do." Mind you, before you even left the school the day before, you had a packet of what you were expected to do for this map skill. They were to go to certain places, once they were in certain places. Let's say they had to go to the library first. One group had one hour at the library and they had to watch the time. They had to get from the train station to the library and do these activities at the library. From there, then they were to meet back at this other place and they had a check point for where their homeroom teacher was. That was reading a map; that was following skills.

In addition to her admiration for the expectation of student responsibility imbued within this lesson, the relationship that Ellen witnessed between students and teachers in Japan moved her to want to change her own teaching.

When I came back the first time, I had admired the way the teacher in Japan communicated with those kids. I loved it when they would knock on the door and they'd say, "Excuse me" [in Japanese]. Then they'd go over and say to the teacher, "I brought all these books for you." . . . A teacher's job was to go to the home with the kid and look at the house and say, "This room is not conducive for learning. You don't have a dictionary over here. That poster is distracting. Put the poster over here near the bed." Rearrange furniture for a home. I mean, they really got involved in the child's life.

In spite of her graphic examples of teacher-student violence and abuse of teachers, one of her most lasting impressions was of the respect for education she experienced in Japan.

I mean, when you walked into a Japanese classroom, there was such eagerness to learn, such a respect for those who could get the most education. Even with the bad kids, the communication with the teachers, they would walk into a teacher's room and they would talk to them like a big brother or something. There was a bond between the teacher and the student and that bond was because the teachers were there all the time for those kids. The teacher was their coach in a club of some sort. Their teacher was there to help them. They didn't give A, B, C, D on their report card. They would say, "This child is having difficulty in associating with this student and these are the methods that we took to get this student to merge as part of a Japanese child." That's the kind of critique that these teachers had and they would go away on weekends, a week at a time sometimes if you're in ninth grade, and spend that whole week as the mother or father to these children. It was almost like a family.

The teachers I interviewed expressed a variety of impressions and observations about the schools in their host country, but Ellen is the only one to describe such a wide range of feelings: from disgust about the treatment of Burakumin children and their actions to this last impression of a warm, family-like relationship among students and teachers in the schools. Although she greatly admired the relationship the teachers developed with their students, that relationship did not come without cost, especially with regard to time commitments. The ambivalent reactions that Ellen discusses about the exhausting schedules of Japanese teachers express the dilemma she faced. While admiring the results of that extra time and effort, she found that being a Japanese teacher working such long hours was intolerably exhausting and intense.

The tension within Ellen about these interchanges was part of the reason she felt extremely tired, leading to her hospital stays for stress and exhaustion. She found that being expected to perform on the time schedule of a Japanese teacher was very difficult for her. Her perspective on the demands of teaching in Japan ranges from its being impossibly time-consuming, almost precluding the possibility of a social life for teachers beyond school, to its social role of caring and responsibility for students. The ambivalence she felt about what she observed in Japanese schools is reflected in her discussion of the treatment of unruly children juxtaposed with her adulatory description of the emphasis on music in the schools. Ellen's impressions reflect the complexity of her long-term international experience in the ambivalence she was still feeling when I last interviewed her in March 1996.

THEIR LEARNING ABOUT SCHOOLING ABROAD

"I must respect my teacher." A student in China

The experiences of these teachers allowed them to learn and make some observations about the schools in their host countries. Their learning differed because of the different context and content of their teaching experience abroad. Ellen's long experience in Japan offered her an unusually rich array of positive and negative reactions. Mary Ehrhardt felt the frustration of the older Chinese teachers who had been thrown into teaching regardless of their interests or desires. They had gone through the cataclysm for education called the Cultural

Revolution (1966-1976), when all the schools were closed and intellectuals were sent to the countryside to shovel manure, among other things. Ed Donovan learned why his Chinese students were so motivated in comparison with many American students. Ellen Stacey was amazed at the violence she witnessed in the schools and the treatment of troubled, rebellious Burakumin and Ainu children. Denise Green witnessed the sense of belonging and identity with a school community, which she identified with the use of school uniforms and insignias.

Ed Donovan and Mary Ehrhardt expressed very different observations about their teaching experience in China, perspectives different from each other's and from those of teachers in Japan. Each of them was assigned to only one school (in Ed's case, one classroom) for the duration of his or her stay in China. Ed had more to say about his experience on the English corner in Kunming and connections he made there than about his formal teaching experiences. He was fascinated with why "everybody is so dead set on getting educated in English" where he was teaching in China. He analyzed this question and came up with three reasons. First, they saw it as a means of leaving China to go to a foreign country to study. Second, if they spoke English, they could go to international conferences. The most predominant reason, however, was that they could then read and understand better English journals in their field. As a result, Ed noted, "All of the people that I taught had at least ten years under their belt. Some of the older ones had been taught English by missionaries before the war [World War II]." Ed observed that their proficiency was mainly in reading and writing, not speaking the English language: "They didn't hear it and they spoke it oddly. And I don't mean that a British accent makes it odd. It's just that odd construction of phrases, very standard types of English. You don't know the idioms, or if you know what the idiom is, you don't know how to use it."

Ed was aware that education beyond high school was available to only a very elite few, perhaps two-tenths of 1 percent of the population of China, with the result that those students were extremely motivated, perhaps even more so than Paul Vandemere's Fortune 500 CEOs. This elite aspect of education in China puts the university teacher in an elevated role, as Ed describes it, a god like role. "I think that in Chinese education, that the teacher is God and they're puppets. And God infuses them with everything." He also noticed that Chinese students seemed adept at memorization:

They can repeat back volumes of poetry. They can repeat back chemical formulas. They can repeat back lessons that they had in physics ten years ago. Practically verbatim. An American student doesn't do that. The American student says, "Where do I find the information?" In China, the student can't say that because the library system practically precludes that. So they are not involved in the process because it's just not available to them.

Ed, like Ellen Stacey, thought about the issue of respect for teachers and education in general. He noted that "there is at least a more outward respect in China. There is an adherence to certain kinds of manners that must be exhibited to a teacher. Those manners seem to reflect a system of respect." His students greeted him with a short bow at first. "I'm not sure that this surface respect was always indicative of an internal respect," Ed said. When they told him that they must respect their teacher, he asked them why. "They would say things like, 'I must respect my teacher.' I would say, 'Why must you?' 'My parents say I must respect my teacher. I must respect you because you are a teacher.' " Ed attributes this respect mainly to the small number of young people who have the chance to go to the university.

By contrast, one of Mary Ehrhardt's greater concerns was the fatigue and depression she witnessed among middle-aged teachers in China. These K-12 teachers were faced with tremendous demands and personal reprisals if their students did not perform well on the university examination track. This is the major difference between the professors who taught at the university with Ed and ordinary teachers in China. The tiny elite who worked so hard to pass the examinations might well consider university professors akin to gods. The strain this puts on K-12 teachers almost reduces them to a condition of servitude by U.S. standards. Many of these teachers felt trapped in their jobs and had not wanted to become teachers in the first place, having been forced into these jobs by the government. They had not been introduced to the great philosophers of education, such as John Dewey, but were taught to mimic their teachers, having received little training in their field. Mary described the background to this situation.

I'll just say that maybe two-thirds of the English faculty were people in their 40s, and these are people whose educations were disrupted in their early teen-age years by the Cultural Revolution. They were sent to the countryside to be reeducated by the peasants and they were away from their education for five or six years. When they were allowed to return to Beijing, they were assigned a career. By that time, the higher education system was restructured using the Russian model so that there were mostly science institutes and manufacturing or engineering institutes. People wanting to become teachers were schooled in a particular subject area, but Mao Tse-Tung and the planners of that period had no need for the social sciences. These teachers had no idea of what educational philosophy was or how it impacted on classroom practice or educational psychology. . . . They only had been taught to mimic the teachers; as a matter of fact they had had one or two years of training in their subject and then were assigned schools. Twenty years later, many of them maybe didn't want to be teachers in the first place. They are caught, they have no alternative other than remaining in their positions.

She found that many of these teachers seemed bored and fatigued. They were the least receptive to the new ideas brought by the Americans that seemed to inspire the younger teachers.

We saw such fatigue on the part of these middle-aged teachers and wondered why they napped during their lunch hours. Actually it was depression rather than fatigue. Because of perhaps boredom in the way that they were expected to teach and the fact that they didn't have an alternative, they didn't have a choice of anything else to do. However, one of the teachers who was really exhibiting physical ailments, physical problems related to teaching, we discovered this year, took a sick leave but has really found another career and has taken advantage of the commercial real estate boom with his brother.

Mary hoped that the exchange program might make a difference in this key school, even among these demoralized teachers. She felt that if young teachers in disciplines other than English, who might be more receptive to cultural aspects of the exchange program rather than strictly English proficiency, were chosen to participate in the exchange, the impact might be greater. Students could be chosen as much for their outgoing attitudes as for their academic achievements, thus increasing their impact as cultural "ambassadors."

These teachers were keenly aware of the differences between their perceptions of education in the United States and education in Japan and China. They learned about what it means to be caught in a system in which the teachers feel they have no control. Some of their assumptions about the schools were debunked, especially Ellen's, when she was confronted by violence and what she saw as discrimination in Japanese schools. They learned how some schools operated in their host countries. Ellen especially admired the teaching of music and map skills, emphasizing student responsibility. It is apparent that the U.S. teachers were often learning while they were modeling and teaching American English.

Their learning about conditions in the schools, different approaches to curriculum, and the work of teachers was influenced by their different contexts. Ed's perspective about respect for teachers is affected by his teaching in the university. Mary understands a very different reality for the middle-aged English teachers who are burdened with tremendous responsibility and little authority to improve their situation, except to leave their teaching jobs.

Denise Green believed that the purpose of her trip was to expose Japanese teachers and students to a U.S. middle school teacher on a short-term basis. She seems to have accepted and enjoyed this role. Ellen Stacey's experience in Japan was as complex as her reactions to it. The demands of such an intense experience could overwhelm many people. Ellen has a great deal to teach us about how an extremely long-term, in-depth experience can affect the pedagogy of a veteran teacher.

These four teachers made positive contributions in the arenas in which they taught. Two of them also expressed concern that their short time in each classroom made it difficult for them to develop long-term, in-depth relationships with students and teachers. Mary Ehrhardt did not express this thought, perhaps because living with a family and riding a bicycle ten miles to and from school every day probably gave her a feeling of immersion in the culture that even Ellen Stacey, who lived in Japan for three and a half years, did not seem to experience.

These American teachers brought a different style of teaching to China and Japan. It is easy to imagine the frustration felt by the Chinese monitor when Ed Donovan refused to stay behind the podium as was expected, and the confusion of students who put their teachers on a literal and figurative pedestal, when he challenged the Chinese norms on gender by integrating the sexes with a seating chart.

The range of their contributions includes work with teachers planning lessons and holding seminars, modeling lesson plans and role-plays designed to provide more interactions with and among students, and frank discussions with teachers and students about cultural differences. Their contributions encouraged changes in pedagogy and connections with their students and colleagues abroad. The formal seminars with Chinese teachers planned by Mary and Jackie allowed them to address issues of great concern to these teachers. However, their informal exchanges on buses during joint excursions, in which the middle-aged teachers expressed a sense of personal malaise created by the upheavals in Chinese society, may have been even more meaningful. Much learning occurs in the face-to-face spontaneous exchanges among people of different cultures, leading to a kind of cultural knowledge that might not otherwise occur.

This interest in connection leads us to look at the international experience of these teachers through another lens, in Chapter 5 their living experiences in the culture. The friendships they made and keep, their supports, and their general observations on what they learned about the culture will help us understand their experience outside the schools at least as much as their experiences within them.

5

"Only Connect"*

This study does not consider a teacher's pedagogy apart from the way he lives his life. How each teacher constructs his life abroad within sometimes difficult circumstances helps us gain a more in-depth understanding of the learning opportunity entailed in this experience. This is why I have chosen to focus this chapter on the life of these teachers beyond the formal school setting. These teachers talked at length about the experiences that meant the most to them, especially their friendships with individuals in their host countries. What they observed and commented on about the culture in general, not just their school experience, will also help us understand the essence of their cultural experience, the nature of their cultural learning, and how they handled being strangers in a strange land which is the subject of Chapter 6.

The physical and psychological aspects of the context of their lives abroad provide a framework for teacher learning in an international environment. Similar to the six women in Mary Catherine Bateson's *Composing a Life* (1989), each teacher interacts within the constraints of her circumstances to construct her own experience and learning. Evidence of teacher learning abounds in these teachers' observations about their host countries. Sometimes the most rewarding learning occurs as the result of struggling with difficulties on a physical as well as a psychological level.

In four of the six cases, the teachers were exposed to less than ideal conditions from a middle-class U.S. perspective. How these four teachers managed day-to-day problems, such as living in an extremely

---

*Forster, *Howard's End* (1921), subtitle.

small space or being without hot water or heat when the temperature was forty degrees, their commitments to keeping up friendships over long distances, and their comments during these interviews about what they learned are another way of viewing this experience of living in a different culture. How these teachers handle being "the odd man out"—for example, being stared at as if you were an alien from outer space or accepting cultural practices such as slurping soup—will give us some understanding of the nature and impact of this international experience. This cultural learning will make a difference in each teacher's professional life in a U.S. classroom subsequent to the international experience.

LIVING ABROAD

"We bought our toilet paper and milk first from a little man on the corner." Mary Ehrhardt

Living conditions for these teachers ranged from more than adequate (Paul Vandemere) to rather primitive. The reactions among these teachers to their living conditions included the enthusiastic acceptance of difficulties as part of the challenge of this experience, a negative reaction, and passive acceptance. Each teacher interacts differently with her environment and learns in the process, the kind of experiential learning Mary Ehrhardt promotes.

Mary thought herself to be privileged, living with a Chinese family in a four-room apartment, opulent by Chinese teachers' standards (two rooms). However, when the heat was turned off by government decree on March 15, the weather was still very cold in Beijing. Dressing in many layers was necessary, as were quick sponge baths in the frigid air. The water for sponge baths had to be heated in a tea kettle in the evening. Ed and Heather Donovan found their hot water and electricity to be sporadic at best in the foreign faculty quarters they were assigned to; however, the year-round temperature in Kunming is comfortable (in the 70-degree range), it being on a 2000-foot-high plateau in southern China. Ed spoke little about his situation, but he did speak at length about the austere living conditions of some of his Chinese friends. Ellen Stacey showed such dismay about her prospective room that the Japanese authorities moved her to a larger apartment in a better location. Denise Green considered the display of negative emotion to be inappropriate, no matter what the circumstances of her living conditions. Her college experience in Ghana had exposed her to worse living conditions than existed for the exchange teachers in Japan.

Mary Ehrhardt's living situation was the most physically uncomfortable yet emotionally rewarding of these six teachers. Mary's construction of her experience in China is an example of how a teacher might make the most of a physically and mentally challenging international experience. Mary lived with the family of a teacher in Beijing. She had never traveled in a developing country before, so some of the conditions were a surprise to her. She was so elated about her chance to live with a Chinese family, however, that she considered the situation a challenge and grand adventure. However, toward the end of four months some things did begin to grate on her, such as the uncomfortable press of bodies on the buses or the sound of people clearing their throat, just before spitting, a habit caused by the extreme amount of dust and pollution in the air. "It was very challenging," Mary said. "I guess that's the personal part. It was physically challenging and the whole experience had to be faced with the spirit of adventure because there were hardships. We needed to feel that that was part of the adventure."

Riding her bicycle ten miles to and from her school six days a week presented further physical challenges.

Riding a bicycle twice a day probably ten miles each way in some days where the pollution was very bad and the winds were—I've never experienced winds like Beijing in the spring, because there's no vegetation, no grass in that city. The dust blew. By the time you have done this for two or three weeks, you have a hacking cough and are gray with dust by the time you get home. The first thing that my hostess taught me was that we always take our shoes off, never brought them in the house, and then always washed hands. "Xi shou," [wash hands] she would always say.

Traffic flowed seemingly without regulations "even though you rubbed elbows and ran over feet and had fender-bender kind of experiences every day." Her bicycle commute included "grease marks on my pants from wheel marks of other bicycles" and "the only catastrophe that I met with [which] was a head-on collision with either an army officer or a policeman. We literally collided head-on. He knocked me off of my bike. He fell on top of me. He was very angry at me for being in his way although he was driving the wrong way. He was going against traffic."

Conditions within the "sardine can" buses depressed her at times to the point that she wished she had not traveled to China.

I rode the city buses on occasion, which were more like sardine cans. Even standing under someone's armpit or chest to chest, there still was the measure of respect and consideration, I thought, for a fact that this was the way that some people had to get about. I guess one of the times I felt was the most discouraging and I thought, "Well, I really wish I wasn't here," was getting off the bus after having been forty minutes squashed into others. Then to have to step over and try to avoid all the spittle on the sidewalk and just the noise of clearing one's throat and spitting; that cultural custom really bothered me.

Mary tried to put these physical challenges into a more familiar context. It was her way of making sense of such a difficult and demanding life. However, the simplicity of some aspects of Chinese life greatly appealed to her. Thinking herself to be in a time warp of the 1950s in the United States, she remarked about the space-saving simple efficiency of life in China: one bowl and one pair of chopsticks per person; one comforter, no sheets to wash every week; one small refrigerator.

It did not seem like 1995, living in China. What I finally figured out that gave me a point of reference, it felt very much like living in the United States in about 1950, [reminiscent of] my memories of when TV was just new in my home and how everyone gathered around the TV in the evening. Well, my host family did that in China. They watched the evening news during dinner and then relaxed in front of the TV together in the evening. What they enjoyed watching on TV were American classic movies dubbed in Chinese, "Gone With the Wind," "Singing in the Rain." Elizabeth Taylor was very popular. I felt that their level of sophistication was about what my family's level of sophistication was in about 1950. Sunday was a day of rest until May 1. China still had a six-day working week. On Sunday, it was literally a day to nap, visit family, go on a shopping outing—kind of my memories of what Sundays used to be like in my childhood. So I came to sort of think that they were just at the dawn of materialism and all that that brings. That kind of helped me have some kind of reference point for living in China.

Mary described how she did her own hand laundry once a week "in a basin with cold water." Interacting with her host family within restraints provided additional challenges. She was not aware that being supplied with sheets was a luxury in China until her family felt "comfortable" enough with her to tell her this.

After a month or so of providing sheets for me on my bed, my family really became comfortable with telling me that they did not use sheets; that they have a little comforter, so perhaps just a bottom sheet and then a comforter (they do cover, they just pull up a comforter over them), and would that be all right with me? The sheets, they had to wash in the washing machine.

The Chinese authorities had made an effort to make the American exchange students and teachers more comfortable: "In previous generations of the exchange, the first host families were given Western-style toilets so that their American visitors would not be inconvenienced by squatting or in some cases using public bathrooms. The next set of American exchange teachers' and students' host families had a little propane heater so that they could have a shower installed."

When Mary became aware that the four rooms of her host family were "considered quite luxurious" in contrast to the living arrangements of most of her Chinese teaching colleagues in the English department, she was very concerned, especially about the Chinese teachers who had lived in the United States. In China they

lived in just one- or two-room apartments and they had taught for twenty years Since your *danwei* or your work unit is in charge of housing, this is what was offered to them. These were their accommodations. They were discouraged about it. They knew that, in fact they had been to America, many of these people, and they knew the lack of privacy and just the implications of living in cramped quarters. There was malaise about these conditions.

Given her knowledge about how her colleagues had to live, Mary felt very lucky to have a shower.

In my apartment, the little tiny tiled bathroom had a sink, a toilet, and then a shower nozzle overhead. There was a drain in the floor and the sink drained through a hose into this drain in the floor. But when you wanted to shower, you went from the little bathroom into the kitchen, which was on the other side of the wall. And on that wall was a propane heater and there were three valves to readjust, so the flow of water went from the kitchen and was redirected towards the bathroom. After turning the heater on, also ventilating the kitchen with an overhead fan and redirecting the flow of water, then you went into the little bathroom and opened the pipes, turned the faucet on and drained the cold water out. Now the cold water drained into a bucket. You didn't waste that water. It went into a bucket, but eventually when the water that you drew for the tap was warm, then you could turn on the little overhead nozzle and get a little more than a trickle but not the spray of water that we are accustomed to, but a warm shower. In my family, they really showered maybe every other day. I guess I probably showered too every other day.

When the heat from radiators was turned off on March 15, her family "heated water in a tea kettle rather than the shower in the evening. They heated the water, put the kettle in the bathroom and then we would just take a little sponge bath." This is why "all the Chinese people in Beijing wear layers and layers of clothing with long underwear and then just layering out and we did the same. Even in that period after March 15 till perhaps April 15, it was really cold."

Mary found these conditions to be almost a surreal counterpart to the high-tech entertainment technology her apartment contained. She began to construct an understanding of life in China as including extreme contrasts of complex to very simple. It was another way she made sense of her experience.

In my apartment, there were two TVs with VCRs, there was an elaborate stereo system, there was a wall of glassed cabinets which had an extensive video and audio collection. On my second night, the first full night in China, my host and hostess asked me if I didn't want to watch "The Fugitive." The daughter of the family and I sat in one room watching American video while the Chinese husband and wife sat in the other room watching Chinese TV. Not only could I watch the video, but because they have a satellite dish on their roof, I could get English channels from Hong Kong and listen to the news. That juxtaposed with the life in the street. . . . We bought our toilet paper and milk just from a little man on the corner. The construction workers who were working on nearby buildings slept on the sidewalk on a bedroll which they just picked up in the morning as we were going by. They just were amazing to me, those kinds of contrasts. . . . I really learned to enjoy the simpler living and to see that their needs were very well met with many fewer things and that they had time that I often didn't have because my lifestyle was much faster. I came to appreciate all of that.

Another experience involving extreme contrasts was Mary's first facial, something she had certainly not expected. Her hostess insisted that she have a facial and gave her one.

I had never in my whole life had a facial or ever thought about this. My first weekend, this was something my hostess said I must do, is have a facial. She does this fairly frequently, but because of the dryness of the climate, I, first, for a half an hour, had to stay over a steamer and steam my face. Then she had this cream that I had to put my fingers in, so she put a black mask over my whole face that had to stay on a certain amount of time. Then I had to wipe it off and wash and it was followed by oils that you put on your skin. On Saturday mornings, I was not accustomed to this kind of leisure. I was uncomfortable. It took way too long and it was too pampering. And they do this.

The highs, the lows, the surprises, and the contrasts made her experience worth enduring the hardships:

The food would really turn you off, served in gigantic pots and just eating in China is an adventure. You eat every part of the animal. That could really be distasteful to some people. Just the sanitary facilities, the school, two or three years old, but still used squat toilets. And the quality of Chinese toilet paper was like crepe paper. So you would accept the fact that you would be living with some hardships, but every moment of the experience was worth it.

Mary made the most of her difficult experiences, almost always emphasizing positive aspects. She focused on the graciousness of the hospitality she experienced: "As gracious as the hospitality was, I never, never feared for my personal safety ... because there was always this being on a bike, giving enough space; in an elevator, giving enough space."

This chapter, on the international experience of teachers, begins with the experiences of Mary Ehrhardt that were most important to her. How she constructed her life in China provides an example of how a teacher can learn by immersing herself in a culture and simultaneously reflecting on that experience to make sense of it. In some ways, Mary's is the most compelling example of teacher learning in this study. She stretches her mind to put her experiences into a familiar framework, such as a time warp of the 1950s or how the contrasts of technology and primitive conditions abound within one small household. She expresses her depression and frustration at times with being subjected to difficult conditions. However, she dwells on the positive opportunities to learn and make connections with others within her "grand adventure" of experiential learning.

Nevertheless, it is necessary to keep Mary's four months' experience within that context, because in this study, it is not necessarily generalizable to, for example, the three and a half years Ellen Stacey spent in Japan. Mary's U.S. family obligations precluded her spending much more time than four months in China. Had this not been the case, and had her time frame been one year or more, her report might have been different. The context of living with a family, although warm, friendly, and supportive for four months, might have been different if the time had been significantly extended. Nevertheless, Mary's experience can teach us a great deal about how a teacher can learn from the kind of international living such as she actively sought.

During her first experience in Japan during the fall of 1988, Ellen Stacey in stark contrast to Mary, was distraught on being shown a tiny apartment in Japan next to the train station, an extremely noisy location.

> The fifth week of our stay in Japan, everybody was taken by the school district that they were going to be living . . . and shown the place that they were going to live in. They took me to one place and it was smaller than this little condo. I said, "I can't live in this." I had a home, I couldn't live in this little, tiny thing. I started crying. So I went back to my room and plus, my room that they wanted me to stay in was right at the train station. Right at the train station. Every day all the trains were going right by my hotel, my apartment. I couldn't live like that. So they didn't get back with me for a week and I thought, well, maybe I'm not going to stay anywhere. They came to my room and they said, "We've found a place for you to stay." They walked me from the hotel to Mr. Itaro's house, his building. They said, "Here's a place for you to stay." It was about this big, maybe even a little bigger. It had four rooms plus a bathroom and a kitchen, which was quite large. And it was on the fourth floor. It was fine with me.

The colleague with whom she had studied for a year before going to Japan refused to talk to her. Ellen was mystified by this until she spoke with her after they returned from Japan: "Sheila, my study partner, we had studied for a whole year, never came to me, never. . . . She never said a word until she came back from Japan. She was living in a roach-infested place, and she didn't complain. She said she never could sleep without the lights on to keep the roaches at bay. She didn't have a place like I had." Ellen candidly expressed that in that moment she did not understand how most Japanese lived, especially in terms of the lack of space. She also was aware, as was Denise Green, that her facial expression was a important indicator to her hosts.

I didn't complain. I just cried. That was it because I didn't know how to express myself that I couldn't live in such a small place, and a noisy place at that. But I think what had happened is that the superintendent got involved in this location of where I was going to be and he wanted to know my expression. Because Japanese are trained to look at faces. They can tell whether you are happy, sad, sick, or whatever. That was one of the guy's jobs was to watch my expressions. About how upset I was—I can remember going back to the hotel and just crying. They said, "What's wrong?" I said that I can't live like that. Little did I realize that that was the way Japanese people live, but I wasn't ready for it.

Japanese officials were very generous to Ellen during this first experience in Japan because they were aware that she had taken a six-month leave of absence from her school district and was not funded by the state or the district to participate in this exchange:

Money was definitely not a problem. I came home with more money than I left because they kept giving me money for transportation; they gave me money for food. [They were] extremely generous and the transportation money is given to all teachers, but they never let me use transportation. Principals were picking me up from schools, picking me up from my place and taking me to my schools. I never took a train.

During Ellen's subsequent three-year experience, she signed a contract with the prefecture, which paid her contract in yen based on her previous U.S. salary of about $40,000 a year. By her third year, the yen-dollar exchange rate had changed to the point that her pay was nearing $100,000 a year. She had no complaints about her accommodations during those three years, but she did express that one reason she was expected to work so many hours the third year may have had to do with her pay rate. She was asked about what her life had been like in Milwaukee and how many classes she had taught a week there.

I said, "Twenty five hours a week." . . . Little did I realize that I was digging my own grave. . . . The dollar changed. My salary was no longer $40,000. It was up to $70,000 with the exchange rate. They gave me a car plus gasoline allowance, $100 a week. Plus they gave me a free house to live in. I had . . . probably the most deluxe apartment you could get. . . . The deal for the third year was even better, because two years you can live abroad without paying taxes. The third year they said that they would pay me.

Now this is where I really made my money; they would pay my
taxes. I had a choice, pay U.S. or Japan tax. They said they would
pay the Japanese tax. So now they raised my income to compensate
for the Japanese tax. It was that year that the dollar leveled to
the yen. I was making 35 cents on every dollar. I was making
probably close to $100,000 that last year. Because of that, because
of the dollar I was making, they expected me to work that kind of
work.

Mary and Ellen talked a great deal about their living conditions,
Mary from the perspective of the challenge they presented to her
while Ellen talked about her accommodations in terms of what her
needs were, for example, to live in a quiet atmosphere with ample
space. Mary was most concerned about adapting well in the context of a
Chinese person's life. She was concerned about not inconveniencing her
host family, which is reflected in the way she took only as many
showers as they; she went without sheets when she realized this is
how they lived. She did not expect the family to adapt to her needs;
she expected to adapt to theirs even if it meant politely accepting a
"pampering" facial that her hostess insisted on giving her. Mary
quickly became aware that her living conditions were "luxurious" in
comparison with those of most teachers. This deeply concerned her.
Ellen and Mary have very different expectations and thus, reactions to
their living conditions abroad. Understanding this distinction between
approaches to living conditions will help us understand their
observations, the way they learn, and how they adapt to their status
as a foreigner living abroad. This has great bearing on the kinds of
attitudes that they bring back to their classrooms in the United States.
    In contrast to Mary Ehrhardt and Ellen Stacey, Denise Green said
very little about her living conditions. It was apparently not a great
priority to her. However, she did speak at length about what she
thought was her role in Japan, how she felt she had to act in order to
get along there. Expressing negative emotions was something she felt
she should not do. Although she considered it "a bit tiring" to avoid
displays of irritated or impatient behavior, she explains: "But then I
had a mindset to be there a certain amount of time. If the mindset was
for two years, I would have done it for two years." She reconfirmed
these sentiments to her eldest daughter who went to Japan a few years
later. Denise warned her that she must not show negative emotions on
her face because this would be terribly disconcerting to her hosts.

I remember when my oldest one went to Japan, I told her, "You will
not be left alone for one moment." This is a girl that likes some
privacy. You need to get used to that fact, you will not be left

alone. I said, "Don't look sad. Don't look depressed because they are going to be very, very worried about you. Don't roll your eyes, because they'll think you're most displeased about something and will try to figure out what it is and try to fix it because they don't know you roll your eyes anyway."

Denise found that at times her life was difficult in Japan because she was allowed very little time alone. She thought that her Japanese hosts considered it their responsibility to entertain her or generally to keep her busy.

When the only time you can ever be alone is in the bathroom or when you're asleep, and when their culture believes it is rude to leave a guest alone (because we give them some privacy). But they think it's rude to leave a guest alone except when you're sleeping or in the bathroom. Then you have to adjust and it can be a lot to adjust to all of a sudden. You know you can't go in your room and close your door and cry in the bed. You feel like you want to; you can't.

There is a stark contrast between how Ellen Stacey and Denise Green viewed the way one expresses or conceals dissatisfaction in another culture. Denise, like Mary Ehrhardt, thought more in terms of adapting to Japanese culture than Ellen did. To Denise, who went to Japan the year before Ellen on a similar exchange program, physical space was a not an issue. Denise talked about the many festivals she experienced and sometimes participated in, the sense of community and shared culture that she witnessed, and her friendships there. Ed Donovan also treated space and physical comfort as unimportant. He felt he had been well prepared by the program leaders, so he was not surprised that physical conditions were difficult. Mary Ehrhardt considered her hardships part of the price she was more than willing to pay to live as a Chinese person, even though at times it did get her down. She did not, however, dwell on those negatives. She seemed so anxious to learn, to experience what real life was like in China even for just four months that the cold, the dust, the wind, the "sardine" experience in buses, even the bicycle crash were worth it to her. These four different reactions to difficult living conditions demonstrate the interplay of individual characteristics and the context of an experience.

The ways each of them adapted to and constructed their experience show that the more flexible, "other oriented," and connected each teacher was, the more he was able to benefit from this experience, the more he was able to learn and develop relationships with people in that culture. How they prepared for the experience also probably affected their reactions. Each of them stated that the connections they made with Japanese and Chinese individuals were of major importance to them. Sometimes the support they had from other Americans or Westerners helped them deal with loneliness, frustrations, or confusion erupting out of cultural misunderstandings.

SUPPORT, CONNECTIONS, AND FRIENDSHIPS

"Just like bread on butter."   Ellen Stacey

All six of these teachers prized the friendships they made with Japanese and Chinese individuals above all else. They were what made the experience most worthwhile for them. The relationships that developed have continued on a long-term basis. For example, in 1995 Ed Donovan made a special trip to Hainan Island just to visit his former colleagues and students, whom he had befriended during one of his earlier visits. Both Ed and Mary Ehrhardt are keeping up a correspondence with thirty or more friends. Denise Green has visited her Japanese acquaintances when they arrived in the United States as part of the exchange. Ellen Stacey received a phone call from Japan while I was interviewing her. I heard her speaking Japanese and laughing. It was one of her best Japanese friends calling about some things Ellen had sent to her. The importance of these friendships and connections was stressed by each teacher. For example, Paul Vandemere considered his Japanese support system the most crucial aspect to a positive and meaningful experience in a foreign country.

Because, according to Paul, the Japanese company he worked for provided a "great support system" for him and his wife, they were able to adjust easily and enjoy their experience in Japan: "I think any time you spend time in a foreign country, not everyone has a great experience there. A lot of it depends on the support system that you become part of and the company that I was part of had a great support system." The friendships he and his wife made, in addition to their desire to live in an area of Tokyo where there were few foreigners, allowed them to view different aspects of Japan than many other travelers see.

> They went out of their way to make sure that the part-time foreign instructors were included in the family. We met some wonderful Japanese people and made some great friendships. We lived in an area of Tokyo that had very few foreigners. We did that by design. We immersed ourselves as much as we could. My wife, more so than me because I was teaching English during the day

time, but certainly in the evening and on weekends, etc., there was a wonderful opportunity to really get to know people from different cultures, on much more than just a superficial basis that a tourist gets or even from a summer study program. There are different levels that you all get and certainly those who have been there longer have a much deeper understanding than I do. I just scratched the surface in two years, but it was a gracious country, it was a gracious group of people that we dealt with. They opened their doors, their homes. We had a wonderful time.

Bill Notebaum was pleased that "I was able to cross over to a personal friendship with two of the [Japanese] group leaders" during his monthlong experience in Japan. One was an older man "close to retirement" and the other "a younger man just finishing up his university work and in the beginnings of his career. They traveled with us everywhere." These men eventually visited Bill and his family in Cleveland and at his summer cottage in a lovely area of Ohio, "which was a real special experience for them."

SUPPORT

Some of these teachers considered it important to have a colleague, spouse, or friend as a support to them during their experience living abroad. Mary Ehrhardt felt great support from the Chinese family with whom she lived and from her colleague, Jackie, who lived with another family on the ninth floor in her building (Mary lived on the fifteenth floor). Mary who was fifty-four and Jackie who was twenty-eight, "commuted together" on their bicycles to school each day. The program planners were concerned that the people they sent to China would have at least one other colleague with whom they could share this very intense experience, as a support. Ed Donovan and Paul Vandemere felt that being accompanied by their wives had helped them to cope with and enjoy their experiences in a different culture. Although Denise Green was accompanied by five colleagues, she was isolated from her African-American culture. She appreciated the monthly get-together with her American colleagues to share stories and feelings. Ellen, who felt the most isolated, depressed, and lonely by the end of her third year in Japan, was also without much of a support group and with virtually no support from her own American culture.

The emotional support that Denise Green experienced with her group of Americans was very important to her.

The meetings with the other teachers, our little monthly informal get-together, helped because we could just sit down and let it all out, laugh at things, then go on back and not worry about it. We just decided to do this as a group, informally. I even forgot why, what the occasion was for the get-together. Everybody didn't come every time because sometimes you couldn't. Things would be planned for you and you wouldn't be able to. It's just like being with the host family. You really are on display.

Similarly, Mary Ehrhardt found that Jackie was a great support to her, because it would have been difficult to prepare the seminars and presentations, and plan trips alone. Their responsibilities for five U.S. high school students were a challenge.

Because it was an educational exchange where we were responsible for American high school students, and indeed it was only five American high school students, but there were many issues related to the students in our charge. There was personal counseling and even counseling around college decisions and then there were just administrative details. Where we were also responsible for being teachers ourselves, with the planning and carrying out of our classroom responsibilities, it was a very big job for one person to wear all of those hats. In some cases, we probably didn't specifically say, "I'll do this and you do that." We probably just worked in a complimentary way. . . . I think Jackie had terrific language facility. That was always helpful in negotiating, whether it was travel arrangements or shopping expeditions or eating in restaurants. I certainly could not have been nearly as effective as she.

Mary and Jackie collaborated on every decision, even though the Chinese authorities deferred to Mary because of her age.

We did have to make decisions in the country about travel and about putting on a banquet, and we had to negotiate issues with the school administrators. It was interesting because of our age difference. She is twenty-eight and I was fifty-four. I was always deferred to by the principal and the assistant principal. I was always seated next to the principal because I was the older woman. They came to me first for decisions. We certainly talked over every decision.

In contrast to Mary and Denise, Ellen Stacey was treated differently from the other U.S. teachers in her exchange program.

My commission was supposed to be way up in the mountains because my Japanese was the weakest. All three of the city teachers were supposed to be out in the country, because if we were out in the country, our Japanese would improve immensely. Those who were from the state capital were supposed to stay in the big city because their Japanese was pretty good and if they met a lot of Americans or foreigners, there would be no problem. When the superintendent took a liking to me, he changed my whole program. He took me from up in the mountains where I was supposed to be and put me in the middle of the city where he would be close, too. At least twice a week he would call the hotels that we were all staying in and invite us to parties. We were supposed to be studying Japanese and he was inviting us to these parties. He would always sit next to me. Well, the first two times it was fun. I'm a party person and I figured this is my first time in Japan.

Yet this attention by the superintendent had the effect of alienating her from the other five Americans on the exchange and isolated her even before she was the only one who had had her accommodations upgraded.

Then that caused a lot of problems, trust me. Nobody else would talk to me because he was always sitting next to me. He was sixty years old; I was only thirty and he's only half the size of me. I'm five foot nine. He was about five feet tall. They got so upset. They wouldn't talk to me, the other five Americans. They wouldn't talk to me and they would go right by my room and they would go into study groups. They would never knock on my door and ask me to join in their study groups. If we're all going to the bus station or the same destination, they would knock on the doors, but they wouldn't knock on mine. So I had to walk. If it wasn't for the only guy in the group, I would have gone insane.

LANGUAGE STUDY AND CONNECTIONS

In addition to supportive colleagues, hosts, or family members, some teachers in this study relied on internal support. Mary and Denise felt that their work to master enough of the language to be able to communicate with people who did not speak or were uncomfortable speaking English facilitated their connections with those people. Mary Ehrhardt's hard work studying Chinese paid off in the relationships she had with her Chinese family. She felt fortunate to be able to share feelings about her family with them in Chinese, because they did not speak English. They talked about their older children, her host's daughter being twenty-four years old, the same age as Mary's son. It was time for the young woman "to have a serious boyfriend and consider getting married," Mary said. What was "most meaningful to me is that Zhou Li, my hostess, and I could talk about our daughters, our concerns, and hopes. We could, as mothers, sort of giggle about their boyfriends and whether we approved or disapproved."

The daughter of Mary's host family also helped her prepare the speeches she had to give in Chinese every so often to as many as seventy people. She described the kind of speech she would make:

> The setting would be our first sort of official welcome by the principal, the East City District educational representatives, the city of Beijing educational representatives. So I would usually say that we appreciated their initial hospitality, that we had been there a certain amount of time, that we were finding our host families and home settings very acceptable, and that we were beginning to be acquainted with our students and enjoying our students, enjoying their classes and we were enjoying our teaching assignments. We're very grateful to them for providing this opportunity.

The process she would go through before giving the speech involved several steps: "I would write it in English and as much in pinyin as I could. Then the daughter in my host family would really help me fill in the vocabulary and the grammar and put it in the correct word order so that then my job was to learn it so that I could say it." After her speech, "there was always great applause and always beaming faces that we were attempting to communicate in Chinese." Laughing, she described how she had mistakenly used the word *ping guo*, meaning apple, for *peng you*, which means friend: "I introduced our friends as apples." She felt that the Chinese knew she was trying very hard to communicate: "I was certainly nervous and they appreciated my efforts." They all laughed together at this mistake. Learning Chinese at a rudimentary level helped Mary make connections with Chinese people that were important to her social and professional life in China.

> I found that the language study was really worthwhile when I arrived in Beijing because I lived with a non-English-speaking family and I had enough proficiency by then that we could at least talk about the basics of daily living. I think it pleased them that we had that level of communication. It also gave me a bit more confidence that I could find my way around a city. I could shop, and

I could converse with colleagues, teachers, other teachers at school, and students. So I knew when I made the commitment the reason for it. It really was essential for living four months there, that I had at least some level of language.

Denise Green also talked about how helpful her ability to use some Japanese was to enable her to have better discussions with the children about her life in the United States. She also talked warmly of a teacher with whom she had become friends. Denise called her "the New York City lady." She was the mother of the tardy student Denise had called "Yakuzasan," to the delight of the class. Her friend was quite concerned that Denise was single and had no male "significant other," so she arranged a party at her home for Denise to meet four eligible bachelors. During this evening, most of the conversation was a mix of Japanese and English. Her friend's husband and son picked Denise up, and when they arrived,

I was presented with a dozen long-stemmed roses, which cost twice as much in Japan as they are here. She had told her husband to pick out three friends of the appropriate age that had money in the bank. She told me, "I had to make sure they had money," who were not married that could take me out. She said, "If I had known you were leaving so soon, we would have done this earlier." When she did this, I had one week before I was leaving the country. So when I realized what was happening, I thought, "Oh my goodness, what am I going to do about this?" One was an artist and he had a bank account, she told me. And these were some of her husband's drinking buddies. One was a rice merchant. One was an English teacher there who thought he should come along in case there were any translation problems. Then, of course at the meal her 15-year-old son was served some beer. He went in the other room. I said, "You give beer to him?" She said, "But only at home." New York City would be a great city for her. I think she would like New York City. She just has that kind of personality. But she was doing this because she thought I should have a man in my life. She said they were all of good character. They all have jobs and they all have bank accounts. I said, "OK."

One of the four bachelors, a rice merchant who sang to her earlier in the evening, asked if she would join him for dinner. Denise politely declined because every evening was taken up with the "last week activities," such as the farewell banquet. She was quite relieved at the timing of this get-together because it spared her more excuses: "I'm kind of glad she didn't arrange that any earlier because it would have

put me socially in a difficult position for it to be known that I was going
out with men. It would have started a lot of gossip and it would just be
very difficult for me."

SMALL HAPPENINGS

There are different kinds of connections among people, some of which
are close and intense. Others are more acquaintances than close
friendships. Some can be brief chance meetings of strangers on a bus or
train excursion. Denise Green found that small happenings like
laughing at herself as she awkwardly tried a potter's wheel to make a
coffee cup helped her to connect with people in Japan.

> When they took me to this place where this famous pottery is
> made, I had an official escort. So I got kind of a special tour which
> I was glad about later on. One person was taking pictures. They
> were really trying very hard to make a potter out of me, but it
> wasn't working so well. Finally, the master potter shaped it, put a
> little handle on it and let me put my name on it in Japanese on the
> bottom. I was always teased when those pictures were passed
> around about Green sensai's coffee cup because I didn't have much
> to do with this finished project; the master potter did. But they
> were laughing at me and joking. And this is it [as Denise held up
> the coffee cup]. They were having the best time.

Even though Denise taught for only two weeks at a time in a school,
she developed several friendships: "The relationships that were going
to be formed had to be formed pretty quickly because they knew I would
be going on to another school. So this was a teacher who I talked to a
lot when I was in her building. . . . But even after I left her school, I was
invited to her home for a meal more than once. She was someone I was
comfortable with."

> It was just interesting. . . . The Japanese woman, when she got
> closer, talks about men. It sounded like people talking about men
> here or anywhere else. Because you know in public you're supposed
> to save face, yours and other people's face. But in private they
> would talk about, when you got close, they would talk about men.
> Then I remember this one woman telling me she was jealous because
> I was divorced. I said, "Why, you have a good husband?" She
> said, "Yes, but you can make your own decisions. I have to ask his
> permission for everything. He goes out and drinks with his
> friends. He doesn't like it if I want to go out and drink with my
> friends." Doesn't that sound like something you have heard?

Denise, like Mary Ehrhardt, seemed to relish going out among the people to experience the festivals. She often traveled alone and felt that she was treated very well by the Japanese people she met on these trips. She often perused the English version of the *Japan Times* to find out when and where the many festivals in Japan were being held. This is one way she constructed her experience to learn and connect with some of the Japanese people. She enjoyed and admired the community participation in these festivals, with many groups showing their affiliations by wearing *"happi* coats"—not "happy," she explained, but meaning "festival coat." Sometimes she would "jump on the train" during her free weekends and attend these festivals, especially if they were in her favorite city, Kyoto.

It was such a wonderful city, just full of history, and I never did see everything and do everything there was to see and do in Kyoto. But if you want to go someplace for a weekend, there was always something happening. Sometimes just walking around getting intentionally lost in an area you've never been before, I would run into these little parades, these little—I shouldn't say little— parades or ceremonies at a temple or at a shrine, being carried out for some reason. Sometimes I could find out the reason, sometimes I wouldn't be able to. These were fascinating to watch.

She described a favorite festival in Kyoto, the Matsuri, in which adults participated with elaborate floats, the ritual surrounding this festival having been developed over many generations. The community works to assemble floats with all the participants playing certain roles.

There's community participation because those floats have to be assembled, and at least two weeks before the Matsuri you can see strange scaffolding in places in Kyoto along certain streets because that's where the floats are being assembled. The floats may be a couple stories high. They're made with the old-style wooden wheels and to turn corners, they put something under the wheels and you hear the men yelling, calling to each other, but they're not yelling anything. They'd be saying commands that had been used for generations. . . . I just happened to be in Kyoto one Saturday or Sunday afternoon and I was walking along one of the main streets and I saw one of the floats. It was a big, long one that had to be pulled up the street, and people were actually pulling this float to get it in position for the parade. People on the streets were just walking up and putting their hands on the ropes and helping to

pull it. So I walked up and I helped pull it, too. That's a chance
for community participation. They didn't care. Anybody that was
around could just come and help pull. People smiled.

Denise also learned the steps to a dance in the streets of Sapporo,
Hokkaido, the northernmost of the four main islands of Japan.

I was standing there and started talking to someone next to me and
instead of parading through the streets at this point, they were
creating a big circle on this one boulevard. I joined in and they
were showing me how to do their version. I said, "This is how I
learned it in Otsu." They showed me how and once again people
from one organization wore the same *happi* coat or the same
yekhta. I was by myself.

Denise felt that the Japanese made it easy for her to feel welcome and
join in with their social functions, such as festivals. It is as if they
wanted to reach out to her as a foreigner to graciously include her in
their celebration. Perhaps because she was such a willing participant
and ventured out alone, she was able to enjoy and greatly treasure these
experiences.

They make you feel welcome to do that. Strangers will ask you, if
you look interested, if you are watching, or instead they will
motion to you, come on and join. So you feel very comfortable doing
it and people actually show you how to do the dance. If you are
messing up, then they tap you on the shoulder and show you how to
do it the right way or something like that. I guess what I'm saying
is that the *happi* coat reminds me that there are so many of those
opportunities that I saw in the short time I was in Japan that I feel
you know does a lot to preserve their culture and bind the people
together.

Denise, like Mary, created these opportunities for learning and
cultural connections, whether she spontaneously used the opportunity
as in the case of her funny cup or she placed herself in a situation, such
as the festivals, where she was likely to make connections with
people.

Mary Ehrhardt felt she was able to interact and make connections
with Chinese people on an adventure she, her colleague, and five
students experienced taking the "hard-seat" train from Beijing
southeast to Suzhou, Hangzhou, Shanghai, and Huangshan. "Hard-
seat" is the Chinese equivalent of second- or third-class travel. Hard-
seat trains entail many stops and are often very slow. They are much

less expensive than soft seat trains. This was a difficult because, Mary explained, "foreigners are not supposed to travel hard seat." By traveling hard seat, the seven Americans were able to take this long trip for a total of $500 for each of them.

> As far as our hard-seat experience, I wouldn't give it up for the world. We traveled over night seventeen, eighteen hours hard-seat and hard-sleeper, actually. In a hard sleeper we were in open compartments, which had three levels of bunks, so six people in one compartment. We really were like on shelves. We were shelved. We had a mat, a blanket, a pillow, and then we shared a very small table. We sat during the day on the lower bunk. We had a thermos of hot water. There was a lavatory at either end of the car and in some cases the train car was air-conditioned. But we stopped many times and at each, if we wished we could get off and buy our little container of ramen noodles and add hot water. That was the quality of the meal, however, and this is the way the Chinese travel.

As many Americans have experienced in China when they go off the tourist track and interact with ordinary Chinese people, Mary was surprised to find herself, Jackie, and the students a major attraction on the train: "The trains were very precisely on schedule, but we became the entertainment. Families traveling came and sat in the aisle in a little jump seat and watched the Americans and wanted to try to talk to us and wanted their babies to come and see us. We really interacted and interfaced with Chinese travelers."

Ed Donovan had a similar experience traveling hard seat in China, although for a much shorter trip than Mary. It was also an experience that he treasures. During his latest trip back to Kunming to see old friends (1995), he found himself on a hard-seat train.

> It was a ball! It was a ball! The guy that was supposed to get me my ticket, didn't. I mean I never made contact with him. It was an express train, it said, but it wasn't the express train. It was local. It took me five and a quarter hours to go ninety miles. Isn't that something? There were a few people who could speak English, but mostly it was a couple of gamblers here and a couple of gambling games there, and kids peeing on the floor there, just the kind of stuff you see in the street. They had a lot of conversations going on. I had a pair of lovers right next to me. They couldn't keep their hands off of each other except when they pulled into a station. Then they would buy all of the food in sight and sit there and scarf it down. Once the food was finished, they were right back at each

other. It was incredible! Some old lady gave them hell for making out on the train. They were acting sheepish and looked at me.

As Denise describes her connections with Japanese friends and strangers, and Mary and Ed describe their slight connections on hard-seat trains, the juxtaposition of Ellen Stacey's accounts provides a stark contrast. Ellen does not say much about the friendships she developed on her first experience in Japan for seven months, which was structured much the same as the program for Denise. Ellen described her first trip as a whirlwind that caught her up and was over too quickly, leaving her with a desire to return to Japan. She felt she had been "cheated" on the first trip out of learning much Japanese and seeing the country: "It was like being in a whirlwind. What was I doing here? Before I knew it, it was finished." In addition to her language work with tutors in each school, Ellen found that her side trips with administrators to places of interest were opportunities for her to work on her language skills.

When I told you they always had tutors or people that would be my mentor in every school, I would bring my books and they would help me on the days that they didn't have five classes to teach or when they only had one class during that day. They would help me that way and also what I would do is I'd be in the car, on the way to work with the assistant principal or the principal, and they would practice Japanese with me. I would be looking in my dictionary trying to figure out what they were saying.

She appreciated the side trips to Kyoto and Hiroshima, but wishes that she could have seen more of Japan. Unlike Denise, whose school district financed most of her trip and paid her salary while she was in Japan, Ellen's inner-city district did not have the funds to give her anything but an unpaid leave of absence, which put her on a much more limited budget than Denise's.

FRIENDSHIP

One source of friendship and support Ellen developed during this first experience was with a regular Japanese teacher who went out of her way to help Ellen.

I remember the one teacher, she was wonderful. . . . This was a regular teacher and she was in charge of me. . . . Her real name was Hari. She said, "My Western name is Margaret." I liked her a lot. She helped me bridge a lot of gaps in the Japanese society. She was single, but she was also international where she traveled a lot. She tried to make sure wherever I went that there would be men around because I was single. She made sure that I went into Kyoto at least once a month, even though I wasn't at her school any more. She tried her darnedest to practice her English skills, though she was a physical ed teacher. She made sure that I saw every kind of class that was offered to Japanese students in her school. She was a real sweetheart.

Ellen found ways to break the ice with her Japanese colleagues in the schools. Another friend set her up to use a few Japanese words in his phone conversations with her. Her Japanese colleagues thought the whole conversation was in Japanese, which helped to break the ice in each of the schools where she was assigned to teach.

That guy was wonderful, too. A travel agent who spoke beautiful English, he was so funny. He used to call me up at school and he would say, "Whatever I say to you, just say, 'Hai, hai.'" So then he would ask me a question and I would say, "Yes." He'd say, "No, I told you to say, 'hai, hai.'" So I'd say, "Hai, hai." And then he'd say at the very end of the conversation, "Now I want you to say, 'Wo kari mashta.'" It means "I understand." "Wo kari mashta, hai, hai." So when I would hang up the phone, all the Japanese would come around because they thought I had spent fifteen minutes talking in Japanese with this gentleman and I was understanding everything this gentleman was saying. I didn't understand half the stuff that they were trying to tell me. What he was trying to do was make it so comfortable for me in that school and it broke so much ice in every school I would go to.

Ellen also took advantage of chance opportunities to connect with others. She was asked by a woman who helped her on the road to be an English conversation teacher in the mountains on Saturday mornings.

When I drove my car over a cliff, the woman who came to my rescue (this was a crazy story) . . . was studying English and she had been studying it since she was in eighth grade. She was my age. We became very good friends. She asked me to be the English conversation teacher every other Saturday. It was wonderful. So every other Saturday I'd go up to the mountains and I'd be their English conversation teacher. That was wonderful and still today, we communicate.

Ellen viewed relationships between friends in Japanese culture to be almost as important and obligatory as family relationships, thus inhibiting long-term friendships between foreigners in Japan and Japanese people.

> I had so many friends, but Japanese people have a feeling that if they make friends with you, they can't stay friends with you. The reason they don't stay friends is because you move away, your interests change, and you won't be a permanent friend. So they don't make long-lasting friendships with foreigners. For a good friendship, they have to give you part of themselves. I guess that's the bottom line. They gave so much of themselves and got nothing in return [from foreigners].

During her three years of living there she noticed those who were invited to Japanese weddings: "If someone gets married in Japan, they invite friends from their elementary grades, even if they're in university level and they have their professors, their teachers, their instructors, all their lives people who have been mentors for them go to their wedding. A wedding is a really family-friend thing, long term."
This was the kind of friend Sumi was. (Sumi was the friend who had called Ellen during our interview.) Sumi was a substitute in one of the last schools that Ellen was assigned to during her first year there before she went home for her sister's funeral.

> When I went there, Sumi and I just like (snap fingers), bread on butter. We just got along perfectly. They started to abuse her. She said, "What do you mean you want me to stay till 5:00? I'm a sub. I'm only going to stay to 3:00, that's all I'm staying." She became very outspoken. So at the end of that school year (their school year ends in March, and I got to see her in March), and I thought, well, here I meet this great person and now I'll never see her again. She wasn't going back to school to teach because she didn't like the way they were treating her. She started calling me up. She said, "Come on over for dinner." That was the first house I had been invited to for dinner.

In Ellen's three and a half years in Japan, this was her only invitation into the home of a Japanese family: "They would say, 'There's a party and please come to the party.' But they never invited me to their home. As a matter of fact, for two and a half years, Sumi's home had been the only home I had ever been invited to." Unfortunately, Cathy Davidson's *36 Views of Mount Fuji* (1993) was not available for Ellen to help prepare her for the fact that the lack of space in most city apartments makes the entertainment of foreign guests in the home difficult and rare.

Ed Donovan made many friends in China, some thirty-five of whom he had been communicating with for nine years: "I've written all of them. They've been responding. They all want to come here, of course." During the summer of 1995, before Ed began his teaching assignment at a teacher's college, he visited many of these friends.

> I went to Hainan Island. This is about the first of July, last of June. I met friends that I hadn't seen for nine years, that I had been writing and they had been writing me. That was quite exciting. From the time I was first in China, that was ten years ago. I saw a former university professor who had been an exchange scholar here at the university. I saw a gal who was a former colleague in the English department at the medical college, who was also a student, who is now a travel agent in Hiko city. Another who had been a former student of mine who was in the physiology department at the medical college, who is now selling construction stuff. She sells things like waterproofing for cement.

He subsequently returned to the medical college outside of Kunming to visit many friends there: "I saw many, many people that I knew before, many of them who live off of campus. I mean, they don't have anything to do with the school at all and were just delighted to see me and had dinner for me." He also made some new friends with whom he communicates now in addition to the others from prior visits, some of whom live in the same cities and share his letters with each other: "My stamps for foreign letters are—I spend a lot for them every month. Some of them are stamp collectors so I usually put a packet of domestic stamps in with them so that they've got a copy of them. So it's kind of interesting." Asked how he felt about this visit with old friends, Ed answered with gusto: "It was a ball! It was a ball!"

During his year in Kunming, the English corner on Sunday morning is where Ed made some of his first meaningful connections with Chinese people. Just the challenge and adventure of breaking out of his "cocoon" constructed by the authorities at the medical college and venturing a few kilometers by bus into the city center created a sense of excitement for Ed: "One of the things that was really surprising to me was going to English corner on Sunday mornings." A teacher from the teacher's college in Kunming, whom Ed still writes to occasionally, had started the corner to allow English-language students in the city to converse in English with each other. Ed had been in China for only one month when he heard about the English corner. He made his queries about the corner part of his English lesson.

I decided I'd go and find it. I didn't know anything about the town; it was my first month there. I hadn't even been downtown except by being transported down, and in the back seat of the car, you don't pay attention to where you are going. So I asked one of my students, "How do you get there?" In order to use their English, I'd say, "How do you go downtown?" They would say, "Oh, you catch No. 5 bus; it takes you down to the center of town." Then I started asking about what was in the center of town. "Oh, the park was at the center of town." "What happens in the park?" "Well, they've got a merry-go-round and some of this other stuff." And I said, "Do people walk in the park on Sundays?" "Yes, people walk in the park on Sundays." You have to repeat. And when they'd talk to me, I would repeat what they said so that they were sure I heard what they said. I think that's a pretty common technique when teaching a language.

When he mentioned to a colleague about wanting to go down to the English corner, she was concerned about his going there alone.

I asked one of the other foreign-language teachers about it and she said, "Oh yes, I go down there sometimes." I said, "Well, I'm going to go down Sunday." She said, "Oh, someone should go with you." And I said, "OK, if somebody wants to come, that's fine." Sunday morning nobody was at the apartment door, so I walked out, went down and got the No. 5 bus, went down to the center of town, found my way into the park and just kind of strolled around and came on [the] English corner. People flocked around me, literally. So for three hours we held forth and finally everybody had to go to lunch. They all invited me back for each Sunday thereafter, and as often as I could come.

The people in the park asked him about the city he was from and his family.

People would say, "What city are you from?" I would say, "I'm from the city of Detroit." They would say, "Oh, that is the automobile capital of the world." And I would say, "Yes, that is." They want to know about your family. They want to know about things that they're familiar with, that they can respond to you with. I would say, "My father is deceased." "What's deceased?" "That means he is dead." They understood that. Then I would say, "Is your father still alive?" "Oh, yes, my father is well." I would say, "My mother is still alive, she is seventy-eight." "Oh, isn't that a wonderful age. Aren't you fortunate to have your mother." And then you ask them. It went around, like brothers and sisters.

He went every Sunday, and on the third Sunday

the authorities were waiting for me in my apartment. They were absolutely appalled that I would go downtown by myself. I was surprised that they were astounded at this. They said, "Oh, but we have pickpockets in town." And I said, "Nobody's picked my pocket yet." "Oh, but you are not safe." What they were trying to do was curtail my activity in the middle of town. They said, "Oh, you must have somebody go with you." I said, "I've been going for three or four weeks now. Nothing's happened. I don't expect anything to happen." "Oh, but you must take somebody with you." "If you want to send somebody, fine."

The next Sunday his "doctor" students were supposed to escort him into town.

Well, they weren't there when I got on the bus, so I went anyway. They showed up about an hour later huffing and puffing, saying they had really been scolded by the authorities for not going downtown with me. I said, "Well, the bus was there, so I just took the bus." They stayed with me and they walked back uptown with me and they showed me a couple good places to eat. We sat and had lunch. I bought lunch for them. That went on for about three or four weeks. Then finally, they decided I could get along OK on my own.

On the fourth Sunday Ed learned what some of the town's people thought of the people connected with the medical college. He, his wife, and Dr. Wong, one of his English students, were confronted by a very angry Chinese woman.

Heather was off buying pencils or pencil holders. This huge crowd gathered around her, to watch her bargain for these pencil holders. I'm standing off to the side, kind of leaning up against the building. I've got jeans on and tennis shoes, a hat and just a sports shirt on. This lady (you know how the Chinese orate in a classroom; their voice off the back wall of the building), she started this, and very soon I had a very large crowd around me. And I said to Dr. Wong, "What's the big deal?" "She wants to know who you are." I said, "Tell her I'm a teacher up at the college." He said, "Well, I did, and she doesn't believe me." I said, "Ask her to ask the question through you." So he repeated what she asked and I said, *"Lao shi at Long Yi da xue"* [professor at Long Yi University]. She paused a minute, and said, "Well, he's dressed like the rest of us." She said this in Chinese and Wong was translating: "I guess he can't be all bad. He doesn't look like one of those stuffed shirts." So from there on in, in town I could do no wrong. People would wave and say, "Hello, Mr. Ed." What happened was that I had established a contact between the college and the town, something that had never been done.

Ed used his sparse Chinese vocabulary to break the ice with this woman. In doing this, Ed feels, he broke a barrier between the town's people and the university. A clerk in the store who was trying to learn English would often accompany them back from the park.

He was just struggling to learn English. He had a limp. He was a heavy smoker. He used to walk back with us from the park on Sundays. We invited him back to the apartment a couple of times. He came up and sat and talked with us for a bit. One evening he showed up. Usually we had students in. We invited him in. He was very embarrassed because he recognized that these were all scholars from the college. I said, "Come in, you are a friend of mine." And so he came in and sat in a corner. He didn't say very much. He was watching the conversation going on. About 10:00 he left with everybody else. I said, "Gee, thanks for coming. I really enjoyed having you here and having your company." He just looked at me.

When the year was about to end, this man arrived at their apartment along with quite a few others who were there to say good-bye.

People from all over town were coming into the apartments to say good-bye to us. This guy showed up on one of our last days and before my students and some of the college leaders and whoever else was there, he stood up and said, "All my life, I was taught to hate Americans. I have found out that it is not right to hate all Americans. Mr. Ed has taken me as a friend. He is a very educated man. I don't have an education. But he does not see that as a barrier to friendship. Now, no longer do I." You could hear a pin drop in the place. He left after that. It was very touching.

During a visit with an artist whose work he admires, Ed, with little facility in Chinese language, enjoyed (and endured) five hours of pointing at things and struggling to learn the words.

Yeah, we get along, it's amazing. I can't speak Chinese, he can't speak English except for a few words (he of English and me of Chinese). We get along fine; we don't need anybody around. We can communicate. It's very interesting. It's hard, but we've been left alone for like a day at a time and when you're done, you're completely exhausted because you've gone through this pantomime routine and the grunting and pointing, but we enjoyed it. Heather had gone with my friend who was a friend of his. She and her husband had taken Heather some place else in Kunming I think to buy a dress or to get a dressmaker to make a dress for her. I say we were left a day, it was probably five hours or something. So the artist and his wife and I were in his apartment and he was doing some painting. His wife cooked a meal for us and we would point to things and make the word for it in English and Chinese and we'd say, "Hen hao" [very good]. But I picked up a lot of words. We went around pointing at things and he'd give me the Chinese name and I'd give him the English name. I've got to say that he learned more English than I learned Chinese I think. But it was a delightful afternoon, it really was. [Nevertheless], it was very tiring. I got out of there and we finished dinner and we got left alone. Heather and I were talking and I started going to sleep. She said, "What's the matter with you?" I said, "I'm exhausted!" The culture antenna is up the whole time. It's tough. Yeah, he hung out a lot of stuff for us and art magazines, a lot of art magazines. Really some beautiful, beautiful things this guy has done. But you know, he's retired now and the last time I wrote, he was not in good health.

In spite of the language barrier, Ed has kept in touch with this artist through a friend for nine years: "He doesn't speak English or read it, so I have to write to somebody that knows him who can translate for him. I've got a good friend of mine who lives in Kunming who was a scholar here in '85 at U of M [University of Michigan]. So when I write him, I always enclose a note for the artist. That's kind of neat."

Ed has done much more than maintain contact with another of his colleagues at the medical college, a divorced woman.

She has a nine-year-old daughter and she's backed into a job that she'll never escape as an English teacher at the college. She'll never get a promotion; her pay will probably stay with the cost of

living. Then she's got an elderly mother that she cares for and she
lives in a place that's awful. It's so awful that she wouldn't even
invite me. She would always meet outside on the street some
place.

Divorce still is anathema to many people, and it would count against
her at work as well as in her personal life. Raising a child under these
circumstances presents even more serious problems.

She's thirty-six I think now. Her chances of remarriage are pretty
slim, even though the ratio of men to women is way out of whack.
They've got about 5 percent more men in China than they do women
because of the practice of abortion and child abandonment and
things like that. This gal will be productive all of her life, but
she will never rise in the hierarchy of this school at all. She was
married to a guy in the school. He's no longer there. He went back
to his home town wherever that is, nine hours away. He doesn't
even make contact with her anymore. Just to kind of make sure
that she has some kind of cushion to work with, I've been helping
her along periodically and I want that kid of hers to have a decent
education. She knows it. The kid is only nine; it's a little girl.

Ed has decided to help this woman and her daughter out financially
once in a while to be sure that this little girl will have a chance for a
better education.

I just make sure that she gets a little cushion once in a while to be
sure that the kid can get enrolled in a decent school. I send her
some money periodically—$100 at a pop, which isn't an awful lot
of money. It's 800 yuan, 830 yuan. But for her it goes a long way
because it's back in the interior of China. They pay fees now to
send them to school. The fee level depends on the school. So if
this kid wants to go to the key school in Kunming, she's going to
have to pay a higher fee than in the neighborhood school.

Ed, like Denise and Mary, worked hard to make and maintain many
friendships with individuals in China. It was these relationships
that were most meaningful to him.
    A few days before my last interview with Mary Ehrhardt, she had
called her host family in Beijing and had a forty-minute conversation
with them just to catch up.

Just on Saturday, I called my host family in Beijing. Bob and I sent
a fax; actually, he made the first phone calls and found that fax is

an international word. My [host] family could understand that a fax was coming. We set up a time, so that Saturday morning it was close to my hostess's birthday, and I called and I invited my wonderful friend who taught with me to come because her Chinese is so much better than mine. We had probably a forty-minute conversation and caught up. This is a very warm friendship. It's really—I know that we will meet again.

The connections and friendships that these six teachers made in their host countries, at superficial as well as deeper levels, were the highlights of their experiences in Japan and China. The experiences discussed in depth for the four teachers highlighted in this chapter are illustrative of the convictions of all six. Paul and Bill concentrated much more on the effect of their experience on their work in the United States. Their narratives will be explored at length in Chapters 7, 8, and 9. Those who were able to establish connections in classrooms as well describe a rich and meaningful experience. Some of these teachers exerted a tremendous effort to establish relationships that have lasted. Mary Ehrhardt's work learning Chinese paid off in closer relationships with her family. Ed Donovan's correspondence, followed up with visits to his friends nine years after his initial experience, shows his deep commitment to them. Ellen's ambivalence about her Japanese experience seemed to fall away when she talked with and about her very close Japanese friend. The stories they tell about challenges—traveling on hard seat trains or attempting to create pottery or dancing in a festival—are told with a spirit of delight and wonder. The importance of these connections are crucial to an understanding of the impact of this experience on their personal and professional lives.

What seems to be the most meaningful aspect of their international experience is their connections with individuals in the culture, their friendships. When Mary Ehrhardt talked about living in the cold, the difficulties of showering and riding to school, it was not as a complaint. Her eyes sparkled with the spirit of adventure. She expressed her concerns about the families, the women teachers and the struggles she sees in the future for young people, especially young women with a sense of compassion and empathy. She does not blame the middle-aged teachers for their feelings of hopelessness. She is concerned about them as individuals who have difficulties, that many U.S. citizens would have trouble understanding. Ed Donovan also evidenced worry and concern about the future for some of his Chinese friends. He has made a financial investment to help the child of a friend, to make some difference in the child's life. The connections and friendships they have made encompass the most meaningful aspects of their international experience.

Teacher learning occurs at the intersection of the disposition of each teacher with the international experience. This experience includes many variables such as living conditions, support, small encounters and friendships that affect the educative nature of the experience. The character of each teacher greatly affects the learning potential of the international environment. Their reactions to being an outsider in another country, the subject of Chapter 6, provide another context for what they learned abroad, their observations about the culture in which they lived and worked.

6

Strangers in Strange Lands

You felt just like you had stepped into the painting. —Mary Ehrhardt

The observations of each teacher provide a window into what they thought was important to know about a culture and their surprises. Sometimes their assumptions were debunked. Mary Ehrhardt was amazed to see an old woman sitting on the curb making a broom by hand next to a Mercedes. She was jarred by the construction workers sleeping in bedrolls on the sidewalk next to her building which was equipped with a satellite dish. Ed Donovan expected to find poverty, but was surprised to participate in a wedding party in which the bride, groom, and celebrating family and friends wore no shoes. While Denise Green described in great detail the festivals in which she participated, reflecting an admiration of the community spirit she witnessed, Ellen Stacey described her frustrations with Japanese ways and a fear of gangsters, the Yakuza. Paul Vandemere chose to talk about learning cultural customs, such as why Japanese people paint in the eye in a Daruma doll or what the tea ceremony signifies.

Paul Vandemere considered his two years in Japan a much more meaningful experience than his post-college, two years of teaching in Cairo, Egypt. Although none of the other teachers in this study lived and worked separately from their host cultures in what Paul calls "*gaijin* [foreigner] ghettos," there are many foreigners who live this way in another country or who travel to see sights without experiencing a culture more authentically. According to Paul, it would be better for people to study a culture in the United States than become a part of the "*gaijin* ghetto" and generalize from that experience as an authority, especially as a teacher. From this perspective the international experiences of a teacher could result in more harm than good.

Not everyone would be able to necessarily spend that time overseas. Not every educator may have that opportunity. I think it's a whole lot easier to get that in-depth knowledge by doing it firsthand. Clearly, it's a whole lot better to get, to do the in-depth study, on the Internet or electronically, or in libraries and talking to others on campuses—to avail yourself of those opportunities—than to do the *gaijin* ghetto approach that I mentioned. That always just amazed us. Like I said, it's not being critical, as long as they're not passing themselves off as experts or forming judgments, making sweeping generalizations based on their limited exposure, and very inaccurate exposure probably, especially if they're coming back to teach in America. If they are coming back to teach American kids about those countries based on that kind of experience, that is not just unfortunate. It's probably damaging to our goal to have students have an accurate understanding of the world.

Paul describes the experience of "a pleasant lady from New York City" with whom he and his wife became friendly as a counterpoint to his perspectives on international experience.

At the end of her year, she said, "Oh, I probably ought to finish up my roll of film. This is my first roll and I need to get a few more shots." She would leave the classroom and go to an English tea parlor she had found near where she lived, where she could order her English tea, sit down and read her American newspaper, go back home with her bilingual television and get the American shows, and have an American experience. There are *gaijin* ghettos; *gaijin* is Japanese for "foreigner." And in many countries around the world where there is a strong American presence or any foreign presence, . . . it's possible for someone to spend virtually all their time within that ghetto area and really never tap into the culture. It's as if they're not there.

He described an American couple with whom he and his wife were paired on a trip to China. This couple had "been there and done that," a perspective on international experience that Paul indicated was "not for me."

They had been to the Great Wall, been there, done that. Did the Bund in Shanghai at 6 AM, doing the Tai ji, been there, done that. They did Nepal and they did others, etc. They spend two years at the American compound in Saudi Arabia with the oil companies. They were living with other Americans, had American food, had

American television, will go back to America for vacations. It's as if they were not in that culture. You will find that in a lot of places where there is a large enough concentration of foreigners. It's a shame. I can tell you exactly where those places are in Cairo and Tokyo. You could probably tell me where they are in Beijing, in China. . . . I guess I shouldn't be critical of them. It's not for me. Maybe that's all they're comfortable in experiencing. Maybe that's the extent of how much they really want to get into the culture. For them, that's OK.

Paul tolerates this, as long as these people do not claim to be authorities after this experience.

It's certainly not for me and as long as they don't pass themselves off as being knowledgeable about China or Japan. You and I know after our time overseas, we've met tourists who've done the ubiquitous two or three weeks in Shanghai, in Beijing, in Xian, in Suzhou, etc., and now they know China. That's just like saying a Japanese or Chinese person that comes to America and does New York, Washington, D.C., Vegas, and Los Angeles, and they've done America. All of a sudden they form opinions on the basis of that. That's equally ludicrous.

For a different person, Bill Notebaum's one-month study tour could have been the kind of experience Paul warns against. Instead, the trip was a powerful learning opportunity, as Bill became aware of how little he had learned about Japanese culture because he had concentrated so exclusively on economics and trade relationships. Bill described his observations of Japanese business practices involving team work and cooperation. He was trying to understand changes he was reading about and observing in the United States similar to the changes that were happening in Japan, partly because of the work of the industrialist, W. Edwards Demming, there. "When I traveled in Japan, observing Japanese secondary education and then watching Japanese businesses or organizations in operation where they conducted meetings and so forth, rightly or wrongly, I came to the conclusion that Western understanding of Japanese sense of team and cohesiveness is very misleading."

He was surprised to find that instead of viewing examples of extreme efficiency in Japanese organizations, he found a great deal of time being spent unwisely on ritualized functions.

Their sense of team and cohesiveness is fairly hierarchical and authoritarian in nature and a lot of the process time that they put

into this team is not really a building of consensus nor an achieving
of understanding of consensus. It's more a constant reinforcement of
the existing cohesion that's already there. It is cultural and
unique to each organization. So they spend an inordinate amount of
time on what I would consider to be an organizational ritual in
which the obvious is said over and over and over again.

One example of this was the team that was responsible for their
group, two members of which he had befriended. "They'd say, 'We
were meeting last night.' I'd say, 'What do you mean you were meeting
last night? You got back into the hotel at 10:00, when did you have a
meeting?' 'Oh no, at 11:30 we were in so-and-so's room and we worked
on the agenda for today until 2:30 in the morning.' " These experiences
confirmed Bill's belief that there were many misconceptions among
Americans about the economic system in Japan, misconceptions that Bill
wanted to challenge.

Ed Donovan, like Bill Notebaum, was interested in debunking
stereotypes that his Chinese students had about Americans; for
example, that there was little sense of values like honesty and
integrity in the United States. Ed sends one of his Chinese colleagues
who teaches teachers English in China materials such as *Reader's
Digest*.

I always send him these value things to show him that American
teachers also must have values. Chinese are very skeptical about
America as a nation having a value system that's worthwhile. . . .
If I can get something like that, he will translate or have his
students translate. They know that the value system is here for
things like honesty and different kinds of proprieties.

He would respond to people like travel agents who would say: "Oh, in
America everybody would steal that."

"I'd say, 'Not exactly. You have to understand that I still have this
wallet. Even though I left it someplace [in the U.S.] and forgot about it
actually for a couple of days.' " When Ed returned to the store near his
hometown in the United States, "somebody had picked it up and set it
aside and said, 'When this guy comes in, give it back to him.' "

EXPECTATIONS

"It was so removed from what we were led to believe." Ellen Stacey

While Ed and Bill were working to dispel misleading stereotypes on
both sides of the Pacific Ocean, Ellen Stacey's observations related to

her difficulties in coping in a society different from her own. Ellen's learning may be viewed through the lens of her struggle to adapt to different mores and procedures, and her fears. In describing her experiences, Ellen used a word she heard fairly often in Japan, *muzukashi* meaning "difficult." She described it this way: "That is their way of saying it is too difficult for you to understand what's happening. Because you wouldn't understand it, you're a foreigner. You don't understand Japanese minds. If I asked for things and it was something I asked on my own, *muzukashi disho*, too difficult." She did not understand this until the third year of her experience.

> I had not been invited to any one's home other than Sumi's. If I invited people to my home, dinner could not be until after 9:30. I'll give you a perfect example of what happened to me my third year. I invited ten people to my home for dinner. When I got this apartment, it came with a microwave, it's called a *dinshi rangi*, it's an oven-microwave. You can cook and you can bake in it and it's a microwave also. I put my twenty-five-pound turkey that cost me almost $200 into this machine and it died. It broke. I got these people coming and it's now 3:00. They're coming at 9:00. That gives me six hours. I called up my boss and I said, "I need a *dinshi rangi*. The one that's in the building is busted and it's not going to work. I need one today. Can I go out and will you buy it for me?"

She pointed to a microwave on her kitchen counter, saying, "There's a *dinshi rangi*." She felt she had had no option but to rush out that day and spend $800 on a new microwave that does not work at her home in the United States.

Ellen had this problem, in her own words, "because I didn't follow procedure." A similar experience helped make her more aware of why she was frustrated by this kind of experience in Japan. Having destroyed the tire on her car, she called for help.

> I was driving my car and the whole tire—I went over a road division or whatever they call it—and I busted the whole tire, damaged the rim and everything. I can't speak any Japanese at this time. I'm just like freaked out, I'm so upset. All I have is the telephone number for my boss at Haksho. So I called him up and I say, "I'm having problems." He goes, "Where are you?" I said, "I have no idea. I'm in the middle of a street, I have a flat tire, there's a pachinko parlor in there." He said, "Find someone, flag them down, and ask them to come speak to me on the phone." So I go down the street and I see this man and I say, *"Tes kota, tes kota."* So he comes over, he's helping me. I give him the phone.

Now my boss knows where I am. In the mean time, I'm feeling really guilty because I know it was my own negligence that busted this tire, right? So I go to the gas station and tell them to fix it. I need the tire fixed. So he fixes the tire and it's costing me about $300 to fix this tire because I need a rim and a tire. By this time, my boss is here. So I said to my boss, "I have to go to the bank to get $300. Please come with me." So he walks me to the bank, teaches me how to use the ATM machine. I get $300, I go back and pay this guy $300. I walk away, I got a tire fixed, no problem.

Ellen was surprised then when her boss handed her an envelope full of cash.

As soon as the tire is in my possession, I paid the bill, I turned to him and he hands me an envelope. In this envelope is $2,000. I said, "What's this for?" [He said], "This is $2,000 for your airplane ticket." I said, "Why didn't you give it to me before I went to the bank?" You know what I'm saying? He's going to give me this money, I'm going to pay for this tire. So two weeks later, I get $300. I said, "Why are you giving me $300?" "To pay for the tire." I said, "What do you mean pay for the tire? I already paid for the tire." They said, "But that's Honda's car. Next time you have a problem with your car, call me. I have to do all the negotiating and it's a company that this Yaksho sends us to fix the tire." I was too American, too Westernized. I had to take care of the matter right away.

Ellen acknowledged that her "American" proclivities bumped up against the Japanese way of handling problems. The Japanese had wanted to take care of her in their own way, but she admitted: "I didn't allow them." Probably the most poignant example of Ellen's "American" impatience with the Japanese bureaucratic way of doing things was the experience she had trying to gain permission to leave Japan a few days earlier, after her teaching responsibilities were over, to be with her dying sister.

Denise focused on fitting in with the culture gracefully and was far less judgmental than Ellen in her observations about these differences. Bill Notebaum was most interested in understanding Japan in his area of inquiry and debunking stereotypes and misinformation about Japan. Ellen did not discuss these kinds of difficult experiences on her first seven-month experience in Japan. Had Denise or Bill lived there longer than their respective seven months and one month, the emphasis in their observations might have been very different.

Within the context of Ellen's tension and frustration in Japan, she expressed great concern about the Yakuza, Japanese gangsters:

> The Yakuza are the Mafia. I would go to a gas station every day, or once every couple days, to get a tank full of gas because I had a car. One day, they wouldn't wait on me, no one came out. I waited and waited and waited and no one came out. I looked over in the corner and there was a black Yakuza automobile. I looked inside and there were the Yakuza inside.

She learned from a foreign friend who worked for Honda about how the company informed its foreign employees about the Yakuza. "They gave him a charge card, a telephone card. . . . If you're harassed by the Yakuza, you put it into the phone. It will automatically tell Honda where you are located and they would come. Honda personnel would come to your rescue." Within this discussion about the Yakuza in Japan, Ellen described her fear when she happened on a struggle between a man and a woman in the post office.

> I was in a post office, waiting to get some stamps, and there was this man arguing with—he wasn't saying anything, his girl friend was trying to find out, because the post office and the bank are one and the same, she was looking for money in her accounts. She didn't have any money. He became very belligerent and started beating her up in this post office. I had walked from the school to the post office so I didn't have a car. He looked at me and he became real nasty in his gestures and everything toward me and he grabbed his girl friend by the hair and he pulled her out of the post office. When he went out into his car, he took his car and just smashed into the car that was behind him and then took off.

The people in the post office were afraid the damaged car was Ellen's. "I said, 'No, I walked.' They didn't call the police. And that was the end of the situation." Ellen also described an American friend who had been hit in the head with a chair by some "young hoodlums."

> He had eighteen stitches in his head. . . . He was in the hospital for almost two weeks. He had a concussion. The school system didn't know how to handle it because they would have lost face with the exchange program. They would have lost face among themselves because no one was there to protect these foreigners that were representing another country. He said it was a very difficult time for him.

These examples of Ellen's are a stark contrast to her positive observations about Japanese schools and the description of her "bread on butter" relationship with Sumi. They also provide a great contrast with the observations of Bill, Paul, and Denise. Ellen's general observations about Japan are overwhelmingly negative, except that she compared the sheltered atmosphere she felt in many Japanese schools with the similar atmosphere she experienced in Jesuit Schools: "I felt very comfortable in the Japanese school system." It appears that the only time Ellen felt secure and experienced some pleasure during her three years in Japan was in the schools and with her one Japanese friend.

Part of her concern for safety was fueled by her assumptions about Japanese society as being nonviolent and relatively crime-free: "In Japan, I had this false confidence, false sense of safety, because everything you read in the newspaper said it's the safest country in the world. So when I saw the anger of these young kids, and I saw the— what do you call it when you abuse the kids—it was like, where did this come from? This isn't really supposed to be here." When her nieces visited Ellen in Japan, she observed that they, too, had accepted these assumptions and were surprised by the reality, just as she had been: "They again had the same false sense of security as I did. We went to the airport and I went to say good-bye to them and while we were waiting in line to get into the airport, there was this man literally kung-fuing this other man in front of our car. My nieces went, 'Wow, is this TV? Are there cameras?' It was so removed from what we were led to believe."

In our interviews, Ellen, a teacher in what is considered a dangerous area of inner Milwaukee, seemed more sensitive to violence and crime in Japan. Ellen's expression of her learning in these observations demonstrates the power of assumptions and fears to affect observations and thus learning. Paul Vandemere, who lived in Japan two years, does not mention the Yakuza.

Denise Green emphasized the sense of belonging to a community. She felt that American kids "are missing out on this" because of the fun, the community spirit, and the way "it keeps history alive." She described how the children take part in Japanese festivals.

> Koni is built around a castle that was built around 300 years. Then elementary school children, if they're in their elementary school's marching band, will march in a parade playing their instruments in their school uniforms. Also, they will make their own models of the castle that the city's built around. They will carry them in a traditional style, where the model is on a long pole and kids each side of each pole will carry them on their shoulder. Each group

will wear the same *happi* coat. It's just a wonderful festival. I remember the year that I was there, it rained but the parade went right on, including the paper reproductions of the castles that were going by. I took a lot of pictures which really came out quite well. . . . Then at castle festival, they had children dressed up from Samurai, those eras in Japanese history, the members of the nobility and the lower classes, to get the period of Japanese history. Some of them were walking, some of them were on horseback but in full costume of that era. That was appropriate. I'm sure for the children, it was quite exciting to be picked to be one of those costume people or to have your castle replica be one that was in the parade or to be playing an instrument in a marching band. I mean, the whole town, the whole city turned out for it.

Denise enjoyed the way that children in Japan wore uniforms, comparing this to the group identification and expectations entailed in wearing *happi* coats during festivals.

The attire that goes along with it. You play a certain role and you dress for that role. When you go to school, you wear a uniform in the public schools, secondary level. Of course, you're expected to behave in a certain way, the hairstyles are regulated, along with the shoes you can wear and the socks, etc. Your group is recognized by what's written on your *happi* coat. You had a certain role to play in the festival, you play it. "Oh, that's the group from such-and-such, or that's the group from the Board of Education, or that's the group from GM, or that's the group from Toyota or something like that, or whatever business was in the group in that parade or that festival." You'd be able to identify them.

The impressions of Japanese society described by Denise and Paul were very positive. Mary Ehrhardt and Ed Donovan evidenced generally a positive, nonjudgmental learning stance in China. They chose very similar issues to talk about in their observations about their experiences in China. Both were surprised by the level of poverty they witnessed in the country. They were concerned about and commented on gender inequities, particularly the burdens that many women faced. They both greatly admired Chinese artistic and cultural traditions, including brush painting, calligraphy, *wushu*, and *tai ji juan*, Chinese martial arts. They also commented on the traditions of respect for education and age that they observed in China.

While Ed was more an observer of the arts, Mary learned by plunging into her experiences, not content to just watch a Chinese master painter paint peach blossoms, but intent on trying it herself: "Another

wonderful part of the exchange was being able to be a student and after
our full morning of teaching, we took several classes in the afternoon,
teachers and students together. The school provided for us a class in *wu
shu/tai ji*, a class in Chinese history taught in Chinese, Chinese which
met twice a week, calligraphy, embroidery, and painting." She carved
her own "chop" (a seal with the owner's name inscribed in characters on
the bottom), finding it difficult to sand it down to make it even. She
worked by imitating her master teacher to construct peach blossoms.
She reveled in her "chance to be a student again" in China. These
efforts made Mary feel that "this experience just got richer and richer,
day by day, overwhelmingly rich."

Mary's description of learning brush painting allowed her to
experience Huangshan, the yellow mountains, as if she were "stepping
into a painting."

> Through the classes that I took in China, I really learned a
> tremendous amount about brush painting and calligraphy and even
> embroidery so that now my appreciation for especially Chinese
> painting is much greater. I really learned how the job of a novice is
> to emulate the master and my experience was making many
> attempts and only getting a *"keyi,"* being OK, possibly OK, but my
> bamboo rarely measured up to the teacher's bamboo. I understand
> now that there is an essence, and that the job of the Chinese
> painter is to paint it as lifelike as possible. But there is a very
> prescribed way with only three strokes or that each peach branch,
> plum branch, can only have blossoms that come with one petal,
> three petals or five petals. So, in a way, it's a bit formulaic but on
> the other hand, this is the way that the master artists saw it so
> this is the way one has to copy. One has to emulate the master.

When Mary traveled to Huangshan, the yellow mountains, that had
served as the setting for many famous landscape painters, she was
overwhelmed by the possibilities of art and by the feeling that she
was in that setting, a part of that art.

> Going to Huangshan, climbing Huangshan, one of the nine sacred
> mountains where there are clouds and rock and pine trees and
> water, all the elements in Chinese landscape painting. That was
> just a remarkable experience because you felt like you had just
> stepped into the painting. Then you can really see why these are
> the things that the landscape painter paints. They have to have
> each of those elements. And so when you attempt a landscape
> painting, you paint rocks as the master did, but the master
> actually saw the mountain. I certainly now can show my feeble

attempts, but also can explain to my children when they're brush painting that our way is to be expressive and to use our imaginations and to create; that's not the Chinese way. The Chinese way is to emulate the ideal, to emulate the master.

Ed Donovan talked enthusiastically about paintings and calligraphy scrolls that his artist friend had given him. This was the friend with whom Ed had struggled to communicate for five hours one afternoon in China.

That lotus blossom, that's one that he's given us. We've got several calligraphies of his and a couple of them that I like very, very much we gave away. Even my kids or my in-laws like the stuff and so we just gave it to them. They display it, so it's kind of neat when I walk into their houses and see it. I've got a very traditional set of paintings that my daughter just had to have. She took them and one's of spring, winter, fall, and summer. Which is a very traditional kind of thing for artists to do. Of course, it's got the traditional things in it like the mountain and the water and the trees and the people are about the size of— they're just minute, they're so small. It's a very Daoist type of school. The clouds, that was the other thing. Clouds and mountains and water and trees. You've got all of that and you've got everything.

Declaring that he loved Chinese art, Ed said:

I've watched this guy paint with a brush and with his fingernail. I've watched several artists do that sort of thing. I've got another artist friend of mine from Kunming who is a more modern artist. I suppose we'd call him a commercial artist. But now he wants to get into more traditional painting because there's more status to it.

Mary and Ed learned by observing Chinese artists, while Mary took her learning one step further by participating in creating Chinese art forms. Although they appreciated and learned from the artistic tradition in China, Mary and Ed were not prepared for the kind of poverty that they observed there. Mary saw China as a land of tremendous, even "jarring," contrasts.

Even though I had taught about China, I was not prepared for what it means to be a developing country, to be living in a developing country. It was much poorer than I ever expected. The juxtaposition of things that represented poverty, but not even

poverty as much as I knew it, just very basic living, that juxtaposed
with what is now evidence of economic ascendancy, like cellular
phones and luxury cars, always made me do a double take.

At a street market near her neighborhood, she bought a broom that
symbolized the simplicity of life in China, the lack of space for
storage, and centuries of tradition.

> The one thing that I decided to bring back that was a symbol of my
> experience in China was this broom that I bought just on a street
> market in my neighborhood. It's just made out of grass, and this is
> what my hostess used to sweep the floors in their house. But it's
> kind of primitive and it's the kind of broom that I think has
> probably been used for centuries and centuries of time. In China, as
> a matter of fact, in Suzhou, I actually saw a lady gathering the
> twigs and then making the broom. The woman making the broom
> was squatting on the sidewalk beside a Mercedes. But for me this
> is truly a symbol of my daily life in China. This is an implement
> that was used every day and yet it's probably been used every day
> in China for a thousand years. Street sweepers, you might
> remember, used taller brooms but this is the domestic broom. It
> takes up less space. There were no closets in my apartment and this
> could nicely fit in a little corner.

Ed Donovan connected his earlier study of anthropology with what
he observed in China; for example, what he witnessed as a Chinese
way of walking and living on the street. He, like Mary and Denise,
often viewed Chinese tradition and living practices from an American
standpoint.

> Even the whole idea of privacy, anthropologically. Americans
> consider privacy to be when they can get away from everybody else
> and to be shut off. The Chinese consider privacy to be what they
> keep in their heads without revealing it to anybody else. So you'll
> see Chinese walking down the street, they don't even see you.
> They're in a private world of their own. They're avoiding. It's
> kind of a second instinct instead of a conscious effort. Even in
> Shanghai, you'll find people out on the streets with a hose running
> into a basin and they're washing their hair. Not dressed for what
> we would consider to be public viewing. And yet, they're out there
> washing their hair just oblivious to everything going on around
> them.

Mary Ehrhardt, too, was struck by the small living spaces. She looked for a stool to bring back because it also reminds her of how much of Chinese life happens on the street.

> I thought another memento of what I saw every day as I rode my bike back and forth to school was a stool, a tiny stool. So much of life takes place in the streets. I suppose because most Chinese families live in one or two rooms, they do a great deal of everyday living right out in an alley. The little stool is used if you are shelling peas or making dumplings or playing a game of chess that's going to take place over time, or visiting with your neighbor, or knitting. All of those kinds of things went on right in the alley and they used these charming little chairs or little stools. But I didn't find one to bring home with me. I did have photographs, and that's one of the photographs that I enlarged right away. It's just like China to me, China in 1995.

The use of one wok and chopsticks for cooking and serving food made such sense to her when she lived in a small space, even in a luxurious [by Beijing standards] four-room apartment.

> So I think I was really struck by the simplicity of living when you live in one, two, or four rooms as I did. It's very understandable to see why you use one bowl and one pair of chopsticks and the cooking is very efficient. Perhaps a pot of rice and the wok, which is used to make several other dishes. My family shopped almost every day, even though they had a refrigerator. They did maybe a little more extensive shopping early Sunday morning market or later in the day on Sunday. On a weekly basis, I did my own hand laundry in a basin with cold water, even though my family had a small washing machine. Just the details of everyday life were simple.

Ed and Mary showed a sense of empathy with and concern for the people in China who must cope with tremendous difficulties in comparison to middle-class American social and economic conditions. During his 1995 experience in China, on his way to a monastery, Ed observed poverty that surprised him. Although the area of China he and Heather had lived in for a year was quite poor, the poverty in this village shocked him.

> We went through absolutely the poorest village I've ever seen in my life. I don't think any kid under fifteen was wearing shoes. Kids were pretty raggedy. This was at a wedding. It looked like

people who came out of the Cultural Revolution. That's how
poorly they were dressed. The kids in the wedding party, there
were three girls and three guys. The three guys had suitcoats on,
but they were old and shiny. The girls had nice clothes and they
carried pretty flowers, no shoes. They showed me their school.
It's a brand-new school. They were very proud of it. Two rooms;
two teachers who had graduated from high school. Those were
the two teachers. They had six grades in those two rooms and
those teachers had to contend with that. Every kid there was just
a ragamuffin, a dirty little kid.

The mayor and townspeople graciously welcomed Ed and his Chinese
colleagues in the midst of this wedding celebration.

The mayor of the town greeted us. He was preparing the wedding
feast. He was the cook for the town every time they had any kind
of a celebration. He wore a red T-shirt and brown shiny trousers
and open sandals, no socks. He offered us tea. The tea came in—
one was a cup, one was a short thick glass, and one was a pottery
container. Those were our three things of tea. He didn't have two
things that matched or two cups that matched in the village. The
wedding was in the second of three days. This was the singing
day. This was the day when the storytellers get up and tell the
stories that go on and on for twenty-four hours. The first day had
been the dancing day. I guess everybody was pretty ragged at the
end of that day that they had all danced. The third day, which
the mayor was preparing for, was the feast day. That would be
the final day of the wedding. It's in an open-area restaurant with
rough wooden benches and tables. It's cobbled, cobblestone, but
very uneven.

According to Ed, this experience had a "profound impact" on him:
"I've never seen people that poor. Yet they seemed to be fairly happy.
Except the mayor said, 'We cannot keep young people in the town.
They all went to the city.'" Ed explained what he meant by "happy."

They were happy in terms of not worrying about where the next
meal was coming from. They were happy in terms of the
relationships with each other. From what we could see, I don't
think that the young people are happy with that plight in life. I
think that they want something better. There was one black and
white TV in the town. That was it. That was in the restaurant
area. Everybody would go there to watch TV. The picture was
terrible.

Ed was later concerned about how much this generous hospitality might be costing the Chinese, but at the time he had been thinking about answering their questions.

> They extend all of their hospitality to you. I'm sure that we didn't break them and a glass of tea isn't going to break them. But the fact is that we drew a lot of people away from other kinds of things for the forty-five minutes or an hour that we sat and talked with this village mayor. It did [bother me] afterwards. I realized what had happened. I didn't realize it at the time because questions were coming back and forth and you're concentrating on the kinds of responses that you think you ought to give. . . . They wanted to know about America; they wanted to know about what I did, and how many students were in my classes. Just general kinds of things. I was an information giver.

They also wanted to know what Ed thought of their village: "Of course you know I said, 'Oh, it's picturesque.' What am I going to say? It's the poorest village I've ever seen in China? That I enjoyed the storytelling even though I didn't understand the Chinese. But I understood what the process was and what was going on. And the reaction of the crowd and things like that."

At the monastery he took pictures from the roof to capture the scenery: "All you could see is a range of mountains running away from each other from this particular monastery, like the spokes of a hub. Just incredible!" There he learned that the people in the monastery walked two kilometers each day to the well for water. "They'd come all the way down the mountain, walk the two kilometers to the well, get two buckets, and walk back up. One of the ladies was seventy-six years old and still doing that."

In addition to being surprised by the poverty, Ed and Mary learned a great deal about gender issues in China. Ed flatly stated that women were viewed as inferior in China, while Mary focused on the dilemma that talented, young women faced there. According to Ed, despite "the basic assumption being that the law says that women are equal in China, the culture still says that women have to cook and take care of kids. Are there strong women in China? Oh, yes. Are there wimpy husbands? Oh, yes. But by and large the culture looks at women as inferior." This is one reason Ed had insisted on changing the seating arrangement in his classroom.

Mary's concern for the daughter in her host family's household reflects her growing knowledge about the pressures on many young Chinese women in this generation.

She is twenty-one, graduating from college, making important choices for herself. Because on the one hand her parents wanted her to go abroad to experience the world beyond China, but on the other hand she is the only child. The one child, she at age twenty-one, pays a great indebtedness to her parents. They have cared for her from her infancy, and she now will step into the role of caring for them. It's time for her to have a boyfriend, a serious boyfriend, and it's time for her to get married. Even though she prepared to have a career and she would like to further her education, perhaps abroad, but these expectations are so much a part of her life that it's very hard for her to go against them.

Mary considers this situation representative of "a real dilemma for women in that culture. This is a bright young woman who has facility with English and the parents can give her opportunities, but the traditional values and roles will probably prevent her from realizing her potential in many ways." Mary treasures a collage given her by her host daughter's fifteen-year-old cousin, "who dreams of being a fashion designer." This girl lives with her family in two rooms and a detached, "tiny and dirty" kitchen, shared by several families: "The several times that I visited, I had to use the public bathroom on the street which was preferable to whatever they used in their living quarters." Mary felt that this young girl "was a very good artist. In fact, she goes to a high school that emphasizes the arts after school and she dreams, like many Chinese young people, of using her talent to get ahead, to become successful and to break out."

In addition to her concern about gender issues, Mary empathized with the plight of middle-aged English teachers who had been affected by the excesses of the Cultural Revolution [1966-1976], when all schools were closed and they did not receive what they considered to be adequate preparation and training as teachers. On their field trips with the English teachers, several of them opened up to Mary and her colleague about their frustrations and disappointments. To Mary this was a chance for these teachers to "tell us their own stories." They talked freely of the Cultural Revolution, how dramatically it changed their lives, how one married the wrong man because of the Cultural Revolution's pressures and went without love as a result. One woman was accepted by but was prevented from entering Bei Da [Beijing University] because of her father's "political background." Mary witnessed a "kind of hopelessness" in these teachers, who were feeling that "I'm forty-something and change may not happen in my lifetime." They expressed great "worry about the immediate future." Even though they believe "the people will not allow a return to the Cultural

Revolution," they feared the kind of leadership that might emerge when Deng Xiaoping, China's paramount leader, died.

Mary Ehrhardt and Ed Donovan demonstrate a depth of learning that translates into empathy and concern. Their learning has gone far beyond their own assumptions, needs, wants, and desires to a genuine empathy with the struggles of others. Their knowledge also goes beyond cultural differences to affirm a common humanity and represents the kind of concern for human dignity that John Dewey promotes in his work (1900, 1904, 1916, 1938).

The observations that all of these teachers emphasized in these interviews had to do with assumptions they and others had held before the experience and what they felt was most important to report about the culture. Underlying this emphasis was a great curiosity about how people in Japan and China lived and what was different about these cultures that they had not understood before the experience. Only Ellen Stacey, with the longest tenure living abroad, seemed to feel threatened and alienated by Japanese culture. The loneliness she expresses poignantly describes feelings the others felt to varying degrees about being foreign, being what the Chinese call *waiguoren,* an outside country person.

The range of these observations includes negative and positive extremes. We can learn a great deal from them within the context of what we know about each teacher. Mary, Ed, and Denise seem especially elated about their opportunity to learn abroad. This may have been the result of better preparation for their experience, the context of the experience, and their own flexiblility when difficulties arose. Stories abound about the frustrations of travelers in China; for example, the work of Paul Theroux (1988), Mark Salzman (1986), Bill Holm (1990), and Alan Samagalski and Michael Buckley (1984), the two Australian explorers who made a travel book, *China: A Travel Survival Kit,* a hilarious excursion in itself.

Surprisingly, the most frustrated and negative experiences were those of a teacher who lived in Japan, not China. Ellen's characterizations of Japan as a country of rigid bureaucracy and violent crime may be a result of her previous experience with inner-city problem children that influenced her perceptions of her experience. Ellen offers a very different perspective on living and working in Japanese culture than do Denise, or Paul Vandemere, who mainly talked about how his experience in Japan positively affected his teaching and life in the United States. Ellen's perspective should be understood in conjunction with other perspectives and her background and assumptions about Japan. The significance of the great variety of observations in this study is that the way each teacher prepares for and manages the culture shock, being an "other" in a foreign country, is very important.

The quantity and quality of time spent in another culture are also important. The way each teacher reacted to the stress of living in another culture is key to understanding how he learned or failed to learn from this experience.

CULTURE SHOCK

"There goes the United States." Ed and Heather Donovan

How the five people who had more extensive experience felt about this strangeness is reflected in Ed Donovan's expression about "cultural antennae" becoming overloaded, causing the visiting teacher to shut down for a while and regroup in this new and alien environment. Even though they felt they had been well prepared by the program leaders, they were not emotionally prepared for being on display so much of the time. When Denise Green talks about not showing negative emotions, she expresses the pressure associated with representing the United States on an exchange program with Japan, the sense that she bears the weight of representing a group. Heather Donovan felt this sense of cultural responsibility especially keenly because there was rarely a time that she and Ed were not a center of attraction, whether in their teaching, shopping, visiting sights, entertaining students in their home, or just walking down the street. It seemed that there was no place to hide, be alone, or be unobtrusive as a foreigner for a year in an area of China that had been home to few foreigners before 1986. Ed explains, "We felt like we were the showpiece in town. All the time. We represented the United States and people looked at us and said, 'There goes the United States.' "

Since that time, Ed has noticed that many people, even his brother living in Toronto or his student from Britain, go through a cultural trauma when living in a different society for a significant period.

I talk about my brother going to Toronto for two years and coming down with culture trauma. They can't believe it. They speak English and all that sort of thing. But different signals, different body language, different words. You have to be paying attention so you don't foul up. It put him in bed for a week. He couldn't get up. His antenna, everything just shut down. Some people get it very, very badly and it doesn't take much. Can you imagine going and living just in Detroit, where the culture is different than it is in the suburbs? If you have to put up with that stress for a long period of time, pretty soon your antenna shuts down. It can't hold it.

How people handle this cultural trauma varies; Ed experienced it with Heather in China that first year.

One of the things that happens is that you come out and you don't want to face anything. You don't want to look at people, you don't want to talk to them for a good two weeks. It happened to Heather. She walked along looking at the street for two weeks, three weeks after that. She shut down for just three days. I had to bring her meals to her and prop her up and feed her. It was just like she was a rag. She couldn't even get out of bed to go to the bathroom. It just—everything shut down. I can talk about it a little bit and say this is one of the things that you ought to be aware of. It can happen to you; don't panic because of it. It's normal.

Gradually, Heather improved after she and Ed curtailed their activities and slowly re-entered their social life in China: "We shut down a lot of our evening visits. In fact, for two weeks, we didn't have anybody. The third week we had one or two people in that she could tolerate pretty easily. Mei Li was one of them that managed to help a little bit. And a couple of other gals. She wasn't threatened."

Mary Ehrhardt found it tiring to be constantly stared at in Beijing as well: "I think you get very tired of being stared at. You're on stage and there are lots of curious looks, lots of attempts to engage you in conversation. You do feel like you are the goldfish in the bowl."

The conditions for these teachers in Japan and China were radically different, as the countries themselves are very different. It is important that we not confuse the two. The stresses of being an "other" in a foreign country can occur anywhere. In Japan, there is less of a propensity for people to stare at foreigners than in China. There is a great deal more wealth for ordinary people in Japan which, has allowed many of them to travel abroad. China is still emerging from the enforced isolation of the Cultural Revolution and before. In some areas of China, especially the economically booming south, the people are more used to seeing foreign travelers and business people. But few Chinese see a foreigner going to work on her bicycle in February. Kunming is not an area of China where many Westerners have lived and worked. Great isolation and poverty, which Ed Donovan describes, exist there.

Modern Japan is a very different place, an economic powerhouse, with highly educated people, many of whom have studied Western art and literature in greater detail than do some U.S. citizens. The feelings of being a stranger occur within extremely different contexts among these teachers. Cathy Davidson (1993) describes how it feels to undress and carry a container of blue urine, dyed by medications, in front of hundreds of students at the women's university where she would be teaching as a visiting professor for a year. One of her colleagues chided her, "'You haven't made my job any easier. . . . My Japanese students come here already convinced that the Japanese brain is different than ours, that their tongue has a different shape, that their blood is stronger. I can't tell you how many oral reports I've heard this term about how Japanese and *gaijin* look and act so different because *gaijin* have blue pee' " (p. 12). Davidson learned from her experience and went on to enjoy an emotionally intense and fulfilling experience during four years there in the 1980s and early 1990s.

On the other hand, Ellen Stacey was still feeling emotionally drained from her experience in Japan three years after her return to the United States. She attributed this fatigue to feelings of being used, a concern that Denise Green also expressed.

> By the third year, I was mentally drained and this is the part I do not like about the Japanese. They milk your brain. They milk it for whatever they can get. That's why it was so enticing for these young people. They don't take people over thirty-five. . . . They'll take new graduates and they drain their brain. They'll say, "We have a million-dollar project we are working on." They'll pick their brains for all that four-year university where their memory is good and they'll just pick it, pick it, pick it, pick it, till there's nothing left.

She described her first day in Japan, when she was very tired and wanted to be left alone.

> I remember the first day I had gotten to Japan. I didn't know anybody, I was totally exhausted. It was the first day they left me alone so I could get my life together. I had unpacked all my luggage and I was just laying in bed and had finally gotten to fall asleep where I felt like I was getting good sleep. I get this knock on the door and there's this Japanese woman saying, "Hi. I'd like to take you to this place, this place, this place, and let's go here, let's go here. Pack up your things and let's go now." I said, "I'm very tired, I'd like to sleep right now." She never came back. . . . I would only be invited to certain things if they could use me in a certain capacity.

The British evidenced a sense of reserve that Ellen felt Americans would be advised to emulate.

The British refused to share any information with the Japanese. The Americans, "Oh, sure, what else do you want to know?" But that's why I think the Japanese loved the Americans. You see, you are not considered Japanese if you leave the country. So they can save a lot of money. It was cheaper for them to bring over graduates from the university than it was to send their guys over to America.

Like Ellen Stacey, Denise Green wondered whether she was being invited to people's homes because of friendship or because she was wanted for her English skills.

Because we were the model English speakers so therefore people would come over and say, "I'd like to practice my English" or "Will you come to dinner at my house so we can practice our English?" So in that sense, I mean that was our purpose for being there, but in that sense sometimes I wondered, are they doing it because she's a person or because I can spout out some of the English gems of wisdom to their children to say at the dinner table?

While not showing as much bitterness or cynicism about Japan as Ellen, Denise also reflected on the pressures she felt. She considered it her responsibility to try to have empathy for their feelings of people in any culture in which she considered herself a guest. She attached great importance to

learning to read people from other cultures, trying to figure out what they are thinking but not saying. Dealing with their accepted etiquettes. Trying not to let it show on your face, when what's put in front of you [to eat] and you don't know what it is. If you knew what it was, how do you eat it? If you do know how to eat it, do you really want to? And once you do and it tastes awful, you can't spit it out. You know you just must swallow it. Just trying to deal with that and not to insult people. You know they had gone through a lot of trouble.

Denise describes how she handled not slurping soup when she was invited to a Japanese home for dinner shortly before she was to return home.

I was very comfortable being in people's homes and knowing the different kind of etiquette that they had. In fact, when they served the soup, they looked at me funny because I wasn't slurping it. I was going to be going home and I understood the Japanese style of eating and I had enjoyed it but, as soon as I got home and if I slurped some soup, it would be considered just horrible bad manners and I had to break the habit. So I said for the last two weeks I was there, I was going to try not to slurp my soup because of what they thought if I slurped it. Also, I said in America it's bad manners to pick up your bowl and put it to your mouth. So I decided I'll still pick it up in Japan, but I'll not slurp it anymore in Japan just to help me out. So they understood and laughed at me when I did it.

In spite of her warm feelings about these sorts of exchanges, Denise had no illusions about being a stranger in a strange land, an outsider.

I always felt like a stranger because of the generations of foreigners who are still not considered Japanese. But they even look the part physically. I knew that I was never going to be as comfortable as I could be other places simply because I would always be looked on as a *gaijin*, a foreigner. First of all, there was the physical aspect that I didn't even look Asian. At least if you looked Asian, like the Asian people look near Japan and in Japan, then it's kind of assumed you belong unless you open up your mouth and blow it. Because they claim that they can tell if someone is not Japanese yet they've lived in the country a long time and they look Japanese and they speak it fluently, they find that there is a difference.

Exchange teachers in her program were invited to an English-speaking society at a university in Kyoto. The groups asked each other questions, one of which "we had been wondering about" concerning how they would treat a second- or third-generation person of another cultural background, such as Chinese, who spoke Japanese fluently.

"Would you have problems being friends with them?" We knew what they were going to say because we'd asked other people. There was a long silence. They said, "They are different. They may look like us, but they are different. There is something about them that won't be Japanese and we'll always be able to tell." So if that's the way they feel about people that look like them physically, then for those of us who don't, obviously we'll always be looked at as outsiders.

A complication of her status as an outsider could have been the fact that she is an African-American. It was not her African-American ethnicity, however, but her status as a foreigner that she felt put her in this outsider role: "Everywhere I went, I knew that it was obvious that

I was a foreigner. First, because looking at me there was no way they could mistake me for otherwise. I was always aware of that. I didn't always feel like a foreigner. I knew I was always looked on as an outsider."

The strain on her "cultural antennae" tired her at times in a manner similar to Mary Ehrhardt and, especially, Heather Donovan. Denise elaborated:

> Sometimes it bothered me because twenty-four hours a day you didn't always want to feel like you were on display. When you're not working and you have some time off and you go to work Monday morning and you find out where you went all weekend because you were seen different places, that is how your body language and your facial expression have a message that it's difficult to disguise. Sometimes you can get tired of feeling like you're on display, which is an advantage to going out of town for the weekend because when nobody knows you, you can feel a little bit more relaxed. I mean I felt relaxed.

Everywhere she went in the city where she taught, she felt like she was "being watched." The trains to other places were escape routes in a sense, so she could maintain a distance, a little anonymity: "I was glad that because of the trains that I was able to get away, sometimes for a weekend, to somewhere I didn't feel like I was on display."

Denise thought that the Japanese did not think of her as an African-American even when she informed them of this: "Sometimes I don't think they believed me when I said that I was African-American. At that time I said black American because your hair is black, your eyes are black, your skin is black. I would have to explain why we all come in different colors."

She found that in some of her self-introductions at the schools, when she stated that she was a black American, or that she was divorced, the teacher translating would not translate those things. She was surprised that a Japanese exchange teacher who had worked where her father was principal of a school in Indianapolis had told teachers that she was a white American.

> When I would give my introductions, even when I would try in Japanese, I would always tell my race. If I did it in English, sometimes the teachers would translate. I would always pause and many times that didn't get translated and I would say it in Japanese. The teacher didn't say it. I always told them I was divorced, too. That was another thing. The same thing would

happen. Then I would have to tell the children that African-Americans came in all different colors.

She used slides of her family to show that ethnicity in America included complexity and many different shades of skin color.

> Now, depending on the teacher, I did take slides with me. Once in a while I did get to show them and the slides were of my family and family celebrations. They could see that in my family and I would focus on the slides that the people were all different skin colors and that we were all black Americans. I would make this quite visible in the slides. That was something that I would always bring up. I found that my race became the topic of discussion with certain teachers and I heard this from another teacher that was there. He said they were asking him if I was white because of my skin color and hair color and the fact that my eyes are brown and not black. He assured them that I was [white]. It was interesting because that teacher had worked for my father when my father was principal of that school [in the United States]. So he knew my dad from a long time ago.

Even though she was "not sure how they perceived me," she thought that she was not treated differently as an African-American in Japan because her skin color is very similar to that of many Japanese people.

> I wasn't perceived as being African-American and that's the way they treated me. And my skin color was not a whole lot different from some of the Japanese that I ran into, because they had, like everyone else, different skin tones in their race. That I think was a consideration that my color wasn't a whole lot different than some of theirs.   Looking at the eyes and shape of some African-Americans, so there were some physical things there that may not have matched up with their expectations. Therefore, they may not have seen me as being physically all that different. They know I wasn't blond-haired and blue-eyed, so I'm wondering how that affected it. But also considering I was not your ordinary tourist, I was in a special kind of situation so therefore, in the schools I found I was treated quite well and I didn't detect any different kind of treatment than the other female teachers. From the males, yes. But then within their society there's going to be a difference in the way they are going to treat females and males. I think that's a whole different issue. Now I think if my skin were darker and they couldn't help but notice right away, then they may have had a different reaction, I don't know. But I think that

because of my skin color, it didn't turn many faces as soon as they looked at me. . . . I can't help but think that it wasn't a factor because like I said, if you put their arms up against my arms, sometimes the only difference you saw was a little more yellow cast to their skin. But the darkness would be about the same, than for someone very, very fair-skinned. Then if you looked at the noses, some of the noses were more like mine and some were more Caucasian-styled noses and the same with the lips.

Denise has had to grapple with this question because she "had people who are African-American ask me what I think about that. I tell them the same thing. I was treated I think well, but I don't know how it would be if my skin were a lot darker, what the reaction would have been."

Denise felt that her experience in Africa had helped her to be culturally sensitive.

I guess that came from the experiences in Africa. I was an outsider there. Even though I might have been a racial majority, I was a cultural minority. I had to understand just how American I was and I had no right to impose my ways on them. I felt that I did not want to come across as being the "Ugly American," you know, someone who is just going to come and complain and say, "You need to do things this way or you're uncivilized."

The five teachers who lived abroad for extended periods all thought about and experienced being different, not as an outcast, but as a minority, and in some cases, as a minority of one. Ed Donovan's metaphor of overloaded "cultural antennae" seems best to describe their various reactions. It must have been difficult for Denise Green to feel that she must so thoroughly disguise her emotions, but she may have had experience doing this growing up as an African-American child in white middle-class America. She, Ed and Mary seemed most able to deal with this "otherness." Mary might have become much more tired of feeling like "a goldfish in a bowl" had she lived in China much longer than four months. Ellen did not describe this feeling, except to say that she felt used by the Japanese, that she felt lonely in the culture.

The learning of these teachers took many different forms, as expressed in Bill's thoughts about efficiency in Japanese business meetings, Denise's observations about a community spirit demonstrated by festivals, Ellen's concerns about the Yakuza, Paul's interest in the tea ceremony, Ed and Mary's love of Chinese art, and their concern about poverty and gender issues in China. Their learning included unexpected or surprising challenges to their assumptions. Most were actively involved in their learning abroad. Some of them sought out as many learning opportunities as they could. Those who talked about feeling like an outsider in their host country at times did not dwell on this issue because they had managed to cope with that reality, although it was a strain.

Only Ellen appears to have been truly lonely in Japan, which we must consider when we think about her feelings of fear and alienation. Her case could be the basis for more study of how one might construct an international experience for a teacher to prevent the kind of loneliness and alienation she experienced. I believe that her case can be instructive to any teacher who teaches abroad for a significant period of time. Preparation, which encompassed a realistic appraisal of work schedules, living conditions, and support groups and which encouraged a teacher to probe her assumptions and preconceived notions about a culture, might have made a great difference for Ellen.

The observations and feelings that these six teachers have reported reflect a wide range of learning opportunities for teachers abroad. The possibilities include comparative assessments of school and teaching practices and political, social, and economic conditions. Their learning also includes the affective domain of knowing how it feels to live as an "other" in a foreign society. How their learning breaks down stereotypes and affirms a common humanity connects with prior knowledge, as Mary Ehrhardt demonstrates with her foray into Chinese art. The richness and depth of their learning are also affected by their background, preparation, and personality as well as the environmental context of the foreign country. The way each of these teachers perceives his relationships and connections, his feelings of being a stranger, a minority in another culture, will greatly affect his teaching practice, which is the main subject of Chapters 7 and 8.

7

Coming Home

How are we affected by changes in our experiences, especially the radical changes in lifestyle that five of these teachers experienced? What happens when they are welcomed home from such an international experience? According to all six teachers, they felt transformed by the experience almost to the point of feeling like different people. Most of these teachers felt that the experience had enriched their lives tremendously, while in one case there was a loss of important family relationships and spiritual foundations to the point of depression. Yet five of the six teachers considered the experience to be a positive transformation. They all considered it to be a profound experience that greatly affected their personal and professional lives.

In this chapter we will consider their perspectives on how the familiar here in the United States has become strange while the strange had become familiar in their life abroad. Their changes in teaching style, curriculum emphasis, and relationships with students and colleagues are the subject of Chapter 8. The way they share this experience with students and teachers provides a deeper understanding of what they mean by transformation: how this international experience of living in or studying another culture has changed them in ways that mean a great deal to them.

REVERSE CULTURE SHOCK

"Like going to the moon." Ed Donovan

Four of the teachers who lived abroad for four months or more expressed varying degrees of culture shock in the foreign country. On returning to the United States, several described their feelings as being more intense and long lasting than their feelings of culture shock when they initially arrived in their host countries. While they all expected differences in cultures to affect them while they were away, few indicated any preparedness for the difficulties they might face about coming home. Bill Holm, an English professor at Southwestern State University in Minnesota, wrote a book of vignettes about his year teaching in China titled *Coming Home Crazy* (1990). One teacher, Ed Donovan, recommended that I read this because he related to some of the feelings expressed in this book. I found that in some ways it tapped into some of my own feelings on returning home after living and studying in China for ten weeks during the summer of 1981. At that time, I could only imagine what I might have felt if I had had the opportunity to live there for six months, a year, or more. For the teachers in this study who returned from China, there was an intense appreciation of things previously taken for granted, such as the blueness of the sky, the brightness of our supermarkets, of what it means to be an American. Teachers who returned from China became more critical about materialism and wastefulness in the United States. There is no question that all of these teachers looked at some things differently when they returned. How they coped with varying degrees of "reverse culture shock" sets the stage for our discussion of how their experiences influenced their classroom practice.

Many Americans, myself included, have described their first experience in China during the late 1970s and '80s as akin to "going to the moon," to emphasize the tremendous differences between American and Chinese societies. However, when Ed Donovan used these words, he was referring to how he felt about *returning* to the United States after a year in Kunming, not his impressions on going there. While his wife had experienced cultural trauma in China, Ed had more difficulty acclimating to the United States than he had adjusting to China initially.

> The first day back, my son, who had just bought a brand-new Ford Bronco, was visiting. Heather said, "I need somebody to go to the store to buy something." Whatever, it was, three items. I can walk back and forth to this store in twenty minutes and do my shopping in that twenty minutes for three items. My son wanted me to drive his new car. So I did. I was gone for an hour and a quarter. Because when I got in the store, I had forgotten how bright everything was. Chinese stores don't have very much light. Here is this place with fluorescent lamps going, spotlights on things. All of a sudden, I was into a system of organization that I had to learn all over again. I kind of went up and down aisles, just walking. You know, *Coming Home Crazy*. He talks about the same

kind of thing; it's exactly that. Clerks were polite. I wasn't used to that. No haggling over prices. It's just as it's marked. Right. Anyway, everybody thought that I had smashed up his new car because I was gone so long. But it really did affect me, really tremendously. I think both of us, Heather and myself, did not get over the culture trauma coming back, I think, for seven or eight months.

Just as Mary Ehrhardt had felt that life was simpler and less intense in China on her re-entry in the United States, Ed also felt like he was in a different time frame, the pace of life in China having seemed much slower. It was strange to Ed, that everyone was in such a big hurry.

> I didn't feel like I had to rush anything. I could take my time. It didn't make any difference. I think the handling of time in China is so much different. I became very conscious in our culture because everybody was just whizzing by, doing this and doing that. I had the attitude that everybody's nuts. I used to drive, I was a fast driver. I very seldom was within the speed limit. I came back and I couldn't care what the speed limit was, you know 30 or 35 on a 40-mile zone, it didn't make any difference. That didn't catch up to me until probably the next year where I started going the speed limit and all that kind of stuff. So time was one of the real big, big factors and the use of time. The whole idea of intemperate haste is the way I saw it at that time—on the part of Americans.

The hurriedness also included what he felt was "a sense of contentiousness" embedded in a society so dedicated to the selling of materials goods as the United States. He became aware that "we didn't need as many things to live as people were trying to sell us." Advertising, on television and elsewhere, caused Ed and Heather to think about their lifestyle in a different way: "I'm not sure we became minimalists. I think we became a little harder in our judgment about what we bought."

Mary Ehrhardt reflects many of Ed Donovan's sentiments about simplicity in the Chinese lifestyle.

> I really learned to enjoy the simpler living and to see that their needs were very well met with many fewer things and that they had time that I often didn't have because my lifestyle was much faster. I came to appreciate all of that. I didn't really realize what an impact it would have on me when I returned. But the two things that were significant were returning to my school and seeing how intense it actually is. . . . That, plus just being bombarded in

the United States with advertisements, visually and orally. . . .
There was so much that I just had not given too much thought to
before having had this experience: how much we are told we have
to have and how much we buy into that and how intensely we live
compared to the simplicity of the Chinese.

Because "Beijing is so devoid of color (and yet it's more colorful now
than it was in the past) but because it's so devoid of green," Mary often
thought about the lovely place where she and her family have spent
vacations together for more than fifty years, Chautauqua, in western
New York state: "While I was there [China], I really thought a great
deal about the place that has been a regular summer spot for me most of
my life. I thought about the moisture and the greens, the water, the
clean air. That really sustained me a lot."

Upon returning home, Ed Donovan, like Mary Ehrhardt and Bill
Holm, marveled at the blue sky in the United States, something he
had looked at differently in the past: "There were two other things
that really affected us. One was the blueness of the sky. It just is a
different sky altogether. Another thing was the green grass."

Mary Ehrhardt also found that she had become used to a different
diet, which she has continued as a lifestyle change: "I just have
changed my diet. Not having any intestinal difficulties, but just that it
really was a significant change. I don't use butter, I don't eat as much
red meat. I'm more interested in Chinese cooking. I'm trying to do that
a little more."

Mary, and to a much greater degree, Ellen Stacey, felt frustrated
about returning home and to their schools with a wealth of experience
and knowledge that they wanted to share. The frustrations centered on
their feeling that they had changed but were expected to perform
again in the same roles. It was difficult for Mary to return to the same
position without a concrete way for her to share what she had learned
and gained beyond her classroom work.

There was not an awareness of the impact or that this experience
had changed me. I think Walden is a really high-powered school
and the expectation is that I will fit back into my slot and prepare
children to march through the Walden program. The requirements
of doing that really don't acknowledge that I'd bring anything
different than the competent job I did before going. My job is to
prepare children to continue through their Walden education. The
pace quickens from the minute that the fall comes so that there
really isn't even time to have informal discussion with colleagues
or to really say, "Hey, wait a minute." I either would like
different responsibilities or at least some way to express what I've

learned and what I've gained. That's pretty hard because there are some ways. I did teach an elective in shadow puppetry and I did do an assembly program and I did have the opportunity to speak with parents and write about my experience. But the expectation on a daily basis was that I'm back in my slot and I'm doing what I've always done.

Ellen Stacey was so energized after her first seven-month Japanese experience in the fall of 1988 that she explored many new ideas with her students. However, when she returned after teaching in Japan for three years, she experienced a devastating loss of rapport with the teachers and principal of her middle school. While she was in Japan the second time, her school had become a charter school. The teachers had gone to training sessions in Chicago to prepare them for team teaching.

It was the first time we had teaming. Other school districts send the whole staff to these. It was held in Chicago—how to team, what the reason behind teaming was and inspired them to the nth degree. Well, I was in Japan, so I had no opportunity to go to this, but I felt that I had lived first-hand experience. I could fit in and my enthusiasm was really high. I wanted to share, "Well, in Japan they did it this way. Let's try it this way because it really worked well in Japan."

Ellen had hoped that her knowledge about how schools functioned in Japan would help the staff; however, she found that her colleagues did not want to hear about her experiences or her ideas.

The first time Ellen returned, she became aware of a great gulf in the attitudes of respect for education between students she had taught in Japan and her students in the United States. She had not wanted to return to teach in her former school because she knew this would become a problem.

My principal wanted me back there. I was really depressed. After seeing, even the bad students, it was nothing like I was facing again in Milwaukee. I can't explain to you how that was. I mean when you walked into a Japanese classroom, there was such eagerness to learn, such a respect for those who could get the most education. Even with the bad kids, the communication with the teachers, they would walk into a teacher's room and they would talk to them like a big brother or something. There was a bond.

It was her fascination and curiosity about this "bond," this family atmosphere that she found lacking among students and teachers in U.S. schools, that provided much of the impetus for her second experience in Japan.

> Then I came back to Milwaukee and there was "that kid over there" or "that teacher over there." There was no unity, there was no teaming, there was nothing. At 3:00, who could beat out the kids to the parking lot to get to their car and go home. "That's not my problem" or "That kid has a problem, send him out of my room.". . . There was so much I missed and that was the whirlwind. When I went back to Japan, I wanted to know what made that, what caused that bonding.

In spite of the fact that Ellen was asked to present workshops in other buildings and to give a presentation to the state Board of Education, "my colleagues didn't want to hear about it. Not one teacher asked me anything about my trip to Japan. My principal had lived abroad; we only talked once. She never wanted to talk about it after that. 'Welcome back. How was it? Yes, I know what you're going through.' That was the end of that. She never would say, 'Come on in.'"

Ellen was in a state of exhaustion and confusion when she returned in August 1993 after her second experience in Japan: "When I came back, I had lost a lot of energy. I don't know if it was because I was in a state of confusion or what. Or I felt that I was trying to do everything before I went to Japan. When I came back from Japan, I tried to become a little bit more focused on small things instead of the big things."

Because she felt she had missed out on three years of American culture, she used the suggestions of the art teacher to have her students make presentations about famous black people during those three years.

> When I came back the second time, I had missed out on three years of American culture. I really felt deficient teaching these kids. I didn't know what they liked, I didn't know the music, I didn't know the TV programs, I didn't know the personalities. February was Black History Month. (I asked the art teacher and she told me to try this.) I had the kids do a presentation, but I didn't want historical people. I wanted famous black people in the three years that I was gone that they liked: musicians, TV personalities, actors, basketball, sports heroes, anything. Anybody they would like to do a report on. I caught up on three years in one month with the kids doing presentations. I learned the music, I learned the basketball players, I didn't know who they were. "The Dream

Team," who are they? Who's this Magic Johnson? Who is this Michael Jordan? I had no idea who these people were. The kids brought me up to 1993 real fast. It was wonderful, they loved it. They really enjoyed it, so I thank my art teacher for that.

A racial incident occurred in her classroom soon after she returned. It was brought on by her assignment of the story *The Slave Dancer* to her students. She had taken a female student aside, as she had seen Japanese teachers do, to tell the student "one on one, that I wasn't happy with her behavior and she was very rude to all the members of the class." Ellen thought that this student had retaliated by complaining to her mother about the story because it contains the word "nigger."

The Slave Dancer talks about when the slaves were being brought over and what did they call them back then. She told her mother that they were reading a book with the word. "Mrs. Stacey was teaching them this book that had the word 'nigger' in it." I had the NAACP, I had the WCBH [radio station], I had black business all at my school wanting to know what this white teacher was doing using "nigger" in the classroom. I thought stress was bad in Japan. It couldn't even come near to what I was going through at that time in Milwaukee.

This incident, she felt, had irreparably damaged the rapport she thought she had with students in her classroom. To clear the air, she used a methodology that she had observed in Japan to discuss controversial issues.

I went back to the students; I was thinking of using a Japanese technique on this, I asked the students their feelings about the situation. Was the book so bad that I should have banned it from the school? Because that was what NAACP and everybody wanted them to do. The students had a conference and it took a whole period for the students to voice their opinion. I said, "I'll remove myself from the picture. I'm going to put anybody, whoever, your student council rep, that will be the person in charge. And you need to come up with a conclusion." And the kids came to the conclusion after about forty-five minutes that the real problem was, the book was not bad. It was a white teacher, teaching them black history. That was the bottom line. So I asked them to put it in writing, but I did it a democratic way—which I don't think they would have done it in Japan. It was a very difficult year adjusting back in.

She felt a lack of rapport not only with students, but also with her colleagues. Ellen expressed surprise that neither teachers nor the principal asked her to share her experiences with staff or other classrooms: "Not one person, not one person on our staff asked me to do a presentation on Japan. Our social studies department never asked. I had said I would like to. Nobody ever asked. I asked my principal if I could do a workshop at our school to give them an idea of how Japan worked. No, he wouldn't allow me any time to do any presentations." One teacher, whom she had known quite well and who had sent her postcards while she was in Japan, might have provided some support when she returned. According to Ellen, "he saw that he had not grown in any capacity. He had been in the same classroom, teaching the same subject to the same grade level for twenty-five years. He did send me cards while I was in Japan and I would send him letters back, but the year I came back, he moved to another school."

In addition to a general negative feeling about her work when she returned from her second trip, she also felt a sense of malaise and isolation in her personal and family life. She had previously taught full time, gone to school three nights a week, worked out three days a week and "enjoyed a very active social life."

> Before I went to Japan, I was always in the social scene, always. Now I've been back from Japan and I have cut off all my friends. I distanced myself from everything including family. It's safe to talk to my parents because they live in Georgia. But as far as my family itself, there's a big gulf there. Where before I used to be at my sister's house all the time, we'd have dinner together with her family, and I was considered part of her family. There's been a wide gulf there. . . . My dating has gone to nothing.

The "reverse culture shock" and "deep depression" Ellen went through had ramifications on her spiritual life as well. She had become somewhat cynical about Western religions, especially the Roman Catholic Church, in which she was raised.

> I think I went through a period of deep depression when I returned from Japan. They say reverse culture shock is worse. That was true. I didn't think it would have been, but it was and I think in some aspects it still is. I was restless when I came back. I wanted to do everything because I thought money would be able to open all those doors. I had enough money to do all those things then. Right now, I am realizing that it's not the money. I remember when I had my fortune told in China, they told me I need *di chi ti bao*, more

physical strength, to sustain a life there and also a devout, more of a spiritual nature. These days, I've been thinking about the spiritual aspect of my life. . . . I think I tried to do it, but I wasn't happy with what I've seen in Catholicism in America versus Buddhism or Shintoism in Asian society. I'm more cynical about religions, Western religions, than I was about Eastern religions.

Neither Denise Green nor Paul Vandemere discussed any sense of reverse culture shock on returning to the United States from Japan. Denise and Paul had both had what they describe as a very positive experience in Japan. Their experience is in direct contrast with Ellen's more negative descriptions. Mary's and Ed's living conditions in China starkly contrasted with their life in the United States. The experience of Denise as an exchange student in Africa is more similar to that of Mary and Ed in China than her experience in Japan, a modern developed country. Thus, the material living conditions of the people and the teachers may have a bearing on the stress they feel living abroad and in returning from that experience.

Mary, Ed, and Ellen described changes they viewed in their own classroom practice. The trauma some of them described could have presaged a tremendous period of personal and professional growth, or the opposite, or something in between these extremes. For Ellen, and Mary to a lesser degree, it was hard to adjust to an environment in which colleagues were not interested or, as in Ellen's case, were hostile to their desire to share their insights, knowledge, and feelings about their experience. Mary felt a sense of wanting to perform a somewhat different role with her colleagues. There was little acknowledgment on their part that she had changed, that she had been through a transformative experience.

Dewey discusses "educative" and "miseducative" experience, the former leading to a profound transformation and the latter to stunted growth and even regression. Educative experience is accompanied by continuous learning, which is focused, not haphazard, and often very difficult. Ed Donovan became more cognizant of his teaching style and is continuing to change his pedagogy. Paul Vandemere worked to incorporate global studies into the state curriculum guidelines. Mary Ehrhardt began to redefine herself as an educational thinker and leader. Each of these teachers considers these changes a result of his or her international experience. By contrast, when Ellen says she thinks she has "lost what Ellen is all about," she is describing a painful transition. Each teacher's personal trauma and transition has ramifications for the major question of this study. How does extensive international study or experience affect the classroom practice of these teachers?

WORKING AGAINST STEREOTYPES

One of the most significant ramifications of their struggles with "culture shock" was the work of these teachers to debunk negative cultural or racial stereotyping among students and colleagues in their U.S. schools.   Several felt that their international experience had helped them to deal more effectively with this issue. For example, Paul Vandemere felt that Japan has been very successful when judged by the values of Western materialism.   The idea that many high school students consider anything different to be "weird" or "strange" was palliated by the perception of Japan as an economic success story. On the other hand, Bill Noteboem considers this belief to be another misperception or stereotype of Japan; that its economic success is the result of a people more imbued with the work ethic, competitive zeal, and company loyalty than most American workers display.   Paul elaborates his view:

> But always in the back of their [the students] minds, they understood this is a society that has by Western standards been very successful.   They have done very well in terms of the international marketplace.   Clearly, they have a much lower suicide rate and much higher graduation rate, the longevity. You look at different measurements that tend to be used in looking at countries. Japan and other countries in East Asia are clearly way up there in so many of those. So even though you're right, to some the initial reaction was, "Wow this is really weird!" Then, hopefully, the following question is: "Let's think for a minute. Why are they doing this? Why is this there?"

The force of negative stereotypes hit Paul when some people objected to his program around the time of property tax [millage] elections for funding the schools in his district.

> It's the more you know about someone, the more difficult it is to make false judgments about them. You might still not like them, but your reasons for not liking them are hopefully based on honest understandings, not misunderstandings. The more that my kids learned about Japanese and Chinese people from Hong Kong, etc., the less likely they would see them as a textbook enemy, as part of the enemy. To get beyond the idea of Japan bashing and the stereotypes, I early on knew a couple of people supposedly a couple of taxpayers in the district, who said they would never vote for a millage in our district as long as we had the East Asian program because we were teaching them about Japan and China and that

was wrong. Fortunately, they are in the minority and there are lots of others who had a different feeling. But it's a whole lot easier I think to get beyond the stereotypes and the myths because of the knowledge you have when you spend time overseas.

Paul team-taught the social studies course with another Japanese-language teacher. In the first years Japanese teachers who participated in a sister-state exchange program were welcomed into the program until state funding for this program was eliminated. The students who enrolled in the center were generally not racists or Japan-bashers because these students had made a two-credit-hour commitment to learning about Japanese language and culture. However, Paul was sometimes confronted by students in the hallway about Japan's bombing of Pearl Harbor during World War II.

Kids who had those stereotypes, who had the closed minds, were not that likely to sign up to begin with. But what I did get was occasional comments in the hallway, little derogatory things. And I would then talk to those people, not in a confrontational way, because I knew that a lot of times it was based on something their parents had said, someone else, families, family experience, and grandpa. Usually we had the most potential for friction . . . around the time of our discussion of Pearl Harbor and the dropping of the bomb; then also on trade issues with Japan. And those are flash points. That's when someone would come in and say, "Well, my dad said this. My grandpa said this." You could all of a sudden understand some of the feeling, the intensity that someone may have.

Ed Donovan also found that confrontations about his interest in China were more likely to occur with students who were not taking the specialized courses on China and East Asia that he was teaching.

I gave a slide presentation here, I think it was Martin Luther King Day. They were asking for people that had different ethnic experiences. I was talking about China, what a wonderful place it was and how great the people were. One kid said something to the effect, "Did you like China better than you like the U.S.?" A very right-wing kind of question. I said, "There is no question about how that should be answered." Then I went on with my lecture. This kid couldn't stand it. He said, "You didn't answer my question." "Of course, I did." I said, "Which do you prefer?" He said, "Well, I prefer America." I said, "So do I." He was satisfied and shut up. But he could not tolerate the fact that I would praise China for some of the things when he thought that I should be knocking them down all the time. I talked to him afterwards and said, "The question you asked was a very intolerant question." He said, "Well, I didn't know if you were beefing up China so that we'd all want to become Chinese or not." I said, "It's pretty evident that I live here and I do have a choice." That shut him up a little bit. I've given talks to parent groups and a couple of the churches here. They are much more tolerant I think than some of these kids are. The kids are looking for identity and that's part of it.

Mary Ehrhardt was concerned about the possibility of her students' developing negative stereotypes about China's poverty, reflecting a general disdain for poor people in American society. One way she works to defuse this tendency is to show an old film, *Tom and Didi*, narrated by Shirley MacLaine.

It is one of our very introductory experiences to show differences. I remember differences in housing, the American house which has an outside garden and the Chinese house with the garden on the inside and the wall on the outside. Many differences are portrayed. But on the other hand, there are all the similarities. Laughing in both languages, the words for mother and father in both languages. That is a good talking point. It's a good vehicle for launching some conversations.

Mary considers one of the major goals of the study of China and the pen-pal exchange to be reducing "negative stereotyping" among children.

I guess that's probably one of the goals of the whole study . . . to lessen the negative stereotyping. One of the ways of achieving the goal has been to show the richness of the culture and the incredible art and crafts and incredible inventions that this Asian society has achieved. So by making the cultural aspects very appealing, being able to help the children appreciate them, then they are less likely to just go on with their stereotypes, especially with the Chinese children. To interface with the Chinese children in the bilingual class—Chinese-American children or many of them are newly arrived—and they're in the bilingual class because they are just beginning English speakers. But, we do lots of pre-meeting talking and role-playing so that we won't hurt the others. . . . I don't know how we do it. Hopefully, we do. I think they so appreciate the art that they do, the kite making, the pottery. I think that they really can appreciate the culture.

Recognizing and respecting the differences among people is important for all children, according to Mary: "It is interesting on the elementary level, not so much that we were different, but in recognizing the differences. Sometimes I always find a tactile experience, feel this black hair, some of the quality of skin, and just that our curiosity needs to be satisfied about the differences. So I think they too wonder about curly hair."

Denise Green found that her experience helped her students, many of whom were African-American children, dream impossible dreams and expand their ideas of what is possible. Denise became a model to them, her postcards and coins precious symbols of things they might do some day. In 1990, within two years of returning from Japan, she raised money and planned a trip for twelve students and twelve parents from a magnet school in Indianapolis that specialized in English as a second language. Most of the students on the trip were in the sixth grade except for one second-grader who accompanied his older sister and mother. Denise and the families raised $60,000 to pay for the trip. Even though it lasted only two and a half weeks, some of the students were "still corresponding with their host families" when I interviewed her in 1994.

The students came from many different areas of Indianapolis because this was a magnet school. Denise thought that the best and most creative assignment that a teacher gave to the students

was from the sixth-grader's math teacher. The teacher told them to go to a grocery store and make a list of ten things and how much they cost and do the same in Japan and find out how much they cost. Translate the cost from yen to dollars. Compare and contrast, also in packaging size. That made a lot of sense to me. Then report back to class. We also had another teacher that said to keep a diary and then share it.

Denise sent back postcards to each of her students. When she returned, she gave them a writing assignment to "describe the perfect classroom, describe the perfect teacher and the perfect field trip." Her students wrote

about going in a spaceship to outer space. . . . I was just amazed by it. I thought if my going, sending back little postcards, and bringing back the cheap little coins . . . it seemed like they were beginning to believe that some things were possible, that they hadn't thought about before. It does have an impact. And it just gave me more encouragement to keep on providing opportunities for them.

Denise provided these opportunities by inviting Japanese visitors into
her class to talk about Japan: "Of course, they [the students] always
wanted to exchange a few words with them. They would beg me to
teach them Japanese, to teach them a little Spanish. They were just
fascinated by that."

Ed Donovan's method of dealing with negative stereotyping by his
students draws on some of his previous work in anthropology about the
way many people in the world stereotype an American.

> What I do is give them [his students] a stereotype of an American.
> All Americans have long noses. All Americans are rich. All
> Americans are well educated. So I'll take it point for point with
> them and give it back to them how the Americans are viewed and
> stereotyped. All Americans are aggressive. And a kid says,
> "We're not aggressive people." Well, I say, "Take a look at the
> way you walk compared to the way that the Chinese walk. Look
> at the way you point. Look at the way you wave for people to come
> to you." I show them how the Chinese walk and how they wave
> for people to come to them and how they point. Much different. I
> say, "There's a basic assumption here, isn't there? When you point
> like this, you're pointing like a spear. When you point like this,
> you're being gracious." It's a lot different way of looking at things
> and you can get right into the culture just in those kinds of things.
> I'm showing something, but I'm not pointing. It's not like a spear,
> it's more like an offering.

When he talks about and shows pictures of the very poor village he
visited, he is hoping that the students will develop tolerance for the
people and an awareness about what their lives might be like.

> I don't know but I'm hoping that, for some, toleration gets built in
> for the poor around the world. A lot of these kids have never been
> to foreign countries and have never seen anything like that. In fact,
> they've never seen anything except their town. When you describe
> something that's not, it's way outside of their field of knowledge.
> And the only one that I've found that had seen anything like that
> was a gal who had spent some time in Mexico last summer doing
> some church work down there. She was in a very poor village
> where conditions were very similar. So we talk a lot. She can
> connect with me. She understands exactly what I'm talking about.

While sharing his experiences in China with his American students,
he discussed issues like cultural gender differences, an example of

which was the consternation he had caused by seating the Chinese men and women differently. He also planned activities such as Ba Fá Ba Fá (Shirts, 1977), the goal of which was to help his students understand and tolerate cultural differences.

I came here and these desks are all individual and kids would move them around. We sat in circles and there might be a boy, girl, girl, boy, boy, girl. You have a random pattern. It struck me I think the first time that I was in a class, where I had a seminar and I was discussing something. I use a lot of examples of Chinese differences in culture, based on Chinese and American viewpoint of things, today even. They wanted to know if I had ever eaten a dog. Oh, yeah. Whoa! You say, you know it's different. When you are starving, you'll eat anything that's edible. If a dog happens to be nearby, too bad, dog! People get used to that kind of thing. Still, it's tough for them to understand that different people aren't just Americans in different skin or different clothing.

When confronted with students who were showing blatant intolerance, Ed's response was very different after his experience in China.

They know that I don't put up with intolerant kinds of nonsense. I won't let them kid each other at a cruel level at all. I just don't put up with it, particularly if it's ethnic. I think a lot of things that probably went on before are the same things that are happening today in places all over the country. I am very sensitive to it now, much more so I think than I was before. I think there were a couple of times, not just a couple, probably many times before I went to China where things were said and I didn't even realize that they were a slam against another kid. [Now] I confront it immediately. I don't give them any quarter on it. They know it so I don't have a problem with it any more, except maybe at the beginning of the year when it's different classes.

Ed's curriculum changed substantially after his year in China and continues to change with each successive teaching experience in China (the summers of 1991 and 1995). In describing how he handles negative stereotypes with his students, he tells the story of his conception of the "ugly Americans" in China.

I think that people who teach in China for any time at all recognize ugly Americans when they see them. We saw a bunch of them. In Xian, a tour group dressed like Americans would dress on

Sunset Boulevard or in Miami: big baggy shorts and floppy T-shirts with a lot of print on them, walking as though they are on the muscle, very aggressive walk. They expected things to be like it was in America and it wasn't. . . . I know what they talk about when they talk about the ugly American. . . . They drove up in this air-conditioned Mitsubishi bus that was brand-new I'm sure. They were a California group, probably from Beverly Hills. They were dressed to the nines: the men in yachting outfits, like duck trousers, boat shoes, and blue blazers with captain-type yachting hats. Women were dressed in safari outfits, with hiking boots and the stockings, and knickers, jodhpurs they were. They had the fan out to here along the sides, the silk scarf with a safari helmet. As they were walking along the Wall, they were walking as Americans do, kind of apart from each other, giving each other space. Because they were not walking quickly, the Chinese who were, go in between them and sometimes would touch them. The one lady turned a little bit one way and say, "Well, I never." Then she turned the other way and said, "Well, I never." This went on all the way down the Wall. She was expecting people to say, "Oh, excuse me for bumping into you." Nobody was having any part of that, except her. You could hear them talking about how rude the Chinese were with no concept in their heads about the space that they were taking up or about how rude they were because they expected people to conform to their particular culture.

When his students react by laughing, sure that they would never behave this way in another country, Ed cautions them.

Mostly they laugh and see it as a funny story. Then what we do is come back to it and say, "What are our basic assumptions here? How would you behave?" None of them believe that they would behave that way. My comment is that "you are a product of your country. Unless you have that winnowed in some way or leavened in some way, you're going to continue to be a product of your culture. You are going to express your culture in exactly the same way that these people did that were on the wall in Xian." "Oh, I'd never do that." "Don't say never."

EMPATHY IN THE CLASSROOM

In discussions of their efforts to eliminate negative stereotyping among U.S. students, several of these teachers talked about their heightened empathy with students in their classrooms, especially those from immigrant and ethnic minority backgrounds. In their study of teacher behavior, anthropologists George and Louise Spindler (1994) documented that middle-class white teachers often favor students with similar ethnic backgrounds to their own. How these teachers feel their international experience affects their relationships with their students may add another aspect to the Spindlers' analysis. A teacher's in-depth exposure to another culture, such as these teachers experienced, can lead to a more sensitive and empathetic relationship with students of different ethnicity and backgrounds.

Ed Donovan described how international experience may help a veteran teacher become more sensitive about negative stereotypes.

> I am very conscious of where they are coming from. Extraordinarily conscious. I think the same thing is true when I have kids coming in from European countries. All of a sudden your antenna goes up and you are very attentive to what the differences might be. Even kids from Canada. There's really a difference and we don't realize it until you have been in a different culture: [to understand] the oddities of the American culture.

His heightened consciousness about what these young people from other countries may be experiencing is often evident in Ed's teaching. The experience he had with Heather's extreme reaction in China has helped him understand what some young people, who have been brought up in different cultures, go through when they emigrate to the United States.

> I think you just pay more attention to them. If they don't understand something, you're there so that they can say, "I don't understand it." Try to explain it to them. I have a kid now from Korea who has been here maybe three months now, from September. When she first came into the program, she was just lost. She couldn't understand why kids behaved the way they did or knew where to go or anything else. I kind of took her by the hand and led her through until she became comfortable. We have a kid from England that just came in January and we're still kind of leading her around by the hand and saying, "Don't worry about it. Just relax a little bit." She's gone through the culture shock. She was here up until last week; last week she crashed. She couldn't get out of bed. Her antenna had been so alert that her psyche just had to take a rest. She came back today and I was talking with her, and she said, "I don't know what happened. I thought I had the flu. I couldn't move." I said, "I know exactly what happened. You have culture shock." "Oh," she said, "this culture doesn't seem to be so much different." I said, "It's way different, and your

antenna has gone out." So I think just the fact that you are aware
of the kinds of ways they're affected has a lot to do with orienting
them into the culture so that they can get along a little bit better.

Ed believes that his relationships with students in general are closer
and, similar to Bill Notebaum, he feels there is a more relaxed
atmosphere in his classroom: "I'm not sure it's just me, because of the
experience that I had, but one of the things that I have noticed is kids
seem to be a lot more comfortable with me, than they were before. I
don't know if it's because I've slowed down and tolerate a lot more or
because I am more sensitive."

Paul Vandemere also felt he was much more sensitive to ethnic
diversity in his classes, often taking a pro-active stance with his
students about their differences.

> One of the things that I tried to do was to, as I became aware of
> students' ethnic backgrounds in my classes, I would try to use that
> knowledge at different times when we were discussing different
> topics. . . . If I knew that I had a student whose family was from
> the Middle East, I would ask them if they knew about it, what
> their understanding was of what things were like in their country.
> It gave that person hopefully a sense of pride. . . . I would always
> try to have it presented in a positive light, so that kids were
> respecting that person's family background, so that person would
> not be seen as weird.

Just as Ed Donovan dealt with these issues head-on, Paul let his
students know exactly how he felt about ethnic slurs.

> I'm tired. . . . I become frustrated when we do these knee-jerk
> reactions and categorize people. We really are cruel. The ethnic
> slurs that go on, that are based on ignorance, that are based on
> maybe one or two experiences. For someone to condemn an entire
> country for Pearl Harbor. For someone to condemn an entire group of
> people because of Saddam Hussein. On and on and on, it is just not
> fair. I think the more you can make people feel proud about the
> positive things of their country's accomplishments, of their family
> background, the better off you are.

By comparison, Mary Ehrhardt worked in a more concrete way to
celebrate culture and diversity in her school. She had brought back
some leather shadow puppets from China. Seven or eight girls, five of
whom were Chinese-American, worked very hard to put on a shadow
puppet performance for grades four, five, and six. Mary felt that the

Chinese-American girls "relished in the experience, in the aesthetics, in the telling of Chinese tales. It was a celebration for them." The sixth-grade girls had chosen to do this project as an elective and Mary was very pleased with the results: "We sewed our puppets first and we examined the leather puppets, especially the sixth-grade girls, they hinged the hand, the wrist. They just did an excellent job."

Mary had gone through a multicultural training course at her school in addition to "this wonderful China experience." She feels she still needs to work on her own awareness about diversity issues: "I think that there are subtle issues that I still need to work on. I think all of this experience raised a great deal of consciousness. Sometimes in order to protect a child or nurture a child, I realize I still don't give enough credence to who they are." Mary believes that the China curriculum helps make the diversity issue authentic, especially for Caucasian American children.

The connections that the children made with newly arrived Chinese children in the pen-pal exchange may have been the most meaningful demonstration of promoting ethnic understanding and respect among these six teachers. It would be impossible to quantify what these second-graders get out of such an exchange, especially under the tutelage of a teacher who models such a sense of respect and wonder about another culture. A longitudinal study of those children as they travel through their schooling would add another perspective as a follow-up to this study. It would be wonderful to listen to the children evaluate this experience, but that work would be the purview of a future study.

This chapter provides evidence that there is a connection between international study and experience and change in a teacher's pedagogy. The initial reactions of these teachers on re-entry to the United States included feelings of "reverse culture shock," part of the context for the changes they report in their classroom practice. "Reverse culture shock" occurs because these teachers are changed by their experience. They are not the same people who left for an experience abroad; therefore, some of them have difficulties adjusting, in Mary Ehrhardt's words, to their former "slots." Their changed perspectives and new knowledge present great opportunities for each of them, but this awareness does not come without pain. How each of them grapples with new dilemmas in and out of the classroom helps us understand that educative experience involving personal growth can be quite difficult, which is why it is important that positive support mechanisms be in place for them when they return. They have become different teachers with respect to their teaching style, the content of their curriculum, and their relationships with students and colleagues in their schools.

8

Different as Teachers

All but one of these teachers clearly felt they were better teachers for having had the international experience. Only Ellen Stacey indicated that she had been more energetic and creative before her second experience. In fact, in the one and a half years between her first and second experience in Japan, she was named Teacher of the Year for all of Milwaukee's public schools. Promising examples of changed pedagogy occured in each teacher's practice.

Bill Notebaum's change started with his awareness that the traditional methodology in his view was counterproductive to achieving the kind of results he most values in education. Even though he did not feel he had time to change his methods entirely, he gives examples of approaches to specific lessons that are different now than before he began this study. He was grappling with the kind of teaching he would foster in the International High School he initiated just after he returned from Japan and which opened in 1996.

Paul Vandemere and Mary Ehrhardt felt that the experience brought an authenticity and depth to their teaching about East Asia, while Denise Green viewed her experience as providing a model for the children, heightening their perception of what is possible. Ed Donovan described changes in his pedagogy and curriculum choices that he attributed directly to his experience in China. Change in their classrooms includes their methodology, how they teach; their philosophy about teaching; what they teach, the authenticity of their work in the humanities and East Asian history, culture, and language; and their empathy and rapport with their students.

CHANGES IN HOW THEY TEACH

Paul Vandemere found that the content of his teaching changed significantly at the same time as his methodology because he was "studying a lot about instruction and became increasingly aware of the importance of students owning their learning." He knew that his work in debate or forensics was successful "for a reason. We had self-directed learners." After his two years in Japan he decided to incorporate this aspect of his debate and forensics work in all of his classes.

Contrary to the stereotype many people have of Japanese education, Paul witnessed creative examples of pedagogy, especially at the elementary level.

> I saw some innovative teachers who would try some, certainly at the elementary level, try more group projects. Kids were motivated to learn who also worked cooperatively in groups, and they saw the benefits in doing so. I would try to bring that atmosphere into my regular classes. So there were certainly some days where you would come and you would see me teach in the traditional sense. But there were a lot of days where you would come in and see students engaged in group projects and group presentations where I was not fitting the normal mold of a teacher, which is to stand up and talk.

Paul, like Ed Donovan, could construct role-playing and simulation experiences in the classroom based on their deepened knowledge of a different culture. They both used variations of a simulation game, Ba Fá Ba Fá (Shirts, 1977), which allowed students to experience a cultural dilemma that has many ramifications for understanding the complexities of cultural exchanges.

After his return from Japan, Paul hoped to get students to question why cultural practices evolve. Paul started each new class with an exercise to promote cultural understanding.

> Very early on, the very first days of every semester with my beginning students, I would put them in an exercise where they were members of two different cultures, with different norms. They had to send visitors to the other cultures to learn those norms. They had to become observers and then see how they were treated as outsiders while they were doing this. That began their exposure to say you have to suspend your judgments of other countries as you are now learning about them. You have to not be quick to make those judgments. You have to understand.

Paul used this game to get them to think about how and why structures and practices are different outside the United States, with the goal that they would begin to question and understand their own cultural traditions.

> They would begin to all of a sudden examine themselves in America for the first time. I spent most of my time on Japan, second most on China, and a lesser amount on the mini dragons. I would always have them make a comparison to what was going on in the United States and use it as a springboard to reexamine what we do. So after they looked at the Japanese educational system or criminal justice system, I'd have them reflect a little bit on art. Not that I would ever say, "This is what you have to do." I never once told them that the Japanese approach was better and that America ought to adopt. Never once. That's not my role. I would allow them to learn about other cultures. They could then form their own opinions. They would make presentations in which they would learn about the Chinese system of dealing with dissidents or their legal system or other aspects of Chinese or Japanese society. Then they would make some judgments themselves. As long as they were based on what was true, that's all I asked for.

It was not his goal to have students compare U.S. society negatively with other societies. It was his goal that they understand the reasons behind aspects of each of the societies, including that of the United States: "Not that for a minute I was asking them to criticize American society, obviously not. But never take for granted what we have and understand why we have it. There's a reason why our country is organized the way it is. A lot of times, our kids don't think about that."

After his experience in China, and reflecting a similar teaching style to Paul Vandemere's, Ed Donovan wanted his students to experience what happened when members of cultures with radically different languages and values interact also in the simulation role play, Ba Fá Ba Fá (Shirts, 1977).

> You set up two groups; one group is real laid-back. They couldn't care less about money or anything else. The only thing that's important is friendship. The other group is uptight capitalists, who are bargaining with each other all the time to get an upper grip on things. What you'll do is take two people from each culture and put them in a different room with the opposite culture. They can't speak the language. The basic assumptions you have set up in one room are so different from the other room that it's

hard for them to recognize. They have to be able to get along in the culture. There's going to be a representative from this group who are heavy capitalists who want to convert this group so they become a marketplace. These guys will work at it, and finally the laid-back culture will throw these guys out. The reason they throw them out is because they don't depend on friendship. When you take the laid-back group and they come into the money group, they're given so many dibs, or whatever they call those things that represent money, and people come up and start to trade with them, and these guys just give it away. Once they've given away all of their money, they're poor. Nobody pays any attention to them. They want to get out. It's one of the ways that we use to show differences in culture.

He has incorporated this role-play into his course so that students will learn to understand and respect another point of view.

Ed described the changes in his teaching style as a result of his work in China.

I became much more deliberate, I suppose is a good word. Speech pattern slowed down in any case. Less slang, less idiomatic speech. Really, an awareness of when the students here were not getting whatever was in the lesson. I really became aware of that. They were not engaged . . . or they just didn't understand. I don't think I had ever had a doubt in my previous life about a youngster understanding what I said, understanding a concept.

He began to speak more deliberately and carefully.

I had spent a year looking at students that I had to really concentrate on. I think that concentration carried over. It wasn't just a matter of defining words for these people but to get them to understand how a phrase or word was used and could be used differently. Those that seemed to be having trouble, I could approach and talk to them about it. Maybe clarify. It brought in something else that I started doing at that time. That is when I saw a student who didn't understand. In order to clarify, I knew that I was using very standard English; kids sometimes don't understand standard English. I would turn to somebody that I knew had grasped the concept and ask him to explain it. I found out that that was an effective way to get things across.

Ed's teaching practice has also changed in team teaching with a younger man who is still taking courses in education.

I'm doing more team teaching. I'm on an afternoon team now, teaching about Vietnam this semester. I've enjoyed that immensely and with a guy who is still taking courses in education so he's got different ideas that he comes in with. . . . We've done more active things like debates, discussions. I'm using a lot more video with this guy. . . . I think anything that I bring into teaching that deals with differences in culture, the China influence is definitely there. I talk about it and try to get a discussion going about it and try to get the kids to feel what the difference is as opposed to trying to just learn it intellectually.

The experience he had in China, in addition to the creative stimulation he feels in working with a younger teacher who is currently studying different classroom approaches, has energized Ed considerably about his own teaching, even though he is sixty-five years old. There is no shuffling off into retirement for Ed Donovan!

We try to work through things, you know: "Why does somebody say this? What is the purpose of this?" The whole Taiwan exercise, for example. I said, "What's the message here?" Well, they had all read about it. I said, "Well, what's the real message?" We fiddled around with that for a long, long time. We started doing this projection thing, like, "What happens if Lee Teng Hui gets elected?" I said, "Is there going to be a war?" They said they didn't know, they couldn't project that. "Well, what about the United States sending ships?" They didn't know. They thought that was a good idea to protect Taiwan. I said, "Is it our job to protect them since they are a province of China and they see themselves that way?" . . . They went round and round on that. I said, "So what you're looking at is our lack of understanding of what the Chinese see about themselves and what the Taiwanese see about themselves. They share the culture. We're outsiders and we haven't got a clue."

During his international study and just after his experience in Japan, Bill Notebaum developed an awareness of teaching methods that he admired, but felt that he had not changed enough to be satisfied with his own teaching style: "It doesn't look as different as it should, and I'm really frustrated, dissatisfied with that." According to Bill, the reasons for this are the difficulty of changing the expectations of students who are not familiar with a different approach and the time constraints on developing a classroom practice that is more student-centered and inquiry-based.

We all work in a certain culture again, when kids come into your room and expecting a certain thing and already have habits. They're not going to transform those habits just because you want to use a different approach.   So that can be very frustrating. Particularly when your approach more and more relies on kids' own interests, on inquiry and self-motivation, they're just going to abuse it, basically. That's frustrating. And secondly, I'm into so many other different things that I just don't have the time and preparation. Well-constructed, well-thought-out methodology that involves students in the learning process definitely are the best. But they are long and well developed. I would need time to do that. Educational methodology is not what I have right now and it's what I want my teachers to do, and I have views on it, but developing it is not really me right now. I can't do everything.

Bill felt his work to develop a magnet international school including students from ten school districts with an International Baccalaureate degree and curriculum precluded substantive change in his teaching methodology. He felt that to change his pedagogy would require a commitment of time and effort that he did not have in addition to promoting and planning the new school. Bill passionately argues for a pedagogy different from what he considers the traditional lecture-based style and rote learning followed by rigorous multiple-choice tests: "In fact, intimidating students was basically a plus. I mean, that's the way the job was done." He had come to the "educational debate" late, after he returned from Japan. This debate is past tense to Bill because "I know which side is right now and I don't have any patience for those people any more. I'm not going to waste [time on the debate]. I mean, I'd come home too upset about the authoritarian, very torrid, instructional techniques."

This discussion with Bill about his teaching practice reflects his answer to the central question of this study: To what extent does in-depth international study and experience affect the pedagogy of a veteran teacher? In this part of the question, he is responding to how he feels this experience affected his classroom practice. How he responds is not about how he actually changed as a result of the experience, but about how his thinking about pedagogy has changed as a result of many factors, including his international experience. It is the change he hopes to initiate in his international school that he believes has been most affected by his international study and experience. He did not express a desire to adopt Japanese educational practices in American schools, except, like Paul Vandemere, for the homeroom idea. It was in the process of learning about U.S.-Japanese trade issues and business organizational reform that he began to think about school reform, an idea that developed into his proposal for an International High School.

However, within his pedagogy as a classroom teacher Bill seemed satisfied with some aspects of a teacher-dominated classroom.

> I have such a knowledge base and ability to command presence and dominate the classroom. Not dominate in a negative sense, but why not use it? It's kind of a waste if you have, I don't mean this egotistically, but it's kind of a waste if you have what I have to offer, sitting around the classroom watching kids fumbling around on projects. They should be fumbling around on projects, but they should also have the exposure to what I have to offer.

Like Paul Vandemere, Bill has compromised by using a mixture of methodologies.

> What I do is lecture. I don't do anything like a formal lecture, but I have a lot of teacher-dominated instruction. I always have high expectations, but what I do is force my students to blend with traditional academics, an ongoing, almost semester-long project. The best scenario is one that has a public outcome, that they put on a seminar on a topic or they publish a report on a topic and actually deliver it to a public audience. That blends with the coursework, so while I'm teaching economics and giving them the fundamentals, they may be analyzing, for example, the state business climate. Or right now while I am teaching microeconomics, I have my kids each taking a different commodity. . . . My daughter is doing rice because she went to Japan. Other kids are just doing wheat or pork bellies, . . . and [they] do a complete analysis of that product and its history and its current market analysis and future markets.

The key to the change in his classroom is in his emphasis on "engaging students" much more than he had in the past.

> I see the absolute need for engaging students and I also offer much more of a variety of experiences like computer simulation. I have all my kids teach junior achievement classes. They all become junior achievement consultants and teach in the elementary and the middle school. If you were to come into my class maybe three days a week, it would look pretty much like the same old stuff. There's a lot of other things that kids are doing, either on their own that they eventually have to hand in, or is eventually done in

the classroom at the end of the semester. They put on these things and then teach each other. Like what I did the other day is something I wouldn't have done in the past. The topic was England's move to the constitutional problem that started from Charles I and led to the rule of Cromwell, that period in English history ending with the Glorious Revolution. Typically, I would lecture that to the kids or tell them to make it into a story. It can be a good, fascinating story. As storytellers go, I get at least an average.

In this case, his methodology was different.

I just came into the classroom and started with each kid and said that this is the piece of story you have. They'd already read the materials and been prepared. "Now you've got twenty minutes, each one of you, to get your little piece of the story researched and be ready." They were just small pieces. How successful was James I, something like that. Each kid had a little piece of the story. Then after twenty minutes, each kid started telling his piece in chronological order. It accomplished the exact same thing as me lecturing and it was way more effective. They can buy in, and talk and express themselves.

The main change Bill perceives in the classroom atmosphere is that he feels more relaxed, more a teacher than a disciplinarian, focused more on student learning of subject matter than on control.

Just the whole atmosphere in the classroom, I'm much more relaxed and I'm not into control at all. But the funny thing about that is part of my philosophy; it's partly now I think I have the chance to do that. When you are young and when you're being challenged, you have to be in control, you have no choice. But being the age I am now, in sort of a stature or whatever, kids don't mess with me too much. It works to your advantage. You have an aura or whatever and you create an atmosphere in your room and you don't have to be a policeman. Although, I have to say that when I get a particularly bad class, then I've got to switch back to a different mode again. Otherwise, you just can't get anything accomplished. As long as I can be completely relaxed and don't have to play disciplinarian, then that's the way I play it. I also reach out to kids a lot more now by simple things, just normal interpersonal relations.

Bill spoke of this change within the context of how he believed his teaching practice was different after his international experience. Ed Donovan also describes a more relaxed classroom atmosphere in his relationships with his students after his return from China.

Changes in Ellen Stacey's and Mary Ehrhardt's pedagogy included engaging their students in more projects where they took responsibility for the work as well as introducing them to the Japanese practice of standing and greeting the teacher when she enters the classroom. Mary and Ellen adapted their experiences in China and Japan for classroom use. Both were impressed with the practice of standing and greeting the teacher. While Mary Ehrhardt did not require her class to do this every day, she often referred to this practice as an example of the respect shown by Chinese students to the teacher and to each other. In expecting her students to take more responsibility for classroom tasks and their behavior than she had before her experience, Mary invoked the behavior of her Chinese students as a model.

I've especially pointed out in discipline, using my Chinese students as models in discipline, how respectful Chinese students are and what the practices are. When the Chinese teacher enters the room, they rise. And the teacher asks them to sit down. They do not speak unless they are called on. I have many times found myself referring to my Chinese students versus the disrespect it is to the teacher and to their classmates when something that someone says just sets off a general conversation. This class is very much prone to just—they don't have the self-control to listen without just verbalizing their own experiences. I have to model for them what it is like in a Chinese classroom, what the decorum and behavior of students is like. It is helpful. They take it to heart.

Ellen Stacey went further than Mary on this issue, compelling her students to stand and participate in greeting the teacher, a practice she had experienced in Japan.

When I came back I felt that maybe what I should do with my students is make them stand, like they did in Japan when the teacher walked into the room, and greet me, say, "Good morning." Then I would tell them to sit down. They hated it. They literally hated it. "What are we gonna do, say the 'Pledge of Allegiance?'" I said, "No, you're going to say hello to me." Then I made them stand to say, "Thank you." Those kids came back to me now and they say that they remember that the most about my class, that I made them say "Good morning" or "Good afternoon" and "Thank you." It's cute because they hated it, but it was something I was not going to be swayed from.

Ellen was also impressed with the sense of national loyalty she observed in Japan and tried to imbue this sort of feeling about being an American into her students.

> I made them look at our flag and I said, "This is our country." I made them realize that this flag was in my classroom. I never had a flag in my classroom. I made sure I had a flag in my classroom. . . . "You don't know and realize how lucky you are to be in this country. You respect that flag. That's our flag, that's America." I really became patriotic all of a sudden, too. When I came back from Japan, I realized that there was a national unity. They would go shopping and they would pay $200 more for a product even though they could have gotten a cheaper product made in Taiwan, but because this was made in Japan, it had more value to them than this product, the same product, but it just didn't carry the Japanese logo. A strong loyalty. I felt that if we had, if I could create that kind of a loyalty to our country, that maybe the students would feel that "I'm not black," "I'm not white," "I'm American and this is our goal to make America a strong country."

Ellen also tried to incorporate the map skills field trip, which she had thought was an excellent method of teaching map skills, into her curriculum, but the lukewarm involvement of her colleagues and legal realities in the United States thwarted her.

> I tried to get my social studies department to work out a map where we could take our kids in May down to the Cultural Center, and I wanted to do a map and I wanted to plan it where we could go here. "Oh yeah, that's a very good idea. But you do it." I thought, "But you want to take the trip." Right, my goal also was to get this gentleman to help me organize it so the kids would find the unity between us as well as with the kids. This teacher in the city. He said, "Oh that's a wonderful idea. Do it." But that wasn't what I wanted. We ended up taking the trip, but there were no map skills. He told me the city police would not allow seventy children, junior high kids, running through the Cultural Center following maps. I didn't see that there would be a problem.

Ellen's pedagogy, her methodology, and curriculum changed very drastically from the description she gives of herself as a teacher before her experiences in Japan. She is the only one who seems to have become more traditional and book-oriented, especially after her second three-year experience in Japan.

> For some reason I went right into a book. I depended more on the book than I did on my creativity. The only thing I could think of at this point, it's easier. Someone wrote a book, kids' parents paid for it out of their taxes. I've never used it, I think I should use it. I still am teaching out of the book. Now in my classroom, I say, "Bring your English book and open to page 36. Now let's read this and discuss it." Maybe what I'm trying to do is, trying to teach them grammar points, trying to teach them the tried-and-true professional way of writing stories.

Her students "do creative writing [but] they don't like my topics, they tell me." She describes the year I interviewed her as the worst year of her teaching experience. She had worked with her students on the computers for three months. When the system crashed, all their work was gone.

> This year is the worst year for me. The worst year. I wanted to use computers, I wanted to put computers into their world. So we did a lot of research, we used the book, we got the research, we wrote letters, we put all the information in the computers. I didn't back it up and the whole system crashed on us. All their work was gone. That was three months of work and I had nothing. The only thing they had was the artwork that was hanging out in the hall. That happened in November. We still don't have the computers working. I think this year has been, I feel, a total loss.

This hopeless feeling is in stark contrast to the effect she saw on her teaching after the first, seven-month experience in Japan: "The year that I had come back, the full year before I returned to Japan, I won more awards for my students' writings and skills than I had ever done prior to that time." She had used many of the techniques she had seen in Japan, including teaming and group work.

> When I went back into that grouping, making ourselves feel that we belonged together, there were a lot more communications. I was having lunches with my kids in the classroom. We were talking about problems that they were having. I was tutoring, I did it all on my own after school. I had a Japanese program after school two nights a week. I had tutoring two nights a week. I wanted the kids to stay focused and on target. I didn't want them falling behind. We would do writings, we would do stories. We entered

all these contests that the school would send us. I would enter my kids' works. An administrator called me up and said, "What are you trying to do?" She was in charge of the Writing Connection. She wanted to know what I was trying to do because my kids were winning all these awards. My kids were on the radio. They read their writings on the radio. We were personally interviewed by the newspaper.

Linking this enthusiasm with her experiences in Japan, Ellen explains, "When I came back the first time, I had admired the way the teacher in Japan communicated with those kids." The work she did with her American students when she returned from Japan the first time left her feeling satisfied. Ellen felt that she had created something like the atmosphere she had experienced in the Japanese schools.

> I think the kids had a good bond that year, even though it was only half a year. At the end of that year, I walked away thinking, "I did a good job this year." I think I really taught well that year I came back. I think my outlook at the kids as though, instead of being students, they were my children. Almost that kind of a change in my way of thinking and approach to the kids. I made a lot of contacts at home that year. I must have called every student at least three times that year, at their home, telling their parents that their kids are doing great or I was having problems with them, which was something I hadn't done before. I would call and say "I'm having problems with your child," but I had never [before] called a parent and said, "I'm really enjoying your child."

Feeling alienated from her colleagues, Ellen immersed herself in the lives of her students after her first experience in Japan: "I thought since I couldn't get involved with the teacher's lives, I would get involved with the kids. And I did. I submerged myself into the kids' lives. I think that was a very good year for me. Because I was being burned out, and going there and coming back I was renewed. After the three years over there, I think I came back burned out."

In spite of Ellen's feelings of being burned out and tired, she still teaches differently than she had before. Like Mary Ehrhardt, she expects her students to take on more responsibility: "I assigned each student a role, just like they do in Japan. One student's job was to take care of the chalkboard. . . . I gave them jobs, I gave them errands, not errands so much. If someone was sick, it was your job to take that person to the principal's office because he was sick and he needed support. And that was the Japanese way." She used a Japanese motivational style to get the students to take responsibility for something they wanted, a new carpet on the old wooden floor.

> I asked them if they would like to have carpeting. They said yes. I asked for almost three months, "Do you want carpeting?" Then I didn't ask after the third month and the fourth month at Christmas, "When are you going to get us carpeting?" And I said, "So you really want it?" I said, "But if you want it, you cannot chew gum in my room." It was a trade-off. But I wanted them to want it. And they promised they wouldn't chew gum, so I put carpeting on the floor.

When Ellen returned from Japan the second time, she thought about the English language as the tie that binds this country together. This idea led her to "go back to the basics" and teach English diagramming to help her African-American students develop good speaking and writing skills.

> I felt that if the kids could understand the language of English diagramming, that they could then explain some of the culture of America because it lies in the language. These kids had a language skill that was really, if you were to hire them, they would not be the ones that you would hire for an engineer or a scientist because they had very poor language skills.

Ellen found herself returning to childhood values within the context of experiencing a rigorous language program in Japan. A month of testing frustrated her plans for diagramming sentences.

> I went back to my childhood to show the kids the value of grammar and how important it was to diagram sentences. My students were forced to write and had no idea that there was a subject and a verb in a sentence. So that forced me to become more traditional. That part I think I picked up from Japan. Their English skills are really poor. I wanted to diagram this year, but I have no time to diagram for the month of March because it's all testing. I found out that, just like the Japanese, I was more aware of how important testing became in America when I returned.

Ellen said that as she was getting older, she was much more aware of how much these students needed basic language skills, even as a base so that they would understand the structure of another foreign language. Most important to her were, sentence structures [and] the memorization of sentence patterns. If I was teaching them English, I had to give them the ability to really write stories, to be able to really express themselves in writing . . . and instilling in them the love of the English language so that they would want to read more, and that they would want to explore language itself and also prepare them to take another foreign language."

Ellen reflects ambivalence in her use of words to describe changes in her teaching related to her international experience: "lazy," "by the book," "not as creative." Yet these discriptions are juxtaposed with her attempt to create a warm atmosphere in the classroom, integrate more rigor into her classroom, and expect a higher level of responsibility from her students.

All of these teachers have described changes in their methodology as a result of their international study and experience. Mary and Ellen describe changes in their pedagogy by sharing their admiration for the display of mutual respect demonstrated in the tradition of standing and greeting the teacher. Bill and Paul describe a more gradual, evolving change that was affected by the educational reform movement in the United States. However, both connect the experience they had abroad with their greater awareness of the educational debates of the late 1980s. While discussing the central question of this study, they both spoke at length about school reform. Neither explicitly connected international experience to school reform but they felt that they had been stimulated to consider new options about schooling, such as different ways of organizing the school day, which Paul mentions in Chapter 9.

Ed Donovan's change in how he speaks to his students seems more concretely defined. He does not speak about grappling with more fundamental changes involving questions surrounding the teacher-dominated versus student-centered pedagogies. Nevertheless, he does talk about his use of role-plays, which is not in the mode of the traditional lecture approach. In fact, he indicates disapproval of the latter pedagogy, which he considered the norm in China and different from his "Socratic approach." Ed's experience in China seems to have reinforced this approach to teaching while he, to a lesser extent than Paul and Bill, also considered issues of school reform in connection with his discussion of changes in his pedagogy.

CURRICULAR CHANGES

All six teachers discussed changes in their curriculum as direct results of their study and experiences of another culture. Ellen Stacey, Mary

Ehrhardt, and Denise Green consider this the major area of change in their classrooms. They choose not to emphasize differences in teaching style or methods; it is the content of the curriculum they describe as different. Paul Vandemere, Mary Ehrhardt, and Ed Donovan felt that their teaching about East Asia was more authentic and greatly enriched by the stories and artifacts they could share with students. Ellen Stacey became more book- and grammar-oriented to help students appreciate and use English more effectively. Ed Donovan, like Paul Vandemere, incorporated what he considers to be much more authenticity into his curriculum.

Denise Green integrated her experience in Japan within the curriculum, rather than concentrating on a single unit on Japan. She also used this method during her teaching career to share her undergraduate experience in Ghana with her students.

> I still had a regular classroom after I came back from Japan the first time. I was teaching Japanese as part of the school day. Before I went, I remember in classes I had we did an extensive unit on Japan. But after I came back, it was not so much a unit per se, but things as they fit in, but besides the language, the art is more oriented toward Japanese things. It was probably more in-depth. There would be things around the classroom that would fit in and not because this month we're studying Japan, because it related to something else we happened to be doing.

All of the teachers had different examples of how they changed the focus of their curriculum and what new things that they had added. When Mary Ehrhardt was in China, children in grades four, five, and six who had experienced her China curriculum in the second grade sent her questions to answer while she was there, which she did: "I wrote them letters which they shared among their classes which responded to their specific questions about China . . . and the first-graders are just dying to come to second grade to fly to China, to learn about China." In February 1996, when I first interviewed her, she was about to launch the semester-long make-believe China study tour with her second-graders (described in Chapter 3). She is adding two new areas of focus that she had not included before her experiences: "One is this whole issue of what it means to live in a Third World country. Second, is how being a country of 1.2 billion people impacts so much of everyday life" because of "the implications of having to manage the needs of that many people, and how so often" Chinese people told her, "We have just too many people in our country."

One of her examples about Chinese population will be: "Of the twenty-five children, one table (there are four tables in the class) which has five children represents China compared to the other three tables, which represent the whole world, the remaining population of the world. China represents one-fourth of that." She will use her learning about brush painting to help them enjoy this art and understand that the Chinese ideal in this ancient art is "to emulate the ideal, to emulate the master. So perhaps that's the beginning of their appreciation of Chinese painting."

Probably the most radical change of the content in her curriculum is the introduction of Chinese language to her second-graders.

> Rather than asking a Chinese speaker to come do the language component, I've been able to do that myself. I've been able to teach some Chinese and use Chinese frequently during our China studies so that the boys and girls are much more interested in learning the language and so the language is more a focal point. From my Chinese study, my pronunciation is better and my understanding of the language and actually my ability to read a little and write a little has been intriguing to the children, so that we're picking up more books that are written in Chinese and identifying some characters. The language has been much more of a focus. I'm just so pleased with that because I feel that it adds an authenticity to the curriculum.

The language work, the artifacts she brought back to share with students, and the stories she told greatly enriched their work on China.

> We have just recently flown to China, taken our imaginary trip to China. This has been as successful as it has been in other years. It seems that second-graders are still pretty gullible and they do love pretending. They really get into taking the trip and they do believe that they are in China and that their hotel rooms each night look remarkably like their own homes, their own bedrooms at home. But they come back every day willing to travel to someplace different. So this afternoon, we visited the home of a Chinese child and learned about her family and their activities, and we are in Beijing for a few days now. We visited the Forbidden City and the Great Wall through my slides. The whole experience of China for these children is much more real because of my experience. The materials that I was able to collect and bring back including the slides and other artifacts that just really enriched the teaching. I think that at least in this part of the study I am more like their tour guide, and every day we look to see where we are going today. I like that aspect of it. For several weeks we've been doing some comparative geography study of

China and the United States through mapping, using many different kinds of maps. One of the most interesting ones is looking at rainfall and then discovering how that impacts where things grow. Then the children actually create a map on which they apply things like tea and millet and rice. They begin to get a sense of the geography of China. By the time we take the trip to China, we have learned some language so that we can speak a little bit.

The students had learned how to do some calligraphy and how to say some words and phrases, especially typical greetings such as *nihao* (pronounced knee how) for "hello."

We have learned typical greetings and how to say "How old are you?" and how to count. We have learned the basic strokes, calligraphy strokes, and a little bit of the history of Chinese writing and how some characters represent pictures and how other characters are often a combination of pictures. Often the language came out of the celebration of a holiday. So we learned how to give holiday greetings, how to say "Happy birthday," "Happy New Year." And then I guess I have all along used a little Chinese when I say "slow down," "quiet," or "speed up," so perhaps there really has been just all along a little language emphasis.

This year when the students got together with their pen-pal friends in the Chinese bilingual class in Boston, they were able to share a little more because Mary's second-grade students knew some Chinese and enjoyed using the words.

The class is a second-grade bilingual class from a Boston public school. Because of Boston's extensive busing program, most of the Asian children are bused to the school from their communities, which are primarily Chinatown and East Boston. Very often these are children whose families are newly arrived in Boston, so that probably English is not spoken at home. This particular school has the bilingual Chinese program from kindergarten through the sixth grade. But the objective is that each year some of the children will have enough English proficiency to move out of the bilingual program to a regular class.

She also felt that the struggle to learn Chinese would help her students empathize with what many of the seven- and eight-year-old Chinese immigrants were going through in their struggle to learn English.

Coming up next week, we will explore Chinatown with them, their home community, so that I think whereas we're struggling to learn a little Chinese, we have a greater appreciation, our children do, for what it feels like to be a newcomer to America. One or two Chinese children have just arrived from China so that we're aware that these are very new immigrants. I don't know what the chemistry is of this particular class. This particular Chinese class has really been great in that they've not been shy. Even though the language has been a barrier, they have interacted at play and around activities such as tangram puzzles and creating a dragon at the New Year's time so that their comfort level is high.

The two teachers carefully paired the Chinese students who were having the most difficulty speaking with a student who has a better understanding of English to make it easier for them. Because many of the bilingual students speak Cantonese rather than Mandarin, Mary's students became aware of the complexities of many dialects in China, including Cantonese.

On both sides, we try to facilitate that by pairing—being careful about the pairing of children and pairing a non-English speaker with another Chinese child who can almost be an interpreter, one who is a little further along in his or her English. Interestingly, in Boston, most of the families who come are from the south of China, so they speak Cantonese, not Mandarin. The bilingual Chinese teacher does speak both Cantonese and Mandarin. Not only are the children learning English, but they're also being exposed to Mandarin, too. It's interesting for my children to know that even though the reading and writing is the same for all Chinese people, and just as there are many English accents, there are many dialects, so it's difficult in a very large country for people to speak with one another sometimes.

Mary felt that the way she introduced the population issue, combined with her first-hand experience there, allowed her class to be more open and receptive to the Chinese class than she felt her students had been in the previous nine years of the pen-pal exchange program.

One of the focuses that I really wanted to emphasize was what a billion people is like and also what for me were the extreme contrasts between elements of modernization and conditions in a Third World country. So perhaps, the children understood just from the fact that . . . if we were in a group that represented all the peoples of the world, one in four of us would be speaking

Chinese. Chinese is the language most frequently spoken in the world. Maybe this year there has been a greater emphasis on just what the reality of living in China is and the reality of China in the whole world focus. Perhaps that has helped establish an openness, a receptivity to the Chinese children who are our pen-pals. It has been remarkable the way the relationship just got off the ground. Even though their teacher and I both said we have very active and challenging classes this year, when they're together they have been marvelous.

Mary's study of Chinese as a prerequisite to her going to China greatly enhanced her experience there and was a key component in a curriculum change that allowed her students to connect more meaningfully with the Chinese students in the Chinese bilingual class in Boston.

I sought out this kind of bilingual pen-pal experience for my children so they would have an opportunity to hear Chinese, to meet Chinese children, and feel that they had some connection with the Chinese children. The utility of learning the language is apparent both in their greeting and leaving, "good-byes" and "hellos." They notice in their exchange of letters how difficult it is to put together an English sentence and also how eloquent the children are in their Chinese calligraphy. When we write back, there was generally a big emphasis on at least being able to write zai jian [good-bye] or at least some characters to show that we are able to write a little Chinese, too.

Mary continued these connections and enrichment because she had made the effort to learn Chinese. She has in this respect become a model for her students about the connections one can make when the effort is made to learn a language. She was delighted to share with her class the birthday cards sent from two fourteen-year-old students in China: "Just within the last month, on my birthday, two of the students with whom I had a very close relationship sent a birthday card and a little gift; a wonderful birthday card in English which said 'Wishing happiness especially you for.' That was something fun to show my class, that in China, they struggle with English."

Paul Vandemere also considered the authenticity of his curriculum to have been tremendously enhanced by what he could bring back to his students from Japan. When talking about geography and the symbolic significance of Mount Fujiyama, he could speak about it from the perspective of someone who had climbed the mountain. When they studied the tea ceremony, Paul's wife, Ruth, performed it with the

class. Like Mary, Paul used slides and pictures to make Japan come
alive for his students. He had his students perform role-plays about
the proper ways of bowing and presenting and receiving business cards
in Japan for teacher workshops such as the 1992 National Council for
the Social Studies (NCSS) national conference in Detroit, Michigan,
where I observed their presentation.

Paul returned from Japan in August 1986 to direct and teach in the
newly created East Asian Studies Program in his district. Initially,
this program was a magnet center with students being bused there from
three other high schools. Subsequently, the program was expanded to
another site. For the eight years that Paul taught in this program, he
used his experience in Japan and his five weeks of touring China to help
make these areas "come alive" for his students.

> To make these countries come alive is very tough to do. When you
> can bring your own experiences and experiences of others into the
> classroom, not only your knowledge of the culture, etc., which
> you're going to be teaching, but the stories that you can tell and the
> experiences that you can share, it makes your lesson more credible
> with the kids. It brings a degree of authenticity and, hopefully, if
> you do it right, it brings that country and its people to life for
> them. You get beyond the stereotypes.

Paul felt that a textbook-based curriculum would not include the
kinds of cultural experiences that he could offer his students. Ed and
Mary also give concrete examples of how they were able to enrich,
because of their international experience, their curriculum in ways that
went far beyond what could be accomplished in a textbook. Paul listed
the issues that he felt his experiences had enabled him to explore with
his classes.

> I came back with a much greater insight into various aspects of
> East Asia. Even though I only spent five weeks in China, it still
> helped me there and I did visit the other East Asian countries a
> number of times, and it allowed me to have a much greater insight
> and again, not just the traditional areas that are taught, the
> geography, the history and political system, etc. But to me it's
> important that our students know about how a country is organized
> and not just at the government level, but how they related to each
> other; how the individual fits in that society as compared to
> different groups; different relationships, different roles that
> people have. Are they similar or are they different? What is the
> role of women? What is the role of children in that society? How
> are families raised? What role does the community play in that?

These are all things that you don't learn necessarily that much in a lot of the courses you take. They are not in the normal textbooks that students would be getting. That's not the kind of topic that they would get, maybe a paragraph or two, as an add-on or as an extra-credit kind of thing. So I revamped my curriculum to reflect the society as it was, dealing with issues at a much more in-depth basis, topics on a much more in-depth basis. Clearly, my living there allowed me to do that.

He knew the proper degree of bowing and could demonstrate this to his classes, the honored seats in taxicabs or restaurants, for example, dining customs, and many other cultural experiences with which most Americans are not familiar.

The respect that you have for someone else, the deference you give, depends on your position or level compared to that person, either socially or from a business standpoint. Then your language adjusts, the degree of the bow that you give adjusts. I could tell my students, here is a 45-degree bow, here is this kind of bow, here are words that are used, here is a certain deference that's given, and here's how it's done. Here's the favorite seat in a taxicab, here's the honored seat in a business meeting, here is the honored place in a restaurant, here is the place of honor in an elevator. These are all cultural things that are tied in with the society and how they operate with each other. It would have been much more difficult for me to learn that had I not experienced the culture, had I not experienced the elevator operators in department stores, and the affected speech and deferential role that they have had. To learn that traditionally when a kid is disciplined at home, he is kicked outside of the house—the differences that you see as well as a lot of the similarities. But I could go into much more depth as a result of what I was doing. Even the meal experiences. There is a whole culture around food: what you eat, how you eat it, who gets to eat it first. And the bathing rituals, just a whole range of things that would be much more difficult to learn and to bring to life if you were not actually there.

Paul's experience in Japan allowed him to organize his curriculum to include student engagement in cultural practices in addition to his telling them about these practices. In a manner similar to Mary Ehrhardt's experiential pedagogy with her second-graders, Paul arranged for his students to experience such cultural practices as the tea ceremony and martial arts.

My wife will come in and do the tea ceremony. We don't just have to talk about it any longer or show a couple of pictures. She would perform the tea ceremony. I would have students come in and do some martial arts and not just the superficial karate, . . . and then talk of the history behind it. Or I could talk about sumo wrestling and the connection sumo wrestling has with agriculture and the rituals that take place before them and explain those rituals. So virtually every topic that I taught, I could go into much more depth. I could show them pictures of Mount Fuji, because I climbed it. I could show them different parts of Japan or China. I could talk to them about trips down the Yangtze because I did it for five days. So the content clearly changed.

Paul felt he had much greater insight as a result of his experiences in Japan on which he could draw when he developed curriculum. Just as John Dewey taught that a teacher immersed in a subject would be better prepared to plan lessons, enabling her to shepherd a child to a deeper awareness of the field, Paul felt he was better equipped to plan lessons and curriculum about East Asia than he had been before his experience in Japan.

Because I had a much greater insight as a result of living there, I could feel confident in my knowledge and I could design projects for kids that would have them take on different roles. I could bring in slides. . . . That's how it changed also my teaching strategies. I could bring in my walking sticks that I used to climb Mount Fuji. I could bring in the *Daruma* [a good luck doll] and talk about the good luck and how you begin the New Year with these or other symbols. We brought back twenty-six boxes of things. We shipped them from Japan and a lot of them were things that I used. That's how that really affected my instruction. I could bring in the actual artifacts. I can bring in an actual wedding envelope and talk about all the different parts of a Shinto wedding—all the wedding ceremony, all the different aspects—because I attended one. I went to pet cemeteries. Again, so my instruction was changed because I could bring in my experiences and the experience of others directly into the classroom.

Similar to Paul Vandemere, Ed Donovan teaches an Asian studies course in the afternoon in addition to the China segment of the humanities curriculum. He has found a great resource in a Chinese library supported by the Chinese-American community in Detroit.

I've been using the Chinese library. . . . So when I talk about Chinese Opera, I can bring a Chinese opera in and I can bring in the books that do not just describe but also indicate what the position of the masks and costumes are for each of these characters. I make sure that they keep a journal, one article of which must deal with China. They go to an article or newspaper and they pick a current event they want to keep up with for the rest of the semester. Like the Yangtze River is a big thing with the kid who is an ecologist, for example. Somebody latched on to Deng Xiaoping last year. They thought he was going to die last year. There are a lot of things that they have access to that are in regular publications that we get in the States, but the library has been a big help.

Ed now uses more classical Chinese poetry and music in his courses, which he became familiar with during his year in China.

Heather and I put together a bunch of poems from Li Bo and Du Fu and some of the others. I just took down some manuscripts that I had hanging in the room that are calligraphies. I had the translations for them. This is the first semester that I don't have somebody who can speak Chinese in my classroom. When the Chinese read it, it is far different in terms of the cadences. I play Chinese music as my students enter the room sometimes. It's not just Chinese opera, but things that are fairly modern, like the Yangtze River song. The Yangtze River song came from somebody who entered the song in a competition and won the competition with it. It's supposed to represent Chinese feeling for their land. I've got two or three Communist tapes that I play, Communist music like "Our Hopes Are in the Field" and "East Is Red," stuff like that.

As they entered the room, the initial reaction of American students to hearing Chinese opera gradually changed to respect.

The first time they hear, especially Chinese music, the Chinese opera, for example, they say, "How can people listen to that?" My response is, "Well let's listen to it for a little bit. Maybe you can hear something in it that you might respond to." After they have heard it for four or five days, they cease to comment about it. They'll say things like, "Oh, I like that passage." I had one kid two years ago that took a passage and wrote a piece of music around it. It's kind of neat; they did it down in the music room. I don't think he ever published it, but it was just the idea that he could take a piece of it and work it into something that was Western.

In contrast with the experiences of Ed, Paul, and Mary, on his return
from Japan, Bill Notebaum found himself in a classroom role that
deeply frustrated him. He had learned enough to know how much he
did not know about Japanese culture and history. While his work on
economics with adults was fulfilling, he felt that his students were ill-
prepared to understand the nuances of U.S.-Japanese trade because they
had little background in economics. He felt woefully unprepared in
Japanese language, culture, and history.

The year he returned, he worked with a teacher who had studied
some Japanese to initiate and team teach a one-semester Japanese
language and culture class. He was required by the large Japanese
business association that sponsored his study tour to "do something
concrete when you return and you provide them evidence of what you
have done." Bill took this responsibility "seriously, and moving into
that class was the most immediate, most concrete thing that I did." In
the belief that "the best way to learn anything is to teach it," Bill
regarded teaching this course as an opportunity to learn more about
Japan in areas other than economics, the "softer side of things. . . . So I
figured I'd just get right in here and start learning . . . doing literature,
Japanese literature with the kids, rather than just doing numbers and
trade. It's more where I was headed intellectually, not where I'd
really begun my career. I was the humanities-type person. So I wanted
to bring the two back together again."

Within the context of this class, he practiced "words with my
Japanese friends" but was frustrated because "I just never had the time
to devote to it," in addition to his belief that "learning disabilities"
precluded his learning of a foreign language. Bill was disappointed
with his performance in and the outcome of the class, feeling that it
was very expensive for the school district when only fourteen to
eighteen students had enrolled. "A brand-new elective in a school that
already has a saturated elective and advanced placement honors
track" is difficult to sustain, he said. Because his method of teaching
required that he be knowledgeable about the subject, he felt unprepared
to teach this course.

> Quite frankly, I don't think we did all that great of a job. It was
> hard to mix the two together. . . . Her [his teaching colleague]
> language level was well short of fluency. I'm not criticizing her,
> but I think that makes it harder for her to make it natural and
> flowing. My overall comfort level and knowledge base in Japanese
> was sophomore at best. I'm talking about the whole country, the
> political system, etc. I had no formal study whatsoever; I just read
> a couple of history books, read a bunch of econ stuff. But you can't

talk about that forever. A lot of the econ stuff I had was basically useless because the kids needed so much prior econ understanding in order to make any sense out of it whatsoever. It ended up falling more on my weaker area in Japanese, which was more than the Japanese culture piece, which I hadn't gotten that much preparation in. At the same time so many other things were developing in my life and career that I wasn't in that kind of a position like a young teacher or a mid-year teacher, totally into one thing. I had about four or five other major things going at the same time. I could do a little reading and a little prepping, but I couldn't isolate myself and try to turn myself into a total Japanese-literate person. The way I teach, it affects my effectiveness. I don't do worksheets or anything like that.

Bill brings up the problems inherent in veteran teacher learning. This study joins the work of many advocates of school reform, like John Dewey and more recently, Lauren Resnick (1987a, 1987b), Sharon Feiman-Nemser (1983), and Mary Kennedy (1992), who promote lifelong learning for veteran teachers. The reality, with which I am personally familiar, of teaching 150 students a day, giving each of them as much personal attention as is possible, is overwhelming. A teacher who wants to give an essay exam or paper is faced with 150 of these to carefully read, respond to, and evaluate. At ten minutes per paper, one of those assignments takes twenty-five hours. This does not consider time for careful preparation of each lesson. How can we expect teachers to learn new subjects, such as Japanese language and culture? Many teachers, like Mary Ehrhardt, Paul Vandemere, and Ed Donovan, use their summers to learn more about the subjects they are teaching. Bill's frustration about not having enough time to fully study Japanese culture is a dilemma many teachers face, sometimes forcing them to choose between their families and their personal growth and development.

Mary Ehrhardt, like Bill, was also concerned that she did not have the time to pursue her language study on re-entry to the United States. In addition to her regular teaching responsibilities, she was asked to mentor a novice teacher, a responsibility that took substantial time and effort.

The pedagogy and the curriculum of these six teachers who studied and experienced another culture changed in many ways. They all attributed these changes to the effect of their international experience on their professional lives in and out of the classroom. They all talk about changes in the way they teach, in their curriculum, and in their relationships with students. Paul, Mary, Ed, and Ellen give explicit examples of how they have incorporated subject matter they learned abroad or while preparing for their international experience into their curriculum. Cultural knowledge became an integral part of their subject matter. Their international experience has thus been "educative" in the Deweyan sense of having provoked them to continue to learn and *use* this knowledge in authentic ways with students.

Not only did these teachers believe that their international study and experience made a significant difference in their classroom practice, but they emphasized that this experience had a tremendous impact on their professional and personal lives. They constructed and used their experiences to differing degrees to promote their personal growth. In a sense, the pedagogical aspects of teacher change are also reflections of personal transformation, which is the topic of Chapter 9. These teachers believe their classroom practice has changed. For some of them, the impact of the international experience was profound.

9

Transformation

When David Cohen writes about "A Revolution in One Classroom: The Case of Mrs. Oublier [a pseudonym]" (1990), her view of meaningful change in her classroom practice is different from an outsider's perspective. His point is similar to the one he makes in his article "Teacher Practice: Plus CA Change" (1988), about the extreme difficulty of changing teacher practices within this society. Traditional "teaching as telling" (p. 12) is difficult to reform within the context of the human need to perform as an authority figure, such as a parent. In this chapter I analyze how these teachers feel international experience has changed them, not only as teachers, but as humans.

I asked these teachers if they considered their international experience transformative. The answers varied little from an enthusiastic "Definitely!" or "Absolutely!" How they described what this meant to them tended to focus on issues of self-confidence, empathy, and connectedness with others. Examples they gave of how they had been transformed by their international experience include their feelings of increased self-efficacy and self-confidence. They demonstrated this confidence in their leadership work, sharing these experiences with colleagues, and in their attempts to express their understandings in the wider community. Another way they felt they had been transformed was in the way some of them took on the role of advocacy of their beliefs. Most of them spoke passionately and convincingly about the need to foster and improve international education in the United States.

An example of their advocacy in international or multicultural education is their perspective on some aspects of the "culture wars debate" exemplified by Alan Bloom (1987), Diane Ravitch (1983), E. D.

Hirsch (1987), and Chester Finn (1909) among others, who argue that the time spent learning about East Asia, for example, is taken away from the study of Western culture and tradition (Hunter, 1991). The teachers in this study do not agree that studying other cultures somehow undermines our sense of who we are. In fact, these teachers support the idea that international study and experience heighten our self-knowledge and sense of conviction about basic values.

SELF-CONFIDENCE

As a result of their international experience, each teacher expressed feelings of greater self-efficacy as public speakers and advocates. Ellen Stacey considered one result of her first seven-month experience in Japan to be her selection as Teacher of the Year from the City Schools. She had enthusiastically become involved with her students, motivating them to win many district writing awards. Paul Vandemere believed his experience in Japan and as director of the East Asian Center to have been part of the basis for state officials to choose him from some 100,000 teachers to be the state Teacher of the Year. Mary Ehrhardt felt more secure about public speaking and advocating her convictions than she had before her experience of learning Chinese and living in China. Bill Notebaum's experience made him feel confident enough to propose an International High School, which he is now administering full time. Ed Donovan currently advises the local education commission in China on some matters of policy. Delightedly, he says, "They listen to me," perhaps as a counterpoint to his experience in his own district. Denise Green became the district spokeswoman on Japan and has presented programs at national and international conferences.

Mary Ehrhardt, who was reluctant to speak publicly in English, having to give a speech in Chinese to Chinese educators in China was certainly a challenge, especially since she had been studying the language for less than a year. When she returned, she found that speaking (in English) before large groups of people was *mei you wenti* [no problem]. Her work teaching teachers in China had prepared her to think about her beliefs and practices and to be able to articulate them clearly.

> I guess that by teaching teachers, I really had to articulate my beliefs and practices. In faculty work here, because we don't like to enter into debate with our colleagues, we don't really stand up for or are willing to come to blows over something that you hold very dear as an educational practice. Actually having articulated my philosophy and practice for these Chinese teachers, I am much

more secure in doing that in my own school setting. I really feel that having taught for four months before as many as fifty students, I really have developed some public speaking techniques and confidence in my ability to speak to very large groups, so that it doesn't faze me to speak to the whole school of 200 children or a workshop of fifty or seventy-five adults. Those are ways in which I have grown.

Mary believes that she can make a positive contribution now that she feels more confident about advocating her position.

I think that it's giving me more confidence to advocate, to really speak from a point of view of having a firm belief. It's interesting, though. I haven't had a great deal of opportunities to do that. I think that's just circumstantial. I think more and more I will have more opportunities to be directly involved in curricular discussions to which I can make a contribution.

Working with the Chinese teachers had helped to clarify her beliefs.

These Chinese teachers were not aware of child psychology, and by telling them about some of the noted child psychologists, Piaget and Dewey, and how they look at children developmentally, gave them a little foundation for practice. It also makes me see that, yes, this is the basis of our belief, too, especially that young children learn best by being active learners. So there is a basis for our practice and that was missing in their education.

Mary feels that the international experience has greatly enhanced her proclivities to be a learner and has given her the confidence to question and grapple with the new understandings.

In the American setting I continue to feel that I am a learner and I continue to question my practice. As a representative taking American education to China, I felt that I could represent the American ways of teaching based on child psychology. I think that even in my faculty, which is an auspicious group of thinkers, that I have a contribution to make, and I think I can express myself in my own school setting. Right now we are looking at teaching for understanding, with Howard Gardner's *Multiple Intelligences* [1993] as the basis. I feel very excited by that but feel that I can be circumspect and questioning because I am an experienced teacher and I have seen reforms come and go, that I can look at this and think it through and raise questions.

Bill Notebaum woke up one morning before a statewide conference presentation in March 1992 to learn that his colleague, Jack Anderson, would not be there to help him make the presentation The keynote speaker, a well-known Japanese-American economist and U.S.-Japan trade expert from Bernard Baruch College, Yoshihiro Tsurumi, attended this session.

> I was pretty upset, pretty nervous, pretty uptight about that. He came into our session and sat in the back, never introducing himself or anything. But I knew who he was. I had heard him, I think, at one of the prior conferences. And he sat there. Here I had high school kids and high school teachers, and a couple university people, and Yoshi Tsurumi. I was talking exactly on his topic and not close to a Ph.D. in economics and not close to an expert on Japan. But compared to what other people knew, I knew a billion times more. You know nothing, but I knew it was a lot more.

Bill felt buoyed by Tsurumi's "positive facial expressions. . . . Then afterwards, he was extremely complimentary and asked for a copy of the article. We wrote back and forth three or four times. I subscribed to his newsletter and I sent him articles that I thought he would enjoy and vice versa." Bill felt that in the process of studying U.S.-Japan trade issues, working with his colleague at the Federal Reserve Board, sharing his knowledge with teachers, and experiencing Japan, he had experienced a personal transformation: "Getting involved with Jack and doing these speaking engagements, planning all those things, and proposing the school, and all that has been a huge personal growth."

He now interacts with superintendents of school districts on a daily basis as he works to promote and prepare for the opening of the International High School.

> I talk one-on-one now with superintendents and make economic proposals for budgets and stuff, business managers of ten school districts. That would have been unthinkable a short time ago, like 1988, 1989, into 1990. I just didn't interact with those people a lot and when you did, it was more like employer/employee. It's developed or pulled out of me what must have been there all along. It wasn't like I was some repressed person or anything, but I certainly hadn't reached anything close to my potential.

COLLEGIAL SHARING

Several teachers considered their ability to share their experience and new knowledge with colleagues an important aspect of their personal growth and change. The international study and experience of these six teachers also affected the school environment to which they returned. They each sought out ways to share their experiences with colleagues, some more successfully than others. They seemed to have a need to reach out beyond the classroom to express their understandings and sometimes to express their commitment to international understanding and education. The school structures that created chances for sharing varied greatly. In several cases, the school environment was not conducive to sharing insights with colleagues, which thwarted the chances for personal growth.

Sharon Feiman-Nemser (1983), who analyzed why millions of dollars invested in teacher learning centers during the 1970s reaped few rewards, concluded that a major stultifying effect on teacher creativity can be the school environment itself. When Ellen Stacey wanted to share her knowledge with her colleagues and principal, they did not seem interested. Mary Ehrhardt also expressed frustration about being a different person and not having an adequate outlet outside her classroom to express these differences. She did find an outlet by connecting with a network of teachers beyond her school who are committed to the goals of establishing international links between classrooms.

In this section, I will explore how the teachers shared their experiences with colleagues by: modeling their understandings in workshops in and out of school; working to make substantive school curriculum and structural changes; presenting programs to the students, faculty, and community; influencing curriculum and promoting exchange programs at the state level; and finding networks beyond their schools of people committed to international study and exchange programs.

In January 1988, Denise Green returned to her district in Indianapolis and was given a special assignment by the district administration. Instead of returning immediately to the classroom, she was given the full-time responsibility of visiting schools to help "teachers plan and teach units on Asia, with a particular emphasis on Japan." Denise made presentations to the math and social studies steering committees and the Board of Education. Denise expressed none of the frustration about the lack of opportunities to share her experiences that Ellen and Mary had, both of whom went immediately back to the classroom. Denise felt that her full-time work in the schools opened up possibilities for students in other schools. One result of this work was the trip she took to Japan with elementary students and parents from another school in her district.

Denise was also encouraged to present a workshop at the district's "Summer High School," but a minimum of six did not sign up and the session was canceled. Her proposal to present this workshop at a conference in the Caribbean was accepted. She said she presented this workshop to a "standing-room-only crowd of educators from all over the world."

Ed Donovan, like Denise, was asked to present many programs in his school, sometimes co-presenting with his wife, Heather. At times, he was asked to teach units about China in other classrooms or present programs in other schools, especially the junior high schools. He had only one example of a negative situation with colleagues after he returned and no overt examples of professional jealousy. He suspected that jealousy existed "because I have had the experience. They would like to have it without doing it." Ed would defuse this by challenging them when some would say, "Oh what a lucky guy I am. My response is, 'You can be lucky, too. All you have to do is ask.' "

When he returned to the United States to teach in 1987, he found that he was just as sensitive to racial slurs among faculty members as he was among his students. Two teachers, "ex-Army guys," both members of Army Reserves, "still saw Chinese as 'Chinks' and used that term." Ed confronted them, saying, "It's really offensive to hear that when I know these people. What you are doing is depersonalizing people that I've become acquainted with and some of them are my friends. I really resent it." His colleagues "didn't use the term around me after that. It gets into that whole thing of confrontation again. I don't let a lot of stuff go by any more. If they would have used the term 'Chinks' before, I probably wouldn't have said anything. I don't let it go any more. It's an awareness, I suppose." For the most part, his colleagues were "very supportive," many of them writing to him while he was in China.

This unexpected relationship with his colleagues at home mirrored the positive response of his colleagues to his knowledge and experience on his return. They welcomed him into their classrooms and in this process were part of his transformation. He enjoyed sharing his experiences and knowledge with many teachers and classes. He became, as Denise was about Japan, a sort of unofficial spokesman about China. The school was influential in encouraging Ed to develop further as a public speaker and as a strong advocate of international education.

Except for one all-school assembly in which she showed slides and artifacts and talked about her experience, Mary Ehrhardt has had no formal opportunity to present workshops or share her experience with colleagues. A snowed-out presentation to Walden parents was not rescheduled, but she gave an informal slide presentation "on the request of friends and neighbors." Mary was also able to reach out to the greater school community by writing an article for the Walden Lower School parent association paper titled "A Sabbatical Appreciated." In this article, she wrote, "I knew I wanted to learn Chinese and validate my teaching by traveling to China." Feeling fortunate to have been given this opportunity, Mary expressed publicly how much this experience has enriched her life and her teaching.

> My new knowledge of Chinese language and life has enriched me personally and will certainly enhance my teaching. As I prepare to welcome the "New Year" with the current second graders in mid-February, I have newly acquired props and, more important, a deeper understanding of life in the most populous country in the world. Halfway around the world, via letter, fax and e-mail, I have hundreds of new friends and their stories to tell.

In addition to sharing her experience with her school community through this article, Mary has been asked to share with another network of educators that she did not know about before she lived in China. She feels less isolated in the classroom, now that she has joined this organization of social studies educators in New England, Primary Source.

> It's a real clearinghouse for an Asia and China network. . . . I really am now part of a major national China network that I would have never even thought about. I taught for ten or twelve years about China without this experience and without the networking that led to the experience. I don't think I would have had access to this wonderful network of colleagues and conferences and institutes, opportunities to study, that I've now found. So professionally, I also have gained tremendously by becoming aware of this greater network. I now feel that I'm not just a teacher in a classroom, but I'm a part of a whole network of educators who are interested in exploring either ties with Asia or Asian issues through the American school system. So it really has expanded my sense of colleagueship. I don't feel I'm just unique.

Mary facilitated an e-mail account so that students and teachers in the exchange program could continue to communicate with each other.

> Actually in the Huangshan School where I taught, we initiated the e-mail account. . . . We opened an account with the Institute of Astrophysics and then the Huangshan School was very grateful and was willing to take on themselves the monthly service charge.

Then, now a year later, they've just installed a modem so that we
no longer have to hot wire the telephone line to do the e-mailing.
So now this is a real possibility.

She learned at a national English teachers' conference about e-mail
connections among schools in many countries: "At the National Council
of Teachers of English national meeting in March [1996], we actually
had a demonstration of a hook-up of teachers in Russia, in India, in
Japan, in Argentina, and Boston. We were all together through picture
scanned in and voice."

It is in these human connections that Mary felt her most meaningful
experience, and her work with e-mail facilitates those connections.

The correspondence really continues. During spring vacation, the
Carlton superintendent, high school principals, and chairpersons
of the exchange committee went to Beijing and each time that
happens, we send more curricular materials and more greetings.
They brought back this tea that we're drinking. It came from a
colleague in the English faculty at the Huangshan School. There
is this continuing relationship and because I feel lucky that I am
part of this well-established program, that just adds layer on
layer of relationships.

After her first experience in Japan, Ellen Stacey, like Denise Green,
was also asked to present workshops for her school district as a
"spokesperson" for the district. Instead of being a writing consultant for
the state, she "was going around and doing workshops about Japan,
what I saw, what I experienced." The state superintendent of public
instruction asked her to write an article to be published in the union
paper. In addition, the state Board of Education asked her to present a
program with other participants about her exchange program, which
the state had partly funded. She believes this presentation was in
response to critics of the state Board and Department of Education
officials for using state money to pay for their trips to Japan: "That was
the time when they couldn't justify themselves for going over and
spending all that money in Japan." It was at this time that her
colleagues and principal "didn't want to hear about it."

After her second three-year experience in Japan, there were no
opportunities for her to share her experience because she had not
traveled under the auspices of a state program, but through a sister-
school and city program completely paid for by Japan. Ellen expressed
to her principal ideas about asking the students involved in a Japanese-
style competition to take responsibility for keeping areas of the school
clean and free of graffiti.

You have seventh, eighth, and ninth grade. Let them take pride in the school. You have the seventh grade take responsibility for the front of the school. Have the eighth grade take the responsibility for the right side and the ninth grade have responsibility for the other side. Their job is to get rid of all the weeds, their job is to keep the grass cut, their job is to keep the grass edged, their job is to keep the playground clean from debris and everything. And reward them for keeping this and watch and see how you don't get the graffiti on the side of the building. Watch and see how well the school will run. "Oh that's a very good idea." But she never did anything about it.

Rather than working with colleagues in in-service settings, Paul Vandemere, on returning from Japan, threw himself into making the East Asian Center in his school district a success. Like Ed Donovan, he still found time to make many presentations within the school community and at state conferences. He often included his students at the center in these presentations, in which they performed role-plays for audiences of educators. The second year Paul was in Japan, he was asked by his U.S. superintendent to interview candidates to choose a Japanese teacher with whom he would work to help initiate and team teach in the center when he returned.

He felt that the exchange teacher from Japan with whom he team taught the first year of the program had profoundly affected his fellow American teachers because of the friendship that evolved over that year of the exchange.

Shibahara had a profound effect on a number of our teachers. He was someone who, during his spare time, would sit down in the teacher's lounge and his English was good enough that he could easily do that and be understood. He began to talk as he was able to do with anyone and everyone and joke around with them. He had several teachers who at the end of his year came up to him and said, "Before I knew you, I wouldn't talk to Japanese. I remember what my father said and my grandfather said about Pearl Harbor. And I wouldn't talk to you. And I knew that some of my friends were being laid off." These were teachers. And they said, "You've changed us. You've made us understand that there is a human side to the Japanese and you made us see your very good qualities. We can still disagree about certain issues, but we're not going to all of a sudden lump all 140 million Japanese in with the decision to drop the bomb and castigate you." They would go out together and they would go golfing or go have a drink, etc. That had a profound effect on some of our teachers who were normally closed-minded.

Of these six teachers, only Ellen Stacey did not feel that she had influenced her school after her experiences in Japan. The other five found ways to share their experiences with colleagues and the community. Where there seemed to be extensive official and administrative support, for example, in the case of Denise Green, their need to share their insights with colleagues seems to have been fulfilled. They all, including Ellen, functioned to greater and lesser degrees as learning resources in their schools and communities.

Paul Vandemere is an excellent example of how a teacher with international experience can enhance and promote curriculum changes. His influence was felt in many areas in the state because he was asked to participate on a committee to internationalize the state social studies curriculum.

> A group of us has attempted to internationalize the curriculum and to work with different state Department of Education people in social studies to try and revamp the social studies curriculum to include global studies, international studies, and to provide as many international experiences where our students can participate in exchange programs, etc. The two main thrusts that have some potential at the state level are the exchange programs, which we would like the state to encourage and help facilitate more so than they are now, and secondly, a core curriculum that includes the world studies part. I've been a part of both of those.

He also was proud to have succeeded in promoting a world studies course in his district, mandatory for all eleventh-grade students, in spite of his feeling that "it took our district far too long to get there." There are many school districts in his state and elsewhere that have few or no required international studies in high schools. The internationally oriented courses that exist are usually electives, taken by a small percentage of the student body. In 1989 and 1990, Paul was on the state committee responsible for developing core curriculum guidelines to include international studies as part of a broad initiative mandated by state law. Although some parts of the law were repealed by a political movement in favor of charter schools with less state regulation, these guidelines were published and distributed widely throughout the state.

Paul was chosen as Teacher of the Year for the state in 1992. He was given release time so that he could represent the teachers in the state and promote education. In that capacity, he visited schools in one county, where the community supports an initiative in Korean language and culture in the schools: "I went over and talked to foreign-language students in Arden County and congratulated them for their study of Korean. There's a strong Korean component as a result of the college that's there. I would take opportunities like that to congratulate the kids, to encourage them to continue their studies in foreign cultures and languages." Even though as a state spokesman he had to be fairly general in his comments, he included references to international understanding in every speech.

There's no question. It was part of every talk, understanding the world. On my blue marble poster of the world is "A good education will open a world of opportunities." That's been my motto in virtually every speech I gave, whether it be the National Honor Societies or other groups. I'd talk about some of my own experiences and the experiences of my kids who have then gone on to different jobs around the world.

CULTURAL CONNECTIONS AND SENSITIVITY

Several teachers felt that part of their personal transformation was a heightened sensitivity to the feelings of others. They treasure their connections with people in the culture. Mary Ehrhardt believes that as a result of her China experience, "I am a different person. I have had an incredible experience that has really affected me, has changed me." As Elise Boulding argues in *Building a Global Civic Culture* (1990), Mary sees the person-to-person connections as a major enriching experience in her life and as a small effort to palliate what she feels is the deteriorating relationship between the United States and China.

At the official level U.S.-China relations have deteriorated. But what I find on the personal level to be really important is the warmth of the friendships and connections with people so that we can articulate face to face our concerns about our countries' interactions. I think that I really see the importance of the personal contacts and the importance of the shared experiences being educational both ways, for me and my understanding of the larger issues and for my Chinese friends to have asked me concerning their questions about the United States. That has been really enriching, personally enriching, but also I think really important to maintaining connections.

Ed Donovan feels that his life has dramatically changed, partly because he is now cognizant of issues he had not previously thought about.

> It does change your life. There's no question about that. When you spend that long in another culture, your perspective is wildly different from people who have not had the experience. More tolerant, maybe more sensitive to a lot of issues that I was not sensitive to before. Or thought that I was, and wasn't. I think a lot of that depends on the kids, particularly if they realize that you feel very deeply about it.

Paul Vandemere described the transformative effect of his experience, that he could now help students bridge the gap of understanding between cultures.

> Professionally, it is transformative. I never would have been back directing the East Asian program and things that came from the sister-school relationship that we have and an opportunity on a regular basis to interact, to open the eyes of my students and the Japanese students to each other's culture. That would not have happened if I had not been in Japan.

Like Bill Notebaum, Paul incorporated a version of the Japanese homeroom to help create an area where teachers can function more as counselors, as they do in Japan.

> They have a homeroom that is set aside in which they see their students, not always for counseling purposes, but it is an opportunity to touch base with them, to become aware of who they are, the directions they want to head, some of the problems they are having. Too often the counselor design that we have here is tied up in paperwork, in filling out applications and deadlines and jobs, work study and that kind of thing without really knowing the real person, without really seeing them on a daily basis. In looking at the whole person, not just isolated components. So that clearly was an example of something that seems to make sense to try something like that. I certainly reflected about a lot of other things, too, as far as organization of the day, the number of days in which we have instruction, etc. And that's not to say that again, that things in a foreign country can be easily transferred just lock, stock, and barrel. You begin to think about other ways of approaching things, other ways of organizing.

Ed Donovan believes that the greatest value of his work in China and in the United States is to promote tolerance. In one way, the China experience enhanced his core conviction. He admired his father and a favorite uncle because they displayed tolerance. In the interviews, he uses the word "tolerance" many times. Ed simply says, "The people who influenced me were tolerant people. I liked them so I decided to be like them."

I may be more tolerant, more aware certainly of problems that people have from working in a different culture. I work a lot with some Chinese from overseas now and try to explain things, kind of getting it into terms that maybe they can understand a little bit. A friend of mine from Kunming is here now. The first time I've seen him was three months ago, first time I'd seen him in nine years. He was my student. He's working for Ford Motor Company now. The guy's fifty years old and used to be with the space project in China in Kunming. He came here and he fell down, he broke his arm and hurt his back. The poor guy felt like Ford Motor Company was treating him like a piece of dross. I said, "Let's talk about it." So I went down to Westland and visited him for a whole Sunday afternoon and we just talked about the differences in culture.

This talk was very helpful to his friend.

When he came back up to our place the following Saturday with a cast on his arm, he said, "You are my psychiatrist. You make me feel a lot better." I said, "You just have to keep in mind what Americans are like and some Americans are not so nice, just like some Chinese are not so nice." He said, "I didn't think they were treating me in a very humane way." "You wanted some instant gratification the way Americans did to find out if your insurance was going to pay for the whole thing. And if not, who was going to get charged for it. You worried about that. You didn't have to yet." I advised him to go talk to his boss and find out what the disposition was. He said that Ford Motor Company was going to take care of everything. So the big economic cloud was off his back. And the way some people said, "You're not well, go home." That kind of thing. "What are you doing here?" They meant go home to Shanghai. You know, he thought, "I've been doing a good job here. I work hard."

When another friend arrived in Detroit from Kunming, Ed picked him up.

When Ma Wenhua came here, I got him at the airport. The college didn't. I took him to his dormitory and when he and Shiping were headed back to China in 1989 right after Tiananmen, they stayed with us for two weeks because they didn't have a place to live. You become very aware that people are cast adrift literally. Just like the Czech teacher next door to me. He's got a house that he's living in down in Detroit, that is the exchange living quarters, a big beautiful house. But he's isolated down there. He's made a few friends now, but when he was first here, Heather and I had him and his wife and the kids over for dinner and we'd show them around a little bit. He borrowed my car over the weekend to go to Chicago because his car is kind of an old klunker. I don't resent that; in fact, I'm very pleased that he could do it, that he felt comfortable enough to come to me to do it. So, yeah, I'm transformed.

Mary, Paul, and Ed have given examples of how they feel this experience has helped them to be more aware of and sensitive to the feelings of others. Sometimes this sensitivity has included students in their classrooms who have come from other countries, for example, Ed's relationship with the student from Korea, discussed in Chapter 7. Ed's stories about his Chinese friends are examples he gave of how he has been transformed. Paul's examples of transformation include his new work with students as an administrator and his push to include a version of the Japanese homeroom in the school. His idea of the homeroom would make school a more humane place for students, a place where they could communicate regularly with a teacher and other students in a nonthreatening, ungraded atmosphere. Bill Notebaum also hoped to incorporate the Japanese homeroom idea into his International High School for much the same reasons as Paul. Bill's discussion of personal growth and transformation centers on his work to initiate and develop an International High School. This is the subject of the next section and illustrates a particularly powerful consequence of international experience.

BILL NOTEBAUM: A CASE OF PERSONAL AND PROFESSIONAL TRANSFORMATION

Although all of these teachers feel they have been transformed by their international experience, Bill Notebaum is the only one who immediately took action toward the fulfillment of a dream just after he returned from abroad. Within one month of his return from Japan, he put a proposal to initiate and develop an International High School on the desk of his superintendent. According to Bill, his one month in

Japan had served as the catalyst for his decision to pursue this goal. When discussing the issue of personal growth and transformation, Bill saw his transformation as a process within a continuum of experience from the first questions his students asked in his economics class during the early 1980s to the opening of the International High School in September 1996. The apex of this continuum was his experience in Japan, after which he continued his work to debunk myths and stereotypes about Japan.

Although the trip to Japan was, to use his word, a "catalyst" for his action, this was not because he wished to emulate Japanese education in this school. In fact, he indicates that he was "not all that impressed" with what he saw of Japanese high schools in particular. The trip to Japan reinforced his belief that American schools must reform to include curricula and pedagogy that will help students become more effective and aware citizens of the United States and the world. Rather than take the route of more standardized testing, which some promote as an emulation of the Japanese ideal, he would promote authentic performance-based assessments as part of a rigorous International Baccalaureate program.

I have highlighted Bill's work because it is an example of how a teacher who becomes motivated by his international study and experience can use his knowledge to create a better school and thus, a better society. I believe that this is the kind of transformation that Dewey felt is the ultimate goal of educative experience. It is experience that ultimately fulfills a purpose and in so doing has meaning. If that purpose is the betterment of society, the experience is considered educative. Dewey promoted an authentic learning environment in schools, but his ultimate goal was an authentically learning society.

Frustrated after his return home with the superficiality of his knowledge about Japan, Bill felt unprepared to teach a general course about Japan. Nevertheless, he had studied the issue of U.S.-Japan trade relationships enough to feel competent about co-presenting workshops on that subject to teachers. In addition to presenting workshops, "We started our own association of economics teachers and I became president," he said.

He and Jack Anderson, his colleague at the Federal Reserve Board, wrote and published an article that they distributed in their sessions, and the Japanese business association that had sent him to Japan translated and distributed it in Japan. The subject was "U.S.-Japan trade relations. We spun off on the book, *The Japan That Can Say No* [Ishihara, 1989] . . . and called our article 'The U.S. That Can Say Yes.' We basically took a middle-of-the-road, almost pro-Japanese side of the debate." The audience for his article surprised him.

It was more teachers, economists. We got a lot of requests from universities around the world. Jack's office was sending them to Scotland and France. I think they were surprised (Jack doesn't have a Ph.D. and I'm just a high school teacher, you know) that we could bring that kind of insight to the topic. . . . Two versions were actually printed. The text and the graphics were the same, but they published it in Japan on their own paper. It was all in English, though. The Federal Reserve published it as well. We just got so many requests for it that every time we would print 100, they would disappear.

Bill described the prevailing ideas about Japan's economic system, which he and Jack were trying to counteract.

Many American authors, business authors, and economists did not treat the Japanese economy as a dynamic, free-enterprise economy. They treated it more as an economy that is a reflection of deep-seated tendencies in Japanese culture towards identity with a group, for example, that their economy is dominated by large companies that go back to large families that probably go back to dynasties.

The topic was so contentious that Bill and his colleague sometimes had to work hard to maintain decorum in their sessions. He felt good about how he had learned to manage these sessions with teachers, which gave him more confidence to pursue his goals.

Because it is such a super-hot topic at that time, so sensitive, it was just an incredible experience maintaining decorum in the room sometimes. You had to approach your topic with such civility and evenhandedness. . . . We would have a lot of teachers in attendance and there was just so much misinformation about the extent of Japanese trade and whether it was managed and controlled and these large Japanese business cooperatives and how they worked. It was just so fraught with controversy and misinformation that to try to present it and debate it in a civil manner was challenging, but it was fun.

Similar to the stereotypes relating to Pearl Harbor that Paul Vandemere had to confront with students and colleagues, the heated discussions in Bill's workshops encompassed World War II attitudes and subsequent perceptions of a trade war with Japan.

It was more sort of a residue of past views of what Japanese society was like. We're talking about teachers now in their 40s to 50s. They have memories of World War II movies, and I guess you could say that's going to play a role. It's the kind of thing where the Japanese were looked at as mindless worker bees, maybe. That attitude would surface and it wasn't so much like racist criticism or racism, it was a perception of the Japanese and how hard it would be to compete against them. There was almost an acknowledgment that we couldn't compete. It was an acceptance of our inability to compete against them because of the higher priority we placed on lifestyle and creature comforts. Therefore, it was unrealistic to really even talk about the Japanese or to use them as models or to learn from them since we would never want to sacrifice to the extent that they sacrifice in their lives. That point of view came up quite frequently.

Bill believes that we need to look more carefully at Japanese economics and educational practices before we decide to adopt them into our system. He also felt that he and his colleague were promoting a viewpoint at odds with what business leaders such as Lee Iacocca were saying about unfair Japanese trade policies as the basis for the decline in American productivity.

Bill Notebaum's study of the economics of Japan culminated in his one-month study tour there in 1991. Within a month of his return, he had created a three-page proposal for an international school with an International Baccalaureate degree. Five years later, in the fall of 1996, the school opened with Bill as its principal. During five years of planning, Bill developed the school as an academic magnet charter school that includes students and teachers from ten districts in the area, a major feat when one considers the inter-school rivalries and turf battles that such an undertaking would inevitably provoke: "I proposed the international school right after getting back from Japan. I did that in July. Then that fall, 1991, in the fall that's when I proposed the International Baccalaureate program."

Bill describes the basis for this decision:

The link was understanding that public education was a monopoly that was operating like most monopolies do, being fairly inefficient and not always offering what its customers wanted. I'm a strong believer, was and still am, in public education. I thought that for the very salvation of public education we had to look a little bit more from a competitive perspective and offer meaningful alternatives. So that's sort of where the econ fits in. Then the international theme fit in from the point of view that I was growing in experience in that I had just come back from Japan, saw a real void in that area and knew that the economy was generally moving and would never stop moving towards more international integration. And my God, if our students aren't fully and completely prepared for that, it's just going to be self-destructive for our own society and our own well-being and eventually our own pocketbooks.

Five years before this, in 1986, Bill had gone to an International Baccalaureate Conference, where he was impressed with the high standards and rigor of that program.

I'd also been sent back in 1986 to an International Baccalaureate conference, when our school district was exploring that as a possibility, and I thought, hmmmmmm, the public wants accountability, we want world-class standards, but who in the heck knows what they are? What I had seen in Japan didn't really impress me that much, that their schools were all that great, especially the high schools. So, I thought well, maybe there's a marriage that could take place here and I proposed that a school of choice across multiple school districts could have a very targeted theme and could be very focused in its emphasis. . . . I came to the conclusion that smaller schools are better than bigger schools and that . . . any organization without a clear mission and all consensus and commitment to that mission was not going to be a very effective organization.

During the time he was developing this school, he read parts of the controversial work by John Chubb and Terry Moe, *Politics, Markets and America's Schools* (1990), the premise of which he vehemently disagreed with. They argue that private schools are the only arena in which school reform will succeed because the bureaucratic organization of public schools will stultify teacher creativity. Bill said, "I differed with them because I knew what private schools were like. . . . And to think that the lack of bureaucracy in private schools is going to result in innovation is fallacious because the overall culture is not going to allow it."

The purpose of the International High School Bill is developing is to focus on cross-cultural understanding within the context of what Bill considers the realities of world economics: "I put the International Baccalaureate together with the idea that we needed more cross-cultural understanding and a much broader social studies curriculum, and a much heavier emphasis on economics in the curriculum . . . because the world is much more competitive than it used to be, certainly our economy is."

Because he thought of Japan as a counter-example, he looked for another theoretical basis on which to develop the International School. The work of W. Edwards Demming on effective organizations had intrigued Bill, especially Demming's emphasis on a "sense of mission, a general sense of purpose, relying more on things of motivation and moving away from simplistic application of incentives."

> We are constantly measuring them. In fact, we often times see that as a way in which we get the best performance. "Today's a quiz": All of a sudden you have their attention. "The homework will be collected." All of a sudden you have their attention. "A great big hard test coming up." Now you're motivating them. So that puzzled me in the sense that here we are programming our young people with this kind of external incentives and driving their behavior and their learning based on fairly superficial external measurements or rewards, using a combination of carrot and stick. At the same time, I saw organizations shifting and dropping the stick in many cases and the carrot becoming much more humanistic.

The problem of quality measurement in education exists because "we're left without any form of external assessment of the quality of what we're doing. Whereas if a business were willing to go that far and not even use Demming-like measures, they ultimately have some measure that they're going to go bankrupt or they're making a profit."

Like Mary Ehrhardt, Bill is proposing a form of experiential learning.

> I think in terms of measuring academic success, we should pose questions and issues and problems for students that necessitate them drawing on a depth of knowledge. I don't jump to the conclusion that therefore they don't need to know the stuff. I draw the conclusion that we should primarily be assessing them on what they do with this stuff, not the demonstrations of their regurgitation.

Most American schools, as well as Japanese schools, in Bill's view have also relied too much on rote memorization of facts, tested by multiple-choice examinations. One of his reasons for selecting the International Baccalaureate test format was that he believes it is superior in terms of cognitive skills to the Advanced Placement tests with which he was most familiar: "The International Baccalaureate is a test that, while not perfect, went further in testing what was written expression and verbal expression and emphasized the cognitive approach." The International Baccalaureate test is important to Bill because he believes it can help move instruction to a higher level than the traditional carrot-and-stick approach. This traditional approach, Bill believes, fools many people, students included, into thinking that meaningful learning is happening.

> That combination [carrot and stick] works well in both gaining you respect and in creating some from parents, fellow colleagues, administration, and students. Students are some of the quickest ones to be fooled by this. I'd see the structure of American education even in the better teachers. . . . Concrete, they're very concrete, they test on concrete, they cover a lot of things, a lot of stuff and they demand of their students to be able to recall that stuff and their tests are long and difficult from that perspective. . . . If you combine that with an authoritarian classroom structure, your life will be great. Colleagues will respect you, your students will respect you, and there is very little tension in your life. You can sleep easy at night and enjoy every vacation. Other than the fact that you have to grade maybe some papers once in a while. You don't have to do too much of that because you can use mostly matching and multiple choice and true and false. There's a lot of them and they're hard.

Bill states flatly that teachers who rely on these techniques "will simply not get the results" on the International Baccalaureate examination.

He believes that changing the focus and structure of schools will encourage teachers to change their pedagogy.

> I don't blame these teachers because to some extent I was one of them. All you are doing is responding to the environment in which you find yourself. I generally don't criticize people for that. . . . Reasonable, rational, well-intended people are responding to a structure that is producing results that we don't want. Let's change the structure.

The present system has worked for years to create the "worker bee" mentality, an idea with which some Americans had stereotyped Japanese workers:

> The anticipatory set, as it's known in education, should incorporate the big idea and big concepts, the why questions. We've belittled the anticipatory set down to what we are trying to learn at the end

of the lesson of the day, which is creating employees of the future who expect their boss to tell them what to do and pat them on the head when they've done it.

In the International High School, Bill hopes to change what he calls the behaviorist "Jolly Rancher" reward system by motivating the students to work "in what we refer to as self-directed product teams, where they will be the manager of the project and the end product will be academically authentic." He described what the work of these students might look like.

It would have to have a public status. It would be sold to somebody or served to somebody or delivered in a sense that if it has the appearance of being academic in the sense of holding a seminar of some kind, that seminar will have to be organized by the students. It will have to be for other students and/or parents and the professionals in that area. So if the students are really delivering the seminar itself, it demonstrates their knowledge and communicating it effectively to others. If it's a tutoring process, then they're responsible for organizing the tutoring lab and running it, staffing it. If it has a budget, needs a budget, it's budgeted. The authenticness of it is: Is anybody getting tutored? Is anybody getting any benefit from their tutoring?

In the authentic assessment situations, students would not "get the luxury of not performing to their full potential without really experiencing the consequences." If they did not perform their tasks adequately "their tutoring lab would fail. There would be nobody there to tutor the students. . . . Their seminar wouldn't go off because nobody would bother to come to it."

Like Paul Vandemere, Bill admired the Japanese homeroom idea. One of the cross-cultural structures he has built into the school is based somewhat on the Japanese homeroom. The homeroom will meet for twenty minutes twice a week in an atmosphere of ungraded cooperation. A low student-teacher ratio will allow the teacher to more easily get to know these students.

One of the structures we built into this school because of that is that homeroom situation with students at a ratio of twenty to one with a staff member. And part of the objectives of that homeroom section will be cross-cultural understanding. We will basically have a laboratory, if you will, hopefully as soon as we have a diversity of students. It's hard not to have nowadays, so that they will learn some textbook-like things about cross-cultural understanding, but they will have a context in which we will try them and discuss them.

Adapting the Japanese homeroom structure, which Bill had observed as a nonthreatening environment, he hoped to use it as a laboratory for cross-cultural understanding.

> I model this after the Japanese classroom in a sense that homeroom became a nonacademic safety place, a place to become a part of and learn about and discuss the school itself, the organization itself, and their relationship, too. And it's not graded. That's what I consider true of the Japanese homeroom, and in the American sense we would add developing a strong personal relationship for the future. I think that probably happens in Japan, but it's not something they probably talk about. . . . The avowed purpose of the Japanese homeroom is socialization . . . to the school environment.

In Japan, Bill had become aware of the power of culture to influence our lives.

> It [the experience] strengthened just how all-embracing a culture is. How much we walk with our culture. How much of what we are and how we think and how we may approach the world is affected by that? The contrast is just staggering, the whole atmosphere of a meeting in Japan. I just couldn't believe it. The fact that people would come in, a minimum of ten minutes early, five minutes early, no one was late, just the endurance they have for non-entertaining meetings. Official ceremony, everything had to have an official greeting and ceremony.

His basic conviction was reconfirmed, that people "who want to break down some of these [cultural] barriers can do it. It's not that hard. From a theoretical base of knowing everything about the culture you're going into I think is helpful, I believe in putting that in my school."

Bill hopes to offer a varied and challenging curriculum in the school. Many languages, including Japanese and Chinese, will be offered to the students in addition to cultural studies; for example, East Asian studies or Russian studies. European and American history courses will be offered, but none of these courses will be taught in the traditional authoritarian approach. Bill also believes that because long-term learning habits, communication skills, and teamwork have been "woefully under-emphasized," education must encourage "students to be lifelong learners" who will take responsibility for their actions.

I last interviewed Bill in December 1995. An article appeared on April 4, 1996, in a local paper in a city ten to fifteen miles away from Bill's school. The article was titled "District Eyes International High School." Bill is quoted in the article and the school is described as follows:

Instruction will focus on cross-cultural understanding, foreign languages, the international economy and the democratic structure. The school will also emphasize cooperation, character and self-control. . . . Students will have longer, eight-hour school days in an extended 205-day school year.

A further study could entail classroom observations and interviews with students and faculty in this school. How the vision articulated by Bill Notebaum works in practice could be a model for others who believe that internationalizing the curriculum should be a paramount concern in the United States.

In his discussion of how he felt his international experience had transformed him professionally and personally, Bill Notebaum connects the idea of in-depth learning about world issues and cultures to basic issues of school reform in the United States. This sort of school could affirm the cultural heritage of all students in the United States and focus on developing the self-efficacy of students. Educators can learn a great deal from the way Bill connects his international experience to issues of school reform. He is an excellent example of personal and professional transformation within the Deweyan ideal.

These teachers believed that the transforming aspects of their experiences revolved around their feelings of self-confidence and efficacy. At times there was almost an "I climbed the mountain" quality in their accounts of struggles and hardships adjusting to their new environment and back home again. Not one categorically stated that he or she regretted having had the experience, although in the case of Ellen Stacey, the three years may have been too long for her to be separated from her family and culture.

They generally felt more confident in their role as teacher leaders and advocates on various issues. Often this advocacy reflected a passionate commitment to making international education an integral part of the U.S. school curriculum. Their promotion of this idea emerged from many different motivations, from Ed Donovan's desire to promote tolerance to Mary Ehrhardt's drive to establish warm friendships and personal links across borders. In this chapter they discuss how their experience has transformed them as teachers and as humans. Mary Ehrhardt's transformation is symbolized in the e-mail hookup she has expedited that will allow communication between students across cultures. The relationships she made, knowledge of a different language, and the confidence to speak in Chinese or English before large groups all count toward what she and I agree constitutes transformative experience.

In this chapter and those before it, it is clear that international study affected these teachers in their personal and professional lives after they returned home. The effects were different for each of them and sometimes painful. It is clear that they all changed their classroom pedagogy, curriculum, and emphasis to some extent. In Chapter 8, they give many examples of how they handled classes differently, how they "enriched" their curriculum with artifacts, or made their teaching more "authentic" with slides and first-hand "stories to tell." The enthusiasm these teachers showed during these interviews may be enough to wake up many students from their lethargy, a key school reform issue in the United States today.

10

Reform

School reform has been on the political agenda intermittently since the 1830s and '40s, when Horace Mann revolutionized education by promoting universal public education first in Massachusetts and then in the United States. The latest reform movement was epitomized by the *Nation at Risk* report in 1983, decrying mediocrity in U.S. education. Blame for the perceived faltering of U.S. productivity and marketing success in the world, when compared with the emerging competitiveness of Asian nations, particularly Japan, was laid squarely on the steps of U.S. schools. Study after study, financed by, for example, the Rand group (McLaughlin, 1990) or the Carnegie Foundation (Carnegie Task Force, 1986) used international test data, especially in math and science, to bolster their arguments that radical change must occur in the schools to make America competitive again in the global marketplace.

Schools of education throughout the country joined the bandwagon to reform themselves as a precursor to reforming education (Holmes Group, 1986). School-university partnerships were forged to bring "the ivory tower" into the real world of U.S. classrooms, to work with teachers to struggle with and facilitate school reform. Sometimes, however, as has often occurred in the past, the classroom teacher has been ignored. Milbrey McLaughlin (1990) found that school reform will die if there is not substantive change in the individual teacher, and that long-lasting change is as difficult to foster in individuals as it has been in schools (Fullan, 1991; Little and McLaughlin, 1993).

The teachers in this study have taught us a great deal about the relationship of international experience to substantive change in their classroom practice and their lives. Teacher learning that enables change in pedagogy and curriculum is a major school reform issue. In this chapter, I will connect the cultural learning of these teachers to the following concerns of many educators and policymakers: the ethnocentricity among a majority of teachers with narrow cultural experience; internationally balanced perspectives within a teacher's pedagogical knowledge; international experience as a learning opportunity for teachers; international experience to promote a learning environment in the schools; and the personal and professional impact of friendships and connections across cultures for teachers. Based on the data in this study, I will make specific recommendations in Chapter 11 for program educators and policymakers who promote or develop and execute exchange programs among teachers.

LOVING TO LEARN AND ETHNOCENTRICITY

Teachers in the United States often have had narrow cultural experiences, while students in teacher education programs have been described as "culturally insular." Feiman-Nemser and Remillard (1995) describe a "typical American teacher" as "a Caucasian female, married with two children. She teaches in a suburban elementary school. She is not politically active." Ninety-three percent of teacher education candidates are Caucasian; over half are from "small, rural towns or suburbs . . . and prefer to teach middle-class children of average ability in traditional settings" (p. 6). This description of veteran teachers and teacher education students is one reason international study and experience can be considered as a way for veteran teachers to break out of the their cultural ethnocentricity and that of their schools. If the work of these "worldly teachers" is encouraged by educators at all levels, their international experiences can be shared as a learning opportunity for the entire school. Schooling would be less defined by the narrow ethnocentricity of teachers described above.

It would be inaccurate to describe the teachers I studied as typical. Although I did not initiate this study with the thought that I would interview only exemplary teachers, these teachers self-selected themselves into this category by their inquiring minds and determination to alter their lives and work in order to have these international experiences. My first question in this study was about who these teachers were. What were the background influences and characteristics that led them to study and experience another culture in depth? In addition to family, schooling, college, and teaching influences, I found that in general these teachers are people who love to learn. Their personal characteristics describe a teacher who does not share the "typical" cultural insularity. They credit their experiences abroad with expanding their knowledge and understanding and with causing them to reflect on their teaching practices and curriculum. Their increased sensitivity to children of diverse ethnicity provides an example of how international experiences could broaden the minds of teachers.

What kind of teacher would forgo the comfort of his own family, friends, and society to experience risk and vulnerability living and working in a culture different from his own? Are personality characteristics and attitude the key factors in influencing whether a teacher will participate in such an experience and benefit from it? Might these outstanding teachers serve as examples to others who are unable or unmotivated to have an in-depth international experience?

My study suggests that a combination of factors, including personal characteristics, family background, schooling, and teaching experiences, influences the decision to experience another culture. All of the teachers entered into this experience with a spirit of adventure. The two most often stated reasons for this attitude were their desire to become more knowledgeable about a subject they were teaching and to "recharge batteries," to escape the doldrums of teaching the same material to the same age group over a period of years. They wanted to feel the spark of learning again.

Each of these teachers considered certain family and peer influences to have been formative in encouraging their later interest in foreign cultures. Several mentioned that their childhood was shaped with the knowledge of the United Nations as an organization that would work toward international cooperation and world peace. Four of them specifically mentioned the Civil Rights movement as having had a great impact on their thinking. Therefore, there appears to be a link between those who believe in multicultural education, which celebrates diversity, and those who promote international understanding and cooperation. James Lynch (1989, 1992a, 1992b) believes that social justice is the link that can bring these two fields together. Based on the data in this study, there need not be an "either/or" dichotomy between multiculturalism and internationalism. When Ed Donovan confronts two colleagues who use the work "Chink" in front of him, he is providing an example of how deeply his international experience has affected him on the issues of prejudice and racial justice.

A theme that runs through all of these teacher narratives and is a precursor to their decision to study about and live in another culture is their particular learning style. The way they feel about learning is reflected in their exuberance, their curiosity, and their enjoyment of learning for its own intrinsic value, not necessarily for an external goal.

Cyril Houle's (1961) depiction of a person who learns for the joy of it, a lifelong learner, seems to fit these teachers. They are committed to sharing their love of learning as enabled by their international experience, with their students, colleagues, and the community at large. Whereas Houle's continuous learners might keep their passion for learning somewhat to themselves as a solitary exercise, these teachers sometimes exhibit an enthusiasm for promoting a greater focus on international and cultural education in the schools. John Dewey (1904) describes the characteristics of an ideal teacher, who combines a focused, disciplined passion for learning with a sensitive awareness of the experience and capabilities of his students. Such a teacher will draw her students into deeper understandings by developing her own experiences to include an ever-widening base of knowledge and understanding through inquiry. According to Dewey, "Only a teacher thoroughly trained in the higher levels of intellectual method and who thus has constantly in his own mind a sense of what adequate and genuine intellectual activity means, will be likely, in deed, not in the mere word, to respect the mental integrity and force of children" (1904: 329). Teachers who exhibit a love of learning and a deep knowledge base will often motivate students to share in the excitement of learning. Although Dewey does not argue against pedagogical training, he claims "that scholarship *per se* may itself be a most effective tool for training and turning out good teachers" (1904: 327). Teachers must be active learners themselves in order to be effective models for their students. The teachers in this study are exemplary both as learners and as teachers. They model their international knowledge and respect for cultural diversity in ways that changed their school environments.

Although I did not seek out self-actualizing people in the sense of Abraham Maslow's *Toward a Psychology of Being* (1968), all six could be described this way. They often sparkled when they described what they had learned from their experiences and how they felt their experience to have been transformative. Therefore, although more teachers might benefit from an intensive international experience, those who seek it out are most likely to share their understandings and be models for students, colleagues, and community as continuous learners and vibrant, caring adults. By motivating their students and colleagues, they will change the school environment and contribute to fundamental school reform in the process.

CULTURAL CONTENT KNOWLEDGE

Pedagogical content knowledge, the connection of disciplinary knowledge with teaching methods, is a concept that assumes a strong base of disciplinary knowledge domains about which every teacher should know before he tailors this knowledge into concepts that children will understand. It has become a buzzword of the university-based reform of teaching. Within pedagogical content knowledge, however, what knowledge is considered valuable? It is important to integrate knowledge about the world into the curriculum at all levels. For example, diverse cultures have contributed to the domains of math, science, and literature. Teachers in general lack disciplinary knowledge of world history and world cultures. They also display little confidence in their intellectual development (Feiman-Nemser and Remillard, 1995). International experience can not only mitigate the "culturally insular" backgrounds of teachers but also engage teachers in the experiential learning of disciplinary knowledge, which they can then transform into lessons for students. All six teachers, in different ways and to different degrees, changed their methods and curriculum to include what they had learned abroad. They also became more confident about their intellectual ability and development, which they described as part of their basic transformation.

For example, Paul Vandemere and Ed Donovan began to use a version of the same simulation game after their international experiences. This game consisted of cultural role-plays in which students would be faced with having to function in a society with different norms and values. The goal in this experience for Paul and Ed was the same—to promote understanding and empathy in their students by being cast as an outsider. This simulation game was somewhat analogous to the real experience Ed and Paul had in China and Japan, respectively. Neither of them spoke the language and both were outsiders. However, they were treated as honored guests in their host countries. If students become sensitive to each other and to people of different nationalities or ethnicities, it might be interesting to devise an "honored guest" role in a simulation like Ba Fá Ba Fá (Shirts, 1977). This role-play example demonstrates a change in the style and substance of Paul's and Ed's teaching practices.

According to anthropologists George and Louise Spindler (1974, 1994), teachers who are not aware of the way their culture affects their interaction with others will display a proclivity for their own kind—in general, white and middle-class students—in the classroom. This means that these teachers will often ignore minority and poor children, and pay more attention to the white, middle-class children. The Spindlers have devised the concept of "cultural therapy" (1994), which includes ways to help teachers and students become more aware of how their culture affects their behavior before they work on becoming more sensitive to the cultural constraints of others. Four of the five teachers in this study, who lived and worked for a significant period of time (over four months) in Japan and/or China, said they have become, as a result of this experience, more sensitive to prejudice and cultural stereotypes. The international experience served as a kind of "cultural therapy" for them, because they looked at themselves against the backdrop of another culture.

Ed Donovan expressed increased sensitivity in his very strong prohibitions of any sort of ethnic slur in his classroom, after his year in China. His sensitivity to the students from Korea, England, and Canada who have difficulty adjusting to American culture is one way his international experience makes him look at himself and others in a different light. When Ed asks his students to imagine how they might behave if they were starving or when he talks to them about the stereotype of a "typical American," he may be creating a classroom atmosphere that encourages self-reflection among his students, a key part of the Spindlers' "cultural therapy." Stories he tells about the arrogance and ignorance of the American tourists at the Great Wall, and the way many people walk in a society where space has been plentiful in comparison to how people walk in less space, teach his students to look at themselves differently. Engaging American students in role-plays, where they must imagine themselves as minority people with different customs and values interacting with American "capitalists," could be viewed as a method of "cultural therapy" in the classroom. His goal is to help young people to be reflective and tolerant about the peoples of the world.

Mary Ehrhardt's concern that she needs to pay more attention to "who these children are" and their cultural backgrounds has developed because of her international experience. Paul Vandemere highlights the positive attributes of cultures of students in his class and uses role-plays to develop deeper understandings in his students.

This change in the curriculum and their pedagogy was dramatic for all six teachers, from Ellen Stacey's emphasis on grammar and writing skills to Mary Ehrhardt's sharing her knowledge of Chinese language with her second-graders. Paul Vandemere, Ed Donovan, Mary Ehrhardt, and Denise Green all brought back artifacts which they shared with their students to help make their teaching "come alive." One wonders how often Paul pulled things out of the twenty-six crates he and his wife sent back to take into his classes to illustrate, for example, the political significance of a Daruma doll he bought in Japan. Ed Donovan's playing Chinese music as students entered the room and his use of scrolls portraying the words of famous Chinese poets added an authenticity to his subject matter that no text-book could offer. When Paul talked about the significance of Mount Fujiyama in Japan, he could talk about it from the perspective of one who had climbed it.

Teachers like Mary Ehrhardt, Ed Donovan, Paul Vandemere, Denise Green, and Bill Notebaum, who express their cultural learning in respectful terms, have allowed their international study and experience to educate them, to promote their personal growth, and to greatly enrich their lives and their classrooms. Cultural learning has led to the quest for more and deeper understanding and insights in all five of these teachers. However, Ellen Stacey seems to have been somewhat closed down by her international experience. When she decided to introduce more book work and grammar exercises into her U.S. curriculum after teaching for three years in Japan, Ellen explained it in several ways: It was easier and she was feeling burned out; the book should be used, not wasted; her students did not know how to write because they fail to understand the language; and students should appreciate the English language as the unifying element of U.S. society.

When considering the emphasis she put on expecting students to take more responsibility for their actions, like cleaning up the graffiti in the school, the impact of her seeing Japanese students take charge of the cleanup of school grounds and the regimented rigor in the Japanese classroom could have affected her desire to go back to the basics and demand more from her U.S. students. Even though she says she makes curriculum decisions because they are "easier," this does not tell the whole story about the effect of her experience. She is presently teaching Japanese in Milwaukee to seventh- and eighth-grade students, who had previously only had options to take French or Spanish. She is also teaching Japanese at a community college there.

The majority of these teachers discuss their teaching style before the experience in comparative terms, as if they were unaware of some aspects of their own teaching until they learned about different teaching practices in another society with which to compare their own work. For some, this involved changing practice. The three high school teachers, all males, describe their teaching practice before the experience as traditional and somewhat superficial in subject matter. All three made an effort to become more progressive as a result of the experience; they organized fewer teacher-centered lectures, and more group work, role-plays, and student-centered projects. The two female elementary teachers did not describe changes in their teaching style, as both considered themselves progressive teachers before they taught abroad. While they did not see their style as changing, they talked about teaching now in ways influenced by their time in other countries and schools. Cultural knowledge became integrated within their pedagogy and curriculum in ways they all considered transforming.

LEARNING OPPORTUNITIES

In addition to cultural insularity among teachers and effective pedagogical content knowledge, the problem of sustaining motivation and enthusiasm among veteran teachers concerns reformers. In Huberman's study (1989) of the lives of teachers, the most professionally fulfilled teachers had an experience after teaching for some six years that rejuvenated their feelings about their work and motivated them to continue learning and maintain positive attitudes about teaching until retirement. Perhaps we would find in a longitudinal study that the self-described "transformative" international experience of these teachers would qualify as this type of experience and have a similar long-term, positive effect.

Tharp and Gallimore (1988) apply the Vygotskian idea of the zone of proximal development [the moment a child is open to new knowledge, based upon prior understandings], which had initially been applied to the learning of children, to teachers. A study of the conditions in which the personal characteristics and background of individuals interact with new knowledge could include international experience as one kind of learning opportunity for teachers. Self-reflectivity is promoted by George and Louise Spindler (1974, 1994), who advocate exploring our own biases in order to better understand the cultural backgrounds of others. This could be considered a possible outcome of international experience. Most of these teachers returned home, to see their own society in a different perspective, a change that represents a step in the direction of self-reflection.

This study shows that the length of time a teacher is engaged in international experience and the type of international experience that is transformative varies. For example, time spent teaching in the classroom of another country has led four of the teachers in this study to think about aspects of their pedagogy that they had taken for granted. It caused them to be different teachers, with respect to their teaching methodology and their curriculum. Teaching in a different society, such as Japan and China, can function somewhat as a mirror, reflecting a teacher's habits back to her. Things she may have taken for granted, such as clarity of speech, or her background in child psychology, are no longer accepted as a given. I believe that this process engenders a type of self-reflection that is absolutely necessary for school reform in the United States to be effective. Teachers must work to understand their strengths and weaknesses more clearly. It appears that this international experience has accomplished this to differing degrees in four of the teachers who participated in this study.

Those teachers, such as Ed Donovan and Mary Ehrhardt, who were open to the concerns of the teachers with whom they worked, learned through their connections with others. The way the middle-aged English teachers opened up to Mary Ehrhardt showed their trust in her, a trust that she would be sensitive to their feelings. She was very concerned about the plight of these Chinese teachers. Denise Green enthusiastically shared pictures of her home and family with Japanese students and teachers as a form of cultural sharing. Her facility with Japanese made it easier for such a sharing to take place, which was important to her. These cultural exchanges educated the U.S. teachers about the concerns of students and teachers in their host countries.

There were other examples of teachers' learning from their experience abroad. In addition to the eagerness to learn, Ellen Stacey and Denise Green admired the emphasis on the arts, especially the music program, in Japan. Denise wanted her American students to have the same opportunities to learn about music and to play an instrument as in Japan. Paul Vandemere and Bill Notebaum wanted to incorporate elements of the Japanese homeroom into their schools. Ellen Stacey admired the close relationship between many teachers and students in Japan. She also learned about the differences between the workloads of many U.S. and Japanese teachers. These teachers learned while they taught and brought new ideas home with them.

Bill Notebaum offers another example of personal and professional transformation. He felt that his progression from a teacher of humanities and economics to principal of an international school entailed a "huge" amount of personal growth. His international experience was part of his search to find answers for students in his classroom. Each question lead to more study and questions until he began working with an employee of the Federal Reserve Board to help teachers develop different ways of viewing the U.S.-trade relationship with Japan. The culmination of this work was his grant to engage in a study tour of Japan for one month, the catalyst of his work to open an international school. However, it was his previous work and study that set the stage for this final step.

It is impossible to predict how influential a short international experience might be. Others in his group might have only confirmed stereotypes or looked at the experience more as a trip than, as Bill describes it, a transformative experience. A learning opportunity depends partly on what the person brings to the experience as well as the quality of the experience itself. The learning opportunities that these teachers explored abroad enabled most of them to change their school environments, sometimes dramatically.

GUIDING CHANGE IN SCHOOLS

The learning environment in schools is determined by how well educators take advantage of the learning opportunities available to them. The learning opportunities for individuals are best orchestrated by a guide, a mentor, and by example. The modeling of these teachers and their work sharing experiences with colleagues and children puts them in a mentoring role in the school. In the schools where the teachers were welcomed into other classrooms and encouraged to plan and conduct workshops with teachers about their international experiences, the international experience of one exemplary teacher can change the school.

Resistance to change is considered a major hurdle for school reform. Because these veteran teachers are key players in the school, their personal and professional transformations can transform the schools. For example, Bill Notebaum and Paul Vandemere have significantly changed their schools through substantive reform efforts. An apprenticeship of colleagues and students to these teachers, who have a greater knowledge and expertise in one area, could break down some of the isolating tendencies of the school environment for teachers and students. Teacher-to-teacher mentoring in subjects could create a collegial learning environment in the schools.

For most of the teachers, their early schooling was not a major influence on their interest in international or cultural learning. The school environment did not seem to foster curiosity about the world, or anything else, for that matter. The accounts of their K-12 experience include little evidence of intellectual stimulation, except for the occasional exemplary teacher, who is described as being very different from the rest. An example of Bill Notebaum's tongue-in-cheek disdain for most of his education is his praise for a teacher "who actually believed that students should learn for understanding." When these teachers were students, they all exhibited intellectual curiosity and excitement about learning, but the learning generally took place at home, not at school. In fact, Paul Vandemere could not think of one outstanding teacher in his K-12 experience. His "apprenticeship of observation" (Lortie, 1975) in schooling held few positive role models.

After their experiences abroad, all of these teachers felt more secure about expressing their opinions, becoming advocates, joining in the debates waged in teacher meetings and faculty lounges, and thereby creating a more intellectually stimulating environment in their schools than they had experienced as students. Soft-spoken Mary Ehrhardt sees herself in a very different role, as one who can question educational theories, such as those put forward in Howard Gardner's *Multiple Intelligences* (1993). It is clear that she had formerly perceived herself as a listener on many of these issues. Because of her international experience, she has had to think about what she believes in and wants to share these beliefs. She now has the confidence to speak before hundreds of people, because she knows herself and is sure of what she has to say. She will question educational authorities or dogma, feeling she has something to contribute to the debates. She was always a learner, but now she characterizes herself this way and is frustrated that she does not have time to learn more, for example, furthering her proficiency in Chinese language. Mary now feels optimistic about her opportunities to make positive contributions at all levels of the educational process. Those contributions will benefit her students and colleagues in the academic and general community. Her experience in China was the catalyst of her profound sense of personal and professional growth.

Bill Notebaum's work shows how international study and experience can change the school context. Ten years after his district sent him to an International Baccalaureate conference, he is managing the opening of the only internationally oriented public high school in Ohio with an International Baccalaureate curriculum and degree. Bill maintains that it was his work studying the U.S.-Japan trade issue to garner knowledge for teaching economics that started him on this path. He views his one-month study-tour in Japan as a benchmark in his career, a time when he decided to go for a dream. He would work to create a school in which "teaching for understanding" would be the norm rather than the exception, a reverse of his own high school experience.

Within the context of rigorous world studies and cross-cultural understanding, students and their teachers would be empowered to take charge of their learning. In this school, authentic performance-based assessments involving projects with public outcomes would take the place of multiple-choice and fill-in-the-blank examinations, which require rote memorization rather than cognitive learning skills. This public school is in one of the most affluent districts in the state, and students and teachers from ten other districts have applied to study or teach there. Bill's international experience was the catalyst for a major change in a public high school in Ohio.

These teachers demonstrated how their international experience helped them change the context of schooling. Their personal relationships with people from other cultures was the often cited as the most powerful aspect of their international experience, giving each of them a deeper dimension of cultural understanding.

FRIENDSHIPS AND CONNECTIONS ACROSS BORDERS

Although a biased person can accept friendship across cultures as an anomaly, personal connections meant much more to these teachers than sightseeing and shopping. Individuals were accepted as individuals and not seen only as representatives of a race. As in the case of Mary Ehrhardt with her Chinese host family, cultural differences did not get in the way of meaningful human connections The understanding she gained about the hopes and fears of the Chinese people with whom she lived and the Chinese teachers with whom she worked is reflected in her work to facilitate U.S. student and teacher connections with their counterparts in China via e-mail. The work of school reform can be fostered by motivated teachers such as Mary. In China and in her second-graders' pen-pal exchange with Chinese children in the bilingual school in Boston, she encouraged students and teachers to develop their own connections with others. Learning from these kinds of experiences can profoundly affect the school environment with new and different perspectives and the celebration of a common humanity.

When Mary Ehrhardt says, "I am a different person," she means that international experience changed her in ways that were important to her. These changes enhanced proclivities she had displayed much earlier in her life when she felt that homestays in Europe meant the most to her. It is not surprising that Mary thrived in a family setting in China, because what is most important to her are the personal connections and friendships among people in different cultures. She and Ed Donovan personify the sort of teacher who does not want to only learn about and talk about world cultures. Preferring first-hand experiences over vicarious ones, they want to experience life in another culture. Mary, who believes in the Deweyan idea of experiential learning, applies this philosophy to herself as a learner.

Ed Donovan goes to great lengths to revisit friends in China from Beijing to Hainan Island. His correspondence to some thirty-five people while teaching full time seems daunting. However, he enjoys these experiences and describes seeing old friends as: "It was a ball! It was a ball!" When talking about his personal transformation, he describes himself as the sort of person who comes to the aid of foreign students and teachers and others who he says are "literally cast adrift" in our society. He believes he has become much more sensitive and empathetic to these people, because he and his wife experienced these feelings of being an "other" in China. This is probably why he refuses to allow racist remarks by anyone, including his colleagues, to go unchallenged. In becoming more empathetic, he has developed many relationships with Chinese individuals that mean a great deal to him. Twice during this past three years Ed and Heather have hosted exchange teachers from China, each for periods of up to eight months. In 1997 Ed initiated a long-term exchange agreement between his school and a school in Beijing. It is his retirement gift to the students and teachers who will participate in both countries. We can only imagine the future impact of friendships and connections that he and Heather have fostered.

Paul Vandemere, like Ed, gets a great deal of satisfaction in his work to open the eyes of American and Japanese students on the exchange programs he promoted, to let them see and get to know each other as individuals. More than any vicarious experience could, the presence of

Kuniji Shibahara for one year on his staff served to break down the prejudices and negative stereotypes of teachers in his school toward Japanese people because they became friends with him. Here again it is the friendships, the human connections, that make the most meaningful difference in people's attitudes.

The Women's International League for Peace and Freedom, Amnesty International, and Doctors Without Borders are a few of the many organizations that work across borders to establish connections for the betterment of the human race. Breaking down cultural barriers to establish cooperative human relationships across borders is the goal of long-time peace activists like Elise Boulding. The international experience of these teachers puts them in the forefront of this work. That they are teachers who can promote understanding and cooperation in this world among the children ensures that the work will continue in future generations. This is where a Deweyan connection between "The School and Society" (1900) can be the ultimate effect of the international experience of teachers.

Four of the teachers spoke forcefully about internationalizing the curriculum and multicultural issues in U.S. schools. Ed, Paul, and Bill mainly concentrate on the economic argument for improving international education in the schools; however, underlying many of their comments is an optimism about human nature and relationships. Their goal is not only to learn tolerance but to go deeper, and know each other for the intrinsic value and enjoyment of that understanding in itself. These friendships and connections across borders are examples to students and teachers and provide another focus for the relationship between international experience and school reform.

11

Recommendations

The recommendations that I emphasize in this chapter and summarize in the Appendix will clarify how educators and policymakers can work to make international education an integral part of school reform.

WHO SHOULD GO?

I began this study thinking that in-depth international experience would be valuable for every K-12 teacher. However, when resources are finite, choices must be made and some teachers, as exemplified in this study, will benefit from this experience more than others. Therefore, demonstrably exemplary teachers who are willing to put time and effort into preparation and follow-up work should be encouraged to go.

Paul Vandemere, an exemplary teacher, shared his international experience not only with his own students, but with students and educators throughout the state as Teacher of the Year. He has encouraged many students, teachers, and administrators to educate themselves about the world. Ellen Stacey, the teacher who seemed the least enthusiastic about teaching in Japan, took an unpaid leave of absence to participate in the first seven-month, state-sponsored program. She was also actively involved in her students' lives after her first experience in Japan. This change in her work with students was based on what she had observed and admired in the relationships between students and teachers in Japan. It is clear that the experience differs for everyone, but if we can learn from these six people, the fact that they seem outstanding should not negate the potentially positive impact of international experience on any teacher's pedagogy.

However, as John Dewey explains, an experience can have negative ramifications on the creativity and personal growth of some individuals. In this study, it appears that Ellen Stacey, by her own description, had this reaction for several years after returning home. "I had lost what Ellen was all about," she said. Nevertheless, it is possible that Ellen will work through these feelings and emerge as a stronger, more vibrant and reflective teacher. Three years abroad could be traumatizing to many people, especially if they were not prepared for the negative effect of, as in Ellen's case, moving from the status of "honored guest" to "permanent outsider."

All four exemplary teachers who taught in the public sector in Japan or China felt they had made many positive contributions to the host country's schools. They promoted more interaction with students than they felt was the norm. They added humor and flexibility to the teaching of English. They shared many materials and ideas such as role-plays with their English-teaching colleagues in the host country. Delighted to talk about this, they were confident in their methods, often comparing them positively to their perceptions of traditional, formal lecture styles they observed in their host countries. As they worked with teachers, essentially teaching the teachers and students, they were also learning. The discussion that Mary Ehrhardt had with her seventh-grade class in China about American perspectives on age, for example, helped her to define and understand the Chinese reverence for age and think about that cultural difference. This is an example of how an outstanding teacher can benefit from international experience and subsequently share her new understandings with students and teachers in the United States.

PREPARATION

A realistic preparation, including discussions of pertinent reading material, is most important for any teacher who is going to spend a significant period teaching overseas. If the program is ongoing, meeting others who have previously gone is essential. Videotapes and photographs should be taken of the living accommodations, schools, and neighborhoods where people will be. If people need a great deal of time and space alone, China and Japan will be difficult for them. I recommend that any teacher planning to teach in Japan read Thomas Rohlen's *Japan's High Schools* (1983), and articles by Manabu Sato (1992) and David Berliner (1993), which paint a more realistic, less rosy picture of Japanese schools than often emanates from the American press. I also strongly recommend to teachers and educators interested in exchange programs in Japan, Cathy Davidson's *36 Views of Mount Fuji* (1993). This delightfully engaging book delves more specifically into issues of culture and reverse culture shock. Davidson, a college professor who has spent almost four years in four visits to Japan, finds ways to reconcile her ideal of Japan and the United States with the real, to find a place wherein she can combine the best of both worlds. Comparable to Ellen Stacey's emotionally difficult third year in Japan was Davidson's fourth year there. Awareness about the rarity of any foreigner being invited into the comparatively small, cramped apartments of Japanese city dwellers could have helped Ellen to put her experience into a different perspective.

I have often recommended to people going to China that they read Mark Salzman's *Iron and Silk* (1986) and Bette Bao Lord's novel *Spring Moon* (1981) to give a cultural and historical context for understanding their own experience in China. I would add Heidi Ross's *China Learns English* (1993) and Bill Holm's *Coming Home Crazy* (1990) about his year teaching in China. These books and articles should be read and discussed in detail with people who have had these sorts of experiences as a formal part of the preparation. When people are prepared for worst-case scenarios as well as the high points of international experiences and still desire to meet this challenge, they will take the conditions more in stride, as did Ed Donovan.

The Donovans, nevertheless, went through a difficult time with Heather's culture shock. The experience of Heather Donovan and Ellen Stacey has led me to rethink my own experience and offer another suggestion: The preparation for teachers who intend to teach abroad should include the oral and written stories of others who have had a difficult time adjusting to another culture. Accounts of the trauma, painful assimilation and alienation felt by many immigrants to the United States, such as Richard Rodriguez (1982, 1992), could develop a teacher's self-awareness and empathy for others who have faced these difficulties in a context of lifelong change (Ekoneskaka, 1990; Takaki, 1989).

The way these teachers handled their living conditions enabled me to better understand some of their general reactions to living in another culture. Mary Ehrhardt and Ed Donovan, who accepted living in the most difficult physical conditions, seemed to forge the closest and most long-term relationships with people in their host countries. Mary considered her unheated living conditions in March to be a challenge. Ed Donovan did not speak much about the inconveniences he faced: limited hot water, unpredictable electricity. He felt that he had been well prepared by his program leaders, so they were not an issue for him.

Denise Green also does not say much about her living situation. She took the position that one should not show negative emotions to her hosts. She felt it was important for her to be a polite and gracious guest and that it was part of her responsibility in the program to keep her feelings to herself. Denise, an African-American in a white-dominated and often racist world, may have had plenty of practice not allowing her true feelings to show. She felt in tune with Japanese culture, but occasionally she needed to break away on her own.

The importance Ellen gives to space and convenience in her living accommodations suggests that the preparation state officials gave her was inadequate and that she found it difficult to adjust to conditions which were different from what she had expected. Although she felt she was treated very well during her first experience, she was increasingly bitter about her treatment during her second experience in Japan. Ellen was often frustrated by the rule-bound educational bureaucracy, which would not let her return home to visit her dying sister, even though her work was done. Her examples of violence in Japan and apparent fear of the Yakuza are not much tempered by positive relationships with Japanese friends, such as Sumi. Her ideal of Japan did not prepare her for the reality of her experience there.

Three of these teachers experienced extended time in a racial minority status in another country for the first time in their lives. I wonder how much of the psychological trauma of culture shock, which Ed Donovan and Ellen Stacey so aptly describe is based on this minority position. Mary Ehrhardt found that it was sometimes difficult to be stared at so much. Heather and Ed Donovan certainly had the feeling of being on display. Denise Green felt the need to escape her city in order not to feel like she was being watched much of the time. The trauma of culture shock should be explored through readings and discussions with others who have had positive and negative experiences abroad. With thorough preparation we can also debunk stereotypes that make it difficult for the teacher to adjust.

One of Ellen Stacey's young African-American boys in her Milwaukee classroom asked her if she felt strange being the only white person in the Japanese society. She answered that she had not ever thought about this, and yet she expresses the most fear, alienation, and loneliness of these six teachers. Her African-American student was speaking from his own knowledge living as a minority in a white society. This question may have been an opportunity for dialogue on issues of minority status in any culture.

Mary Ehrhardt might have better understood feeling like a "goldfish in a bowl" had she participated in the simulation role-play, Ba Fá Ba Fá (Shirts, 1977). After speaking with school and community officials, who continue to use this simulation, and one of its creators, R. Garry Shirts, I learned that this game has been effective with adults as well as middle-school students. According to Shirts, the game, also developed by Rod Fielder and fifth-grade teacher, Wesley Stafford, who guided his exuberant class to transform itself into an egalitarian society on a different planet with totally different plant and animal species, is still being used at the Carter Center to promote cultural understanding. It could be a valuable exercise for any foreign-exchange program involving students or adults to help them grapple with what Denise Green calls the "outsider" status of living, studying, and working in another culture.

Some of these teachers may have benefited from more careful preparation. In spite of the international orientation of his family and the international relations courses Paul Vandemere took in college, he now feels that he went to Cairo to teach for two years unprepared and ignorant, living in a foreign compound that allowed few meaningful interactions with Egyptian people. The international influences of his youth and his college studies were not enough. Paul acknowledges that he needed a great deal more study and preparation than he had for this experience. Even Mary's preparation seemed to be part of her rich in-depth experience, for example, her work with the Chinese exchange teachers two nights a week to help her prepare and practice the language, and the bonding she felt in meeting with the American students and her colleagues in the semester before she left. I consider her preparation ideal, and her experience reflected the quality of this preparation.

Teachers should be prepared for "reverse culture shock." Four of the six teachers spoke about what Ellen Stacey calls "reverse culture shock," that is, the traumatic effect of fitting back into what Mary Ehrhardt calls her "slot." Because they all felt changed as people and as teachers, four of them spoke of themselves almost as "square pegs" trying to fit back into their formerly comfortable "round roles" in the society and in the schools. Some of them accomplished this quite easily. Ed Donovan, Mary Ehrhardt, and Ellen Stacey all spoke at length about difficulties they had adjusting back into American society and schools.

Ed Donovan looked around when he returned to Michigan and saw everyone moving ridiculously quickly, almost as if they were "nuts." He and Heather were taken aback by the rampant commercialism and materialism in the United States, something they had not noticed as much before. Mary Ehrhardt enjoyed the simplicity of life in China, in comparison with the hectic pace of life in New England. She and the Donovans became more sensitive to the amount of advertising we face in the United States and thought about simplifying their lives by eschewing unneeded material things. This was also the reaction of Denise Green after her year in Ghana as a college student. An American teacher who intends to live and teach in a Third World country apart from isolated foreign enclaves must be especially well prepared for the experience and for a changed perspective on returning to the United States. Ellen Stacey experienced reverse culture shock, not after her first seven-month experience, but after her later three years in Japan. The length of time in a different culture may have been a key determinant of her difficult time there. Teachers who intend to spend more than one year abroad should be carefully screened and their preparation should be even more rigorous than for shorter experiences.

LANGUAGE STUDY

Language study is essential for the most in-depth, richest experiences in another culture. However, because so many American teachers who are not foreign-language teachers have never studied a foreign language seriously, making language study a prerequisite would have eliminated the male teachers in this study. I would call this aversion to language study on the part of teachers a reflection of American society as a whole. The majority of Americans who live in the United States speak only English. Some Americans even seem to revel in this status. Language study is seen in many quarters as a useless frill. Of the less commonly taught, but most often spoken, languages in the world, such as Chinese and Arabic, only a relative handful of Americans not of Chinese or Arab background have made an effort to learn these languages. Therefore, if I limited this study to veteran, non-foreign-language teachers who had attempted to learn the language of the country they were visiting, I might still be engaged in finding participants today. We can learn a great deal from teachers who have made a significant commitment to study and experience another culture, even if they have not chosen to work on the language.

Language learning is possible for all ages at some level of proficiency, given consistent effort. I agree with Mary Ehrhardt that it is worth the effort to be able to communicate with others who do not speak English. Mary's Chinese host family showed that they appreciated her struggle to communicate with them. Americans who do not make the effort do not know what they are missing. A level of intimacy can occur with people that would otherwise be impossible to reach. This is not to say that Paul, Ed, and Bill did not benefit from their international experience. Had they attempted to learn more of the language, their experience would probably have been richer.

There is an arrogance in putting another person in the situation of having to learn your language in order to speak with you while you make no attempt to learn his language. I am aware that with the pressures of teaching, to expect veteran teachers to learn a language as a prerequisite to an international experience is difficult. However, I would strongly emphasize language study for at least six months and preferably one year before the experience, because I agree with Mary. It is worth the effort.

Friendships and relationships with people are generally facilitated when there is an attempt to learn each other's language, even at rudimentary levels. Ed Donovan, who did not formally study Chinese, used quite a few Chinese phrases in his descriptions, which helped him forge friendships. Denise Green also found that her language proficiency eased social situations in general as well as her classroom work. Mary Ehrhardt felt that her stay with a Chinese family who spoke no English would have been difficult, probably impossible, had she not studied enough spoken language at least to get by. Certainly her relationship with the host family, which meant a great deal to her, could not have been as warm and friendly as it was. I am convinced that the experience of anyone living in another culture can never be as rich and rewarding as it would be if that person attempted to learn the language of the people and used it, however awkwardly or haltingly. Mary Ehrhardt is the main support for this argument, in addition to my experiences in China in 1981, 1985, and 1988.

I cannot imagine spending a considerable length of time in any country without attempting to learn some of the language before and during this experience. The scenery was lovely, the art was breathtaking, the food was delicious, but the language facilitated human connections with Chinese people. The connections, the friendships are what most of the teachers talked about in warm and glowing terms. Therefore, on behalf of these human links across borders, I would strongly recommend that any international teacher exchange program include language and cultural learning.

I would not want to dissuade U.S. teachers such as Ed Donovan from living in China because of a language requirement. Older teachers such as Ed (he is sixty-five years old) need a nurturing and nonthreatening language-learning environment and many confidence-building exercises. Many techniques perfected in the English as a Second Language (ESL) programs can be used to great avail for language learners of all ages. Within forty-five minutes I have had adults such as school board members giving commands in Chinese to their colleagues, who followed them correctly. The phobia in this country toward language learning has translated to a lack of support for language and cultural studies in K-12 education, which is going to put our nation at risk in world communication, trade, environmental cooperation, and every arena where we need to understand each other. It is the responsibility of policymakers at every level to encourage language and cultural studies in the schools to better prepare students for the inevitably greater international contacts in the future.

The Task Force for Transnational Competence (1997: 71) recommends that "foreign language competency" be required in "all bachelor's degree programs." (p. 71) The task force prepared this report as part of an effort to improve educational exchange programs between the United States and Japan. For example, during the next five years the Japanese government will sponsor 5,000 U.S. K-12 teachers to go to Japan via the Fulbright Memorial Fund (p. 12). The task force strongly promotes language and cultural studies as major components of all foreign-exchange programs in addition to general education programs at all levels in the United States and Japan.

ADMINISTRATIVE AND COLLEGIAL SUPPORT

Teachers who live and teach for a significant period in another country should be accompanied by a significant other, or colleagues from the United States who could function as a support group for them. Paul Vandemere and Ed Donovan were both accompanied by their wives, who enthusiastically participated in the experience with their husbands. Mary Ehrhardt's program was planned so that the twenty-eight-year-old colleague with whom she collaborated on teaching plans, trips with the American students, and teacher seminars would live a few floors away from her in the same building. This expedited their work together and allowed them to accompany each other on their bicycle rides to school.

It is unfortunate that preparation and a support group did not appear to be a formal part of the program Ellen Stacey participated in for three years. It seems that the other foreign-exchange teachers partly performed this role, but not in a structured or planned manner. This lack of support seemed to contribute to her sense of malaise. Without friends from your own culture with whom you can blow off steam and not feel like an outsider, it is understandable that a person who has not been fully prepared might feel negatively about his experience abroad. I also suspect that this situation may be generalizable to foreign immigrants or students living in the United States.

Mary Ehrhardt was given a sabbatical by her private school to prepare for and take this teaching assignment in China. Because this sort of preparation is expensive, few public schools give teachers sabbaticals to study and develop themselves as teachers. This policy should be rethought in spite of the high cost. Mary's students will reap the benefits of this investment in her professional growth for as long as she teaches. Such a sabbatical program would motivate and revitalize many schools if a well-thought-out follow-up program is developed that promotes the collegial sharing of these experiences among teachers.

All six teachers expressed a need to share their experience in the classroom and especially with colleagues. Ellen and Denise were on state-sponsored programs, where they were asked to make presentations before school boards and in other schools, and to plan workshops for teachers. Ellen's second experience entailed no such institutionalized program of sharing. She returned to the classroom feeling isolated and alienated. Every school administration can find inexpensive ways to promote the collegial sharing of an intensive international experience of one teacher. Ed Donovan's school district did just this. It rearranged schedules to allow Ed to visit other classrooms and school buildings. School officials treated him much differently than school officials in Ellen's and Mary's schools, who essentially ignored their international experience.

Sharon Feiman-Nemser's (1983) work shows that many teachers who are exposed to creative methods and new content will often revert to traditional pedagogies because the school environment is not conducive to change. It is important for the school administration to encourage these teachers to share, not to expect them to go back into their "slots" and do their job the same way as if they had not had the experience. It is the responsibility of administrators to create flexibility for this kind of sharing by giving these teachers release time and offering them as speakers for classes throughout that school and in others. This was done for Denise Green and Ed Donovan, neither of whom felt frustrated because they had few opportunities to share their knowledge.

Teachers As Resources

These teachers became tremendous resources for their schools at very little cost to school districts. It is surprising that a well-endowed New England preparatory school would not use Mary Ehrhardt more as a resource. Mary considers the upper school/lower school split a factor; she believes that perhaps her work may not have been taken as seriously by the general school community because she was teaching elementary schoolchildren. Walden has its own exchange program with China and Chinese language faculty. Nevertheless, her community public school district has kept her active, hosting language study groups, recruiting new teachers and students, preparing them to go to China, and helping to develop curricula about China. In this area the public schools, except for the inner-city school where Ellen Stacey teaches, did a much better job of using this resource and creating a fulfilling, sharing experience for these teachers as well as an inexpensive learning opportunity for their staff.

The key to this issue is follow-up. School districts who ignore the experiences of their teachers remind me of old stories about the Army which had physicists mindlessly digging ditches. These schools are wasting a valuable resource. To encourage a veteran teacher who has made the effort to study and experience another culture in depth to share this experience with students and colleagues is to bring some aspect of the world home into the classroom at minimal expense. The example of this teacher could, as in Denise Green's classroom, broaden the horizons of children and other teachers to include the possibility of cultural learning, a prerequisite for living on this planet, where international interactions will become more and more a part of our daily lives.

School districts should give teachers the choice to return to their former positions or move to another school, if that is possible. Ed Donovan's school administration promised him his former position back when he returned after one year in China. This was also the case with Mary Ehrhardt, Denise Green, and Ellen Stacey, although Ellen preferred not to return to her former school. It is unfortunate that school officials did not give her this choice.

School districts or funding agencies could set up yearly competitive grants to be given to teachers who demonstrate how an investment in their intensive study and living experience abroad will be shared with students and colleagues in the schools. There are many ways districts can encourage their teachers to develop as teachers. This study shows that the impact of a certain kind of international study and experience would be worth the expense.

School districts should encourage cultural connections locally available to teachers, such as pen-pal exchanges, among students of diverse cultures. When the students experience the difficulty of learning a second language, such as Chinese, they cannot help but know a little about how it feels to grow up in a society where children must memorize some 2,500 characters to be able to function normally as an adult. This at least creates respect if not the deeper sense of empathy toward other cultures. In Mary's classroom, the pen-pal exchange is the most striking example of how a veteran teacher's international experience can affect a classroom. She describes the "marvelous" interactions between the Chinese immigrant children and her classes after they have exchanged letters bearing the American children's awkward attempts at a few Chinese words. When Mary's children greet the Chinese-American children with "ni hao" rather than "hello," they create a warmer atmosphere of trying to communicate and caring about that communication.

The impact of this unusual experience could be better gauged in a longitudinal study of these children. The pen-pal exchange in Mary Ehrhardt's class with Chinese students cost her school very little. Mary initiated and participated in this exchange for nine years before she went to China. Her experience made the exchange more meaningful for children. There is no reason why more American schools could not foster intercultural exchanges and opportunities for their children, especially elementary-age children. This might be one small step in a long process to eradicate racial prejudice and bigotry from our society.

Follow-up

After their return, the learning of these teachers during their international experience became integrated into their curriculum via their teaching methodology, stories, different kinds of role-plays, use of artifacts, and their introduction of language into the curriculum. Ed Donovan also became more aware of whether his U.S. students were understanding at a level he had hoped they would. His effort to speak more slowly and use students to help clarify issues shows that teachers in their fifties and sixties can change their pedagogy. Mary Ehrhardt's quest to learn Chinese at age fifty-four, like Ed's, breaks stereotypes about the learning potential of older people, and especially older teachers, when given encouragement personally and professionally. Even though Bill Notebaum felt that at this stage in his life he did not have time to become as knowledgeable about Japan as he would like to be, he still devoted himself to promoting a school atmosphere where courses would be taught by teachers who had found the time to become knowledgeable about many areas of the world that are often neglected in American schools, such as Japan, China, Russia, and Latin America.

This presents a dilemma, the lack of time to study another culture. Time for any professional growth experience is in short supply at most schools in the United States, where there is a lockstep five-hour, fifty- to sixty-minute class schedule during which time most high school teachers meet with at least thirty students per hour and 150 students per day. Doing a good job with each of these students every day leaves many teachers exhausted and little motivated to throw themselves into learning Japanese. Therefore, it is important to consider that those veteran teachers must be given time before and after their experience abroad as an incentive to follow their interests, because the responsibilities of raising families in addition to the pressures of teaching can be overwhelming, as Bill Notebaum describes.

This kind of experience with a clear follow-up could be valuable for many teachers because it might encourage that teacher to engage in further learning. In most cases, these teachers describe themselves as more active learners than before their experience. Ed Donovan found resources in the Detroit area like the Chinese Culture Center, where he could take out materials to share with his classes. Paul Vandemere went back to school in educational administration, so that he could work to change the structure of schools after learning different ways of structuring the school day and year in Japan.   Denise Green offered elective Japanese classes to children at the elementary school where she worked.   She also organized a trip to Japan with homestays for a small group of elementary schoolchildren and their parents.   Denise, Ellen, Ed, Paul, and Bill all shared their experiences in workshops with teachers and educators.   Mary Ehrhardt shared slides and artifacts with an all-school assembly.   Like Ellen, after her second experience in Japan, Mary expressed frustration about not having opportunities to share her experience with colleagues and the school community.

The knowledge of these teachers should be utilized in the development of any exchange program.   For example, the Japanese companies that sponsored Bill and his colleagues also required follow-up work, which encouraged him to co-write "The U.S. That Can Say Yes" with his Federal Reserve colleague.   Follow-ups on how these teachers are using their experience should be undertaken on a yearly basis for at least three years.   This would allow the teachers to gauge the impact of the experience over time.   It is amazing to me that the Fulbright teacher-exchange programs include no long-term follow-up studies, according to my inquiries.   There are many opportunities to learn from these teachers.   Follow-up studies could improve the program from the point of view of long-term advantages or consequences.

Bill Notebaum is my "Abe Lincoln example" of how international study and experience can affect a teacher's pedagogy.   He was a self-motivated learner to begin with, who educated himself informally.   He was driven to know and understand more to feel good about standing in front of students and guiding them to learn and study themselves.   His school administration supported and encouraged him to develop his knowledge.   It sent him to the International Baccalaureate conference in 1986.   Administrators wrote letters to support his quest to go to Japan.   He was given days to do in-service training on economics with teachers.   Finally, they gave him the green light to plan this school and release time to do this.   Many teachers have the spark that Bill carried within himself.   I agree with Feiman-Nemser (1983) that there must be a school environment that encourages these teachers, not isolates them, as was the case with Ellen Stacey and, to a lesser degree, Mary Ehrhardt.

Paul Vandemere, Ed Donovan, and Denise Green were also encouraged by their school administrations to share their experiences with teachers and students in other schools.   This was a full-time responsibility for Denise Green for one semester when she returned from Japan.   District and school administrators supported her efforts to raise funds for twelve elementary children and their parents to go to Japan two years after she returned. Ed Donovan's administration allowed him flexibility in his schedule to visit several schools in the district as well as other classrooms in his school.

Paul Vandemere was recruited by the school superintendent to direct the East Asian Studies Center when he returned. The district had applied for a state grant to train other teachers in Japanese language and culture. The district also qualified to host exchange teachers from Japan to teach with Paul in this center. On returning, he stepped into a ready-made arena in which he could use his experiences on a daily basis. The district and school administration had worked together to use Paul's experience and talents by developing a committee of teachers, counselors, and administrators to promote this program. Paul was also encouraged to work on statewide committees to promote internationalizing the curriculum. Paul would have resigned permanently from his teaching job and stayed in Japan had he not been presented with these opportunities. This is an example of how an enlightened school administration can make use of talented teachers like Paul.

Most of these teachers take an existential leap in the conviction that the international experience is worth the effort and the risk. Risk-taking is rare. It needs and deserves administrative encouragement. School administrations fortunate enough to have such teachers in their midst should do everything possible to encourage them to engage in international study and experience and share their experience with other teachers and students. This small sample of teachers shows that their teaching practice, including their curricula, appreciably improved.

An astute administration might have turned the aftermath of Ellen's second experience in Japan into something much more positive. Some of Ellen's negativism about Japan could have been harmful if she did not balance it pubicly with the positive aspects. Nevertheless, she can talk about problems of discipline and social outcasts in Japanese schools, which might bring more balance to the rosy picture Stevenson and Stigler (1992) and others paint about Japanese schools in comparison with American schools. Ellen's idea about Japanese-style classroom contests to keep the school building clean and clear of graffiti might be useful to many U.S. school administrators.

A sensitive school administration could try to develop an atmosphere that affirms a teacher's experience and encourages others to take the risk of adult learning in many areas. Strained relations between Ellen and her colleagues seem to have been ignored by the administration. This is an unfortunate waste of the potentially positive school-wide benefits of sharing one teacher's experience. The shame of this waste of talent is that it occurs in the inner city, the last place in this country where teacher resources should be ignored, and where there is the greatest need for positive examples.

National Support

An outstanding second-grade China curriculum, augmented by a teacher who incorporates her experience of living with a family in Beijing and who has studied, spoken, and written in Chinese, is a strong argument for the National Fulbright-Hays Program to include early elementary teachers. The current prohibition reflects antiquated American ideas that language and cultural studies are wasted on young children, and that therefore it is not as important for their teachers to become educated in this way. This prejudice diminishes the potential of what young children and their teachers can accomplish. Learning to respect and admire the contributions of other cultures may be even more effective if it begins early in a child's schooling. Young children have been observed to be more receptive to learning the spoken form of other languages than high school students, although, unfortunately, students most often have their first opportunity to study a foreign language in high school. Teachers at the Burton International elementary school in Detroit have provided evidence during conference presentations that students who participated in immersion foreign-language programs in Spanish, French, and Japanese often excelled in other subjects such as math and science (The Pacific Rim Consortium conferences that I chaired: March 1, 1989, November 1990, March 13, 1992).

Until I initiated this study, I was not aware that the Fulbright-Hays grants excluded early elementary teachers. The work of Mary Ehrhardt merits a re-evaluation of this policy. Dewey made it clear that he considered the mind of a four-year-old to be worth the attention of a teacher who has been immersed in his subject matter. Philosopher Bronson Alcott worked with three- to five-year-olds during the 1840s and '50s until his inclusion of an African-American child caused the enraged community to close down his school.

Any professional growth opportunity to increase the subject matter knowledge of teachers through cultural exchange programs and study tours such as the Fulbright-Hays program should not be denied to early elementary teachers on the basis that it will not be useful to the children and the schools. The example of Mary Ehrhardt shows how beneficial a cultural experience can be for the students of a teacher who participates.

Therefore, on a long-term basis, language learning should be required for all American children, starting in the first grade or earlier. Children easily learn language, especially in the spoken form, and especially when English as a second language methods are used. My experience directing K-8 Chinese and Spanish programs in six elementary and middle schools is that children love it. They have fun learning and doing at the same time, the way many of them learned their first language, English. All teacher education programs should require at least two years of a foreign language study, including elementary and preschool levels. This will facilitate the goal of exposing all American children to foreign language at an early age and will encourage them to be culturally sensitive.

The language study in all of these cases must include a cultural component, so that the children, as in the case of Mary Ehrhardt's class, will learn to admire and respect the art, the cuisine, the livelihoods of people from another culture. The goal is to promote positive attitudes in children about people who have different cultural backgrounds. Future connections among the people of the world can promote friendship and cooperation, and prevent racial and ethnic hatred which is still a threat to civil society in the United States and a major problem in this world. I agree with Elise Boulding (1990) that friendship and people-to-people links across borders are some of the best ways to promote peace, cooperation, and good will. Language learning expedites this goal.

QUALITY EXPERIENCE

How does a person experience a culture other than the one in which he was born? There are many different ways of approaching and experiencing another culture. One way would be to spend many hours in a fine library reading quality works about this culture. Another way would be to study the language of a culture. A person who studies this way for a period of years probably has a more in-depth knowledge of the culture than the woman Paul Vandemere describes as having "been there" and "done that."

What makes cultural learning an in-depth experience? It is in the human connections that develop between individuals in cultures. When people drop their guard and talk about what really concerns them in a cross-cultural context, we begin to find the oneness and interconnectedness of all of us on this earth. The power of these exchanges could eventually keep international power politics from fomenting war. When Mary extols the goals of the founders of the League of Nations and the United Nations to promote a worldwide arena in which nations might cooperate rather than fight each other, she sees her work promoting warm, friendly, cooperative relationships with individuals as small steps toward world peace. Mary, Ed, Denise, and Ellen put a high priority on personal relationships that they developed overseas, congruent with Boulding's (1990) model of world citizens reaching across borders to establish relationships. Cultural studies and international experiences can be hollow exercises without human connections. I see the scholar in the library as in a precursor stage to deep and meaningful human relations, which might not have occured without her long-term interest and effort to learn about the culture.

Relationships that these teachers made in the schools with students and colleagues were very important to them. Ellen's best friend, Sumi, was a substitute teacher in one of her assigned schools. Ed Donovan's and Mary Ehrhardt's friendships all emanated from the school community. Denise Green and Ellen Stacey were critical of the programs in which they participated because the short time they spent in each school precluded their developing long-term relationships with people. Mary Ehrhardt and Ed Donovan felt satisfied about the relationships they had forged while in China. Both were assigned to one school, or one classroom, for the duration of their teaching duties.

It is very important for any teacher-exchange program to consider quality of contacts rather than quantity. Except for occasional speaking opportunities, teachers should be assigned to no more than one school and should have continuity in the classes in which they teach. The tremendous awareness and understanding that Heidi Ross (1993) exhibits as a result of teaching a high school English class in China for one year could not have happened if she were assigned a "show and tell role" in a different school each day like Ellen Stacey or in one school every two weeks, like Denise Green. I wonder how Ellen's feelings might have changed had she been assigned to one school every six months or year. A major aspect of a beneficial, meaningful international experience is that this experience must entail opportunities for relationships to develop between teachers in the United States and teachers and students in the countries where they teach. This last point carries over into our understandings of these relationships as part of the nonteaching aspects of the experience of living in another culture.

The changed perspectives that Mary and Ed brought back to their homes and their classrooms reflected their thoughts about values in the United States. These are the prevalence of materialism and commercialism, the need for tolerance throughout society as well as in the classroom, the need for understanding rather than stereotyping, and ultimately the need for empathy, the ability to feel another's struggle, pain, and joy even when that person has been brought up in a culture very different from the United States.

A FINAL WORD: "YES"

The work of these teachers to study and experience another culture has had a tremendous effect on them as individuals and on the many people with whom they come in contact, especially their students. What can we learn from them? That being an exemplary, continuously learning teacher has its rewards in the classroom and in life; that the expression of warmth and friendship across borders can enhance a teacher's life and classroom performance; that loving our brothers and sisters of all races, colors, creeds, and backgrounds need not be empty words in and outside of the classroom; that expressing our friendship the way Ed Donovan reaches out and helps sometimes lonely and distressed foreigners and his own students is a way of showing this respect and love; that the sensitivity that some of these teachers develop to people of other cultures carries over into a sensitivity to ethnically diverse children in the classroom; that teacher learning often leads to more student and teacher learning; that the excitement and enthusiasm of these teachers, ages forty to sixty-five, can be a great resource for school improvement; and that there is a link between the international awareness and understanding of veteran teachers and the educational reform movement in the United States.

Is there an effect of international study and experience on the pedagogy of veteran teachers? To use the words of Ed Donovan; "You bet there is!" This effect is also within Dewey's goal, the lifelong inquiry of a veteran teacher to know and understand his subject matter. Mary Ehrhardt translated this knowledge into a pedagogy that shepherded students toward life-long inquiry.

The goal is to live a meaningful life, to respect, understand and accept those who are different from ourselves, and to engage in cultural learning "to break down cultural barriers," so that the United States and Japan, for example, can both say "yes" together to each other and with each other. Students of every ethnic background in the United States can look at their teachers who have studied and experienced another culture as examples and say "yes" to each other and eventually to students abroad via the e-mail connections that teachers like these establish. Students and teachers would not be limited to perceptions developed in their isolated environment, but within the context developed by their "worldly teachers"; a world of cooperation and human connections that no longer says "no" to those who are different from others, but says "yes" to mutual respect and lifelong learning together.

Appendix: Recommendations Summary

WHO SHOULD GO?

- Demonstrably exemplary teachers who are willing to put time and effort into preparation and post-experience follow-up work.

- Teachers who are more likely to benefit from and share their new understandings with students and educators in the United States.

PREPARATION

- Develop a realistic exchange-teacher preparation program, including discussions of pertinent reading material, for any teacher who is going to spend a significant amount of time teaching overseas.

- Arrange meetings of teachers with others who have taught overseas.

- Share videotapes and photographs of living accommodations, schools, and neighborhoods where the teachers will be living and working.

- Prepare teachers for worst case scenarios as well as the high points of international experiences.

- Include the oral and written stories of others who have had a difficult time adjusting to the culture to be experienced.

- Plan a formal program in which books and articles are read and discussed in detail with people who have had similar experiences.

- Debunk stereotypes that make it difficult for the teacher to adjust.

- Explore the trauma of culture shock through readings and discussions with others who have had positive and negative experiences abroad and through simulation role-plays.

- Give teachers sabbaticals to study and develop professionally.

- Develop a follow-up program that promotes the collegial sharing of these experiences among teachers.

- Prepare teachers for "reverse culture shock."

- Prepare teachers who intend to live and teach in a Third World country, outside of isolated foreign enclaves, for the difficulties and for a changed perspective on returning to the United States.

- Carefully screen the teachers who intend to spend more than one year abroad and make the preparation even more rigorous than for shorter experiences.

LANGUAGE LEARNING

- Encourage teachers to study language for the most in-depth, richest experiences in another culture.

- Expect to learn from teachers who have made a significant commitment to study and experience another culture, even if they have not chosen to work on the language.

- Advocate language learning, which is possible for all ages at some level of proficiency, given consistent effort.

- For funded international experiences for teachers, strongly emphasize language study for at least six months and preferably one year before departure.

- Provide a nurturing and nonthreatening language-learning environment and many confidence-building exercises for teachers of all ages.

ADMINISTRATIVE AND COLLEGIAL SUPPORT

- Encourage the collegial or familial support of at least one U.S. person in the foreign context.

- Consider the quality of contacts rather than quantity.

- Except for occasional speaking opportunities, assign teachers to no more than one school, with continuity in the classes in which they teach.

- Relate the stress of feeling like an "outsider" to the feelings of foreign immigrants or students living in the United States.

- Promote the collegial sharing of an intensive international experience of one teacher.

- Whenever possible, give teachers the choice to return to their former positions.

- Set up yearly competitive grants to be given to teachers who demonstrate how an investment in their intensive study and living experience will be shared with students and colleagues in the schools.

- Encourage cultural connections locally available to teachers, such as pen-pal exchanges, among students of diverse cultures.

- Give teachers time before and after their international experiences as an incentive to follow their interests.

- Utilize the knowledge and experience of former exchange teachers as a part of the planning and execution of exchange programs.

- Conduct annual follow-up studies on how these teachers are using their international experience for at least three years.

- Allow teachers flexibility in their schedule to visit several schools in the district as well as other classrooms in their schools.

- Develop an atmosphere in the school that affirms a teacher's experience and encourages others to take the risk of adult learning.

- Offer professional growth opportunities to early elementary teachers to increase the subject matter knowledge of teachers through cultural exchange programs and study tours such as the Fulbright-Hays program.

- Require second language and cultural learning for all children starting in the first grade or earlier.

- Require at least two years of language study for all students in teacher education programs.

- Integrate culture into all courses that specifically include subject matter about the world, especially at the college level, for example, international relations.

- Encourage the teaching of less commonly taught languages, such as Chinese, Japanese, Arabic, and Russian in addition to French, Spanish, and German at all levels of education.

- Encourage language and cultural studies at all levels of education to prepare students to function in an increasingly interdependent world.

Bibliography

Anyon, Jean. "Social Class and School Knowledge." Toronto, Ontario: John Wiley, 1981.

Ball, Deborah Lowenberg, and McDiarmid, G. William. "The Subject Matter Preparation of Teachers." In W. Houston, Martin Haberman, and John Sikula (eds.), *Handbook of Research on Teacher Education*. New York: Macmillan, 1990, pp. 437-49.

Bateson, Mary Catherine. *Composing a Life*. New York: Atlantic Monthly Press, 1989.

Bateson, Mary Catherine. *Peripheral Visions*. New York: Harper Collins, 1994.

Becker, Howard S. "Persona and Authority." *Writing for Social Scientists: How to Start and Finish Your Thesis, Book or Article.* Chicago: University of Chicago Press, 1986, pp. 26-42.

Bellah, Robert N.; Madsen, Richard; Sullivan, William M.; Swidler, Ann; and Tipton, Steven M. *The Good Society*. New York: Vintage Books, 1991.

Berliner, David C. "Educational Reform in an Era of Disinformation." Paper presented at the Annual Meeting of the American Association of Colleges for Teacher Education. San Antonio, Texas: February, 1992.

Bloom, Allan. *The Closing of the American Mind*. New York: Simon and Schuster, 1987.

Boulding, Elise. *Building a Global Civic Culture; Education for an Interdependent World*. Syracuse, N.Y.: Syracuse University Press, 1990.

Bruner, Jerome. *Acts of Meaning*. Cambridge, Mass.: Harvard University Press, 1990.

Byrnes, Deborah A., and Kiger, Gary. *Common Bonds: Anti-Bias Teaching in a Diverse Society*. Wheaton, Md.: Association for Childhood Education International, 1992, pp. 76-107.

Carnegie Task Force on Teaching as a Profession. "A Nation Prepared: Teachers for the 21st Century." Washington, D.C.: Carnegie Forum on Education and the Economy, 1986.

Casey, Kathleen. *I Answer With My Life: Life Histories of Women Teachers Working for Social Change*. New York: Routledge, 1993.

Chubb, John E., and Moe, Terry M. *Politics, Markets, and America's Schools.*
    Washington, D.C.: Brookings Institution, 1990.
Clandinen, D. Jean, and Connelly, F. Michael. "Personal Experience Methods:
    Methods of Collecting and Analyzing Empirical Materials." *Handbook of
    Qualitative Research.* Thousand Oaks, California: Sage Publications, 1994,
    pp. 413-27.
Clandinen, D. Jean, and Connelly, F. Michael (1996). "Teachers' Professional
    Knowledge Landscapes: Teacher Stories—Stories of Teachers—School
    Stories—Stories of Schools." *Educational Researcher* 25: 3 (April 1996):
    pp. 24-30.
Cohen, David K. "A Revolution in One Classroom: The Case of Mrs. Oublier."
    Educational Evaluation and Policy Analysis 12: 3, (1990) pp. 327-45.
Cohen, David K. "Teacher Practice: Plus CA Change." Issue Paper 88-3 (1988).
    National Center for Research on Teacher Education, East Lansing, Mich.
Conant, James. "Recommendations for Improving Public Secondary Education."
    The American High School Today. New York: McGraw-Hill, 1959, pp. 100-
    18.
Cushner, Kenneth; McClelland, Averil; and Safford, Philip. *Human Diversity in
    Education: An Integrative Approach.* New York: McGraw-Hill, 1992.
Davidson, Cathy N. *36 Views of Mount Fuji.* New York: Plume/Penguin, 1993.
Davis Jr., Sammy; Boyar, Burt; and Boyar, Jane. *Yes I Can: The Story of Sammy
    Davis, Jr.* New York: Farrar, Straus & Giroux, 1965.
Delpit, L. D. "The Silenced Dialogue: Power and Pedagogy in Educating Other
    People's Children." *Harvard Educational Review* 58 (1988): 280-98.
Delpit, Lisa. *Other People's Children: Cultural Conflict in the Classroom.* New
    York: The New Press, 1995.
Dewey, John. *Democracy and Education.* New York: Macmillan Publishing
    Company. 1916.
Dewey, John. *Experience and Education.* New York: Macmillan Publishing
    Company. 1938/1963.
Dewey, John. *Experience and Nature.* New York: Norton, 1929.
Dewey, John. "The Relation of Theory to Practice in Education." In Archambault,
    R. D. (ed.) *John Dewey on Education.* Chicago, Ill., University of Chicago
    Press, 1904/1965, pp. 313-38.
Dewey, John. *The School and Society and The Child and the Curriculum.* Chicago:
    University of Chicago Press, 1900/1902/1990.
DiShino, M. "The Many Phases of Growth: Teaching and Learning." *Journal of
    Natural Inquiry* 1:3 (1987): 12-28.
Ekoneskaka. "Chicapoo Juice." In Walker, S. (ed.) *The Graywolf Annual Seven:
    Stories From the American Mosaic.* St. Paul, Minn.: Graywolf Press, 1990,
    pp. 18-30.
Emihovich, Catherine. "Distancing Passion: Narratives in Social Science."
    International Journal of Qualitative Studies in Education 8:1 (Jan.-March
    1995): 37-48.
Enloe, Walter, and Simon, Ken. *Linking Through Diversity.* Tucson, Arizona:
    Zephyr Press, 1993.
Feiman-Nemser, Sharon. "Learning to Teach." In L. Shulman, and G. Sykes (eds.),
    Handbook of Teaching and Policy. New York: Longman, 1983, pp. 150-170.

Feiman-Nemser, Sharon and Remillard, Janine. "Perspectives on Learning to Teach." East Lansing, Mich.: National Center for Research on Teacher Learning, Michigan State University, 1995.

Finn Jr., Chester E. "A Nation Still at Risk." *Commentary* 87: 5 (1989): 17-23.

Floden, Robert E.; Buchmann, Margret; and Schwille, John R. "Breaking With Everyday Experience." *Teachers College Record* 88 (1987): 485-506.

Florio-Ruane, Susan. "The Future Teacher's Autobiography Club: Preparing Educators to Support Literacy Learning in Culturally Diverse Classrooms." *English Education* 26: 1 (1994): 36-52.

Forster, E. M. *Howard's End.* New York: Vintage Books, 1921.

Forster, E. M. *A Passage to India.* New York: Harcourt, Brace, 1924.

Franklin, John Hope. *From Slavery to Freedom.* New York: Knopf, 1947/1956.

Freeman, Robert E. *Promising Practices in Global Education: A Handbook With Case Studies.* New York: National Council on Foreign Language and International Studies, 1986.

Freire, Paulo. *Pedagogy of the Oppressed.* New York: Continuum, 1970.

Fullan, Michael G. with Stiegelbauer, Suzanne. *The New Meaning of Educational Change.* New York: Teachers College Press, 1991.

Garcia, Ricardo L. *Teaching in a Pluralistic Society: Concepts, Models, Strategies.* New York: Harper and Row, 1982.

Gardner, Howard. *Multiple Intelligences: The Theory in Practice.* New York: Basic Books, 1993.

Giroux, Henry. "Literacy and the Politics of Difference." In Lankshear, Colin and McLarin, Peter L. (eds.), *Critical Literacy: Politics, Praxis and the Postmodern.* New York: State University of New York Press, 1993.

Gitlin, Todd. *The Twilight of Common Dreams: Why America is Wracked by Culture Wars.* New York: Metropolitan Books, Henry Holt, 1995.

Gogol, Nikolai. *Dead Souls.* New York: New American Library of World Literature, 1961.

Goodlad, John I. *A Place Called School.* New York: McGraw-Hill, 1984.

Goodson, Ivor F. "The Story So Far: Personal Knowledge and the Political." *International Journal of Qualitative Studies in Education* 8:1 (Jan.-March 1995): 89-98.

Griffin, John Howard. *Black Like Me.* Boston: Houghton Mifflin, 1961.

Grubb, W. Norton, and Lazerson, Marvin. *Broken Promises: How Americans Fail Their Children.* Chicago: University of Chicago Press, 1982.

Gutmann, Amy. *Democratic Education.* Princeton N.J.: Princeton University Press, 1987.

Heart of the Dragon. Time Life Video. New York: Time, 1984.

Hirsch Jr., E. D. *Cultural Literacy: What Every American Needs to Know.* New York: Houghton Mifflin, 1987.

Hodgkinson, Harold. "Reform Versus Reality." *Phi Delta Kappan.* 73: 1 (Sept. 1991): 8-9.

Holm, Bill. *Coming Home Crazy.* Minneapolis, Minn.: Milkweed Editions, 1990.

Holmes Group. *Tomorrow's Teachers: A Report of the Holmes Group.* East Lansing, Mich.: Holmes Group, 1986.

Honan, William H. "Curriculum and Culture: New Round Is Opened in a Scholarly Fistfight." *New York Times*, Aug. 21, 1996, p. A14.

Houle, Cyril O. *The Inquiring Mind*. Madison, Wis.: University of Wisconsin Press, 1961.

Huberman, M. "The Professional Life Cycle of Teachers." *Teachers College Record* 1: 91 (1989): 31-57.

Hunter, James Davison. *Culture Wars: The Struggle to Define America*. New York: Basic Books, 1991.

Ishihara, Shintaro. *The Japan That Can Say No*. New York: Simon and Schuster, 1989.

Kennedy, Mary. "An Agenda for Research on Teacher Learning." East Lansing, Mich. National Center for Research on Teacher Learning, Michigan State University, 1992.

Kozol, Jonathan. *Savage Inequalities: Children in America's Schools*. New York: Crown, 1991.

Krieger, Susan. "Problems of Self and Form, I and II." *Social Science and the Self: Personal Essays on an Art Form*. New Brunswick, New Jersey: Rutgers University Press, 1991, pp. 187-244.

Lamont, Corliss (ed.). *Dialogue on John Dewey*. New York: Horizon Press, 1959.

Lang, Peter; Schleider, Klaus; and Kozma, Tomas (eds.). *Ethnocentrism in Education*. New York: Peter Lang, 1992.

Lederer, William J. *The Ugly American*. New York: Norton, 1958.

Leland, John and Joseph, Nadine. "Hooked on Ebonics." *Newsweek*, Jan. 13, 1997, pp. 78-79.

Levine, Lawrence W. *The Opening of the American Mind*. Boston: Beacon Press, 1996.

Lincoln, Yvonna S. and Denzin, Norman K. (eds.). "The Fifth Moment: The Future of Qualitative Research." *Handbook on Qualitative Research*. Thousand Oaks, Calif.: Sage Publications, 1994, pp. 575-86.

Little, Judith Warren and McLaughlin, Milbrey Wallin (eds.). *Teachers' Work: Individuals, Colleagues, and Contexts*. New York: Teachers College Press. 1993.

Lord, Bette Bao. *Spring Moon*. New York: Harper Paperbacks, 1981.

Lortie, Dan C. *School-Teacher, A Sociological Study*. Chicago: University of Chicago Press, 1975.

Lynch, James. *Education for Citizenship in a Multicultural Society*. New York: Cassell, 1992a.

Lynch, James. *Multicultural Education in a Global Society*. New York: Falmer Press, 1989.

Lynch, James; Mogdil, Celia; and Mogdil, Sohan. *Cultural Diversity and the Schools: Human Rights, Education and Global Responsibilities*. Washington, D.C.: Falmer Press, 1992b.

Malcolm X. *Autobiography of Malcolm X*. Secaucus, N.J.: Castle Books, 1965.

Maslow, Abraham H. *Toward a Psychology of Being*. New York: D. Van Nostrand, 1968.

McLaughlin, Milbrey W. "The Rand Change Agent Study Revisited: Macro Perspectives and Micro Realities." *Educational Researcher* 19: 9 (December, 1990): 11-16.

Nespor, Jan and Barber, Liz. "Audience and the Politics of Narrative." *International Journal of Qualitative Studies in Education* 8:1 (Jan.-March 1995): 49-62.

Oakeshott, Michael J. "Learning and Teaching." In Timothy Fuller (ed.) *The Voice of Liberal Learning: Michael Oakeshott on Education.* New Haven, Conn.: Yale University Press, 1989.

O'Connor, Edwin. *The Last Hurrah.* Boston: Little, Brown, 1956.

Paley, Vivian. *White Teacher.* Cambridge, Mass.: Harvard University Press, 1979.

Polkinghorne, Donald E. "Narrative Configuration in Qualitative Analysis." *International Journal of Qualitative Studies in Education* 8:1 (Jan.-March 1995): 5-23.

Powell, A.; Farrar, E.; and Cohen, D. *The Shopping Mall High School: Winners and Losers in the Educational Marketplace.* Boston: Houghton Mifflin, 1985.

Ratner, Joseph. *Intelligence in the Modern World: John Dewey's Philosophy.* New York: Modern Library, 1939, pp. 385-417.

Ravitch, D. *The Troubled Crusade: American Education, 1945-1980.* New York: Basic Books, 1983.

Ravitch, D., and Finn Jr., C. E. *What Do Our 17-Year-Olds Know?* New York: Harper & Row, 1987.

Reich, Wilhelm. *The Mass Psychology of Fascism.* New York: Orgone Institute Press, 1946.

Resnick, Lauren B. "The 1987 Presidential Address: Learning In School and Out." *Educational Researcher.* (December, 1987a): 13-20.

Resnick, Lauren B. "Education and Learning to Think." Washington, D.C.: National Academy Press, 1987b.

Rickover, Hyman. *Education and Freedom.* New York: E.P. Dutton, 1959, pp. 311-27.

Rodriguez, Richard. *An Autobiography: Hunger of Memory, The Education of Richard Rodriguez.* New York: Bantam Books, 1982.

Rodriguez, Richard. "Asians." *Days of Obligation: An Argument With My Mexican Father.* New York: Viking Penguin, 1992, pp. 158-74.

Rohlen, Thomas P. *Japan's High Schools.* Berkeley, Calif.: University of California Press, 1983.

Rose, Mike. *Possible Lives: The Promise of Public Education in America.* New York: Houghton Mifflin, 1995.

Rosengren, Frank H.; Wiley, Marylee Crofts; and Wiley, David S. *Internationalizing Your School: A Handbook and Resource Guide for Teachers, Administrators, Parents and School Board Members.* New York: National Council on Foreign Language and International Studies, 1983.

Ross, Heidi. *China Learns English.* New Haven, Conn.: Yale University Press, 1993.

Royko, Mike. *Boss: Richard J. Daley of Chicago.* New York: Dutton, 1971.

Said, Edward. *Culture and Imperialism.* New York: Alfred A. Knopf, 1993.

Salzman, Mark. *Iron & Silk.* New York: Vintage Books, 1986.

Samagalski, Alan and Buckley, Michael. *China: A Travel Survival Kit.* Berkeley, Calif.: Lonely Planet Publications, 1984.

Sato, Manabu. "Japan." In Leavitt, Howard B. (ed.), *Issues and Problems in Teacher Education: An International Handbook*. Westport, Conn.: Greenwood, 1992, pp. 155-68.

Scheffler, Israel. *Reason and Teaching*. New York: Bobbs-Merrill, 1967.

Schon, Donald A. *Educating the Reflective Practitioner*. San Francisco: Jossey-Bass, 1987.

Shirts, R. Garry. *Ba Fá Ba Fá*. Delmar, Calif.: Simulation Training Systems, 1977.

Slobodkina, Esphyr. *Caps for Sale*. New York: Harper Collins, 1940, pp. 47-68.

Spindler, George Dearborn (ed.). *Education and Cultural Process, Toward an Anthropology of Education*. New York: Holt, Rinehart and Winston, 1974.

Spindler, George, and Spindler, Louise (eds.). *Interpretative Ethnography of Education: At Home and Abroad*. Hillsdale, N.J.: Lawrence Erlbaum Associates, 1987.

Spindler, George, and Spindler, Louise (eds.). *Pathways to Cultural Awareness: Cultural Therapy With Teachers and Students*. Thousand Oaks, Calif.: Corwin Press, 1994.

Stevenson, Harold W., and Stigler, James W. *The Learning Gap*. New York: Simon & Schuster, 1992.

Stumbo, Carol. "Beyond the Classroom." *Harvard Educational Review* 59:1(1989): 87-97.

Takaki, R. *Strangers From a Different Shore: A History of Asian Americans*. Boston: Little, Brown, 1989, pp. 21-75, 472-91.

Task Force for Transnational Competence. *Towards Transnational Competence: Rethinking International Education: A U.S. Case Study*. New York: Institute of International Education, 1997.

Tharp, Roland G., and Gallimore, Ronald. *Rousing Minds to Life*. New York: Cambridge University Press, 1988.

Theroux, Paul. *Riding the Iron Rooster by Train Through China*. New York: G. P. Putnam's Sons, 1988.

Trumbo, Dalton. *Johnny Got His Gun*. New York: Bantam Books, 1939.

Tye, Barbara Benham, and Tye, Kenneth A. *Global Education: A Study of School Change*. New York: State University of New York Press, 1992.

Tyson, Harriet. *Who Will Teach the Children? Progress and Resistance in Teacher Education*. San Francisco: Jossey-Bass, 1994.

Waller, W. *The Sociology of Teaching*. New York: John Wiley and Sons, 1967.

Westbrook, Robert B. *John Dewey and American Democracy*. Ithaca, N.Y.: Cornell University Press, 1991.

"What Does It Take to Teach?" *New York Times*, January 7, 1996, Section 4A.

Wigginton, E. *Sometimes a Shining Moment: The Foxfire Experience*. New York: Doubleday, 1986, pp. 11-50.

Wilson, Angene Hopkins. *The Meaning of International Experience for Schools*. Westport, Conn.: Praeger, 1993.

Zeller, Nancy. "Narrative Strategies for Case Reports." *International Journal of Qualitative Studies in Education* 8:1 (Jan.-March 1995): 75-88.

Index

About the Author

MARTHA HAWKES GERMAIN received her Ph.D. from Michigan State University.

ISBN 0-89789-572-X

EAN

9 780897 895729

90000>

HARDCOVER BAR CODE